D0758316

THE CENTURY BIBLE

General Editors

RONALD E. CLEMENTS

M.A., B.D., PH.D. (Old Testament)

MATTHEW BLACK

D.D., D.LITT., D.THEOL., F.B.A. (New Testament)

Galatians

THE CENTURY BIBLE
NEW SERIES
Based on the Revised Standard Version

GALATIANS

Edited by
DONALD GUTHRIE
London Bible College

the Attic Press, Inc.
GREENWOOD, S. C.

Oliphants, Marshall, Morgan & Scott, a member of the Pentos group, 1 Bath Street, London EC1V 9LB. Original edition © Thomas Nelson & Sons Ltd 1969. Revised edition copyright © Marshall, Morgan & Scott 1974. Reprinted 1977. All rights reserved. No part of this publication may be reproduced, stored in a retrieval system, or transmitted, in any form or by any means, electronic, mechanical, photocopying, recording or otherwise, without the prior permission of the Copyright owner. ISBN 0 551 00545 9. Printed in Great Britain by Butler & Tanner Ltd, Frome and London. 77361L20

CONTENTS

PREFACE

Every commentator is faced with initial decisions which affect his approach to his text, and this is especially true of the commentator on Paul's epistle to the Galatians. A nice balance needs to be maintained between philological, historical, and theological considerations. Over-emphasis on any one of these will result in one-sided exegesis. Moreover, in the case of an epistle which is so closely tied to a specific historical occasion it is important to bear in mind the enunciation of principles which can have a more general application. Unless this is done, the study of this epistle would lose all modern relevance. It is part of the timeless quality of Paul's writings that they contain messages which are capable of application in a variety of different ways.

In view of the great amount of literature which has already appeared, no commentator would claim that he is not deeply indebted to his predecessors. Indeed, can he hope to say anything fresh? Since his task is to bring out the meaning of the text, originality of ideas would at once become suspect. Yet in approaching his task, a commentator inevitably projects much of himself. His own experience cannot fail to affect his approach, and to this extent there can be no two commentaries on this or any other epistle which are alike. To this extent, there is some justification for the present commentary. To think through the exegesis of an epistle such as this is no easy task, but it is certainly enriching. My own appreciation of the fundamental character of Paul's theology and the dynamic faith which launched a Martin Luther on his reforming quest has been deepened.

There is much in this epistle about the true gospel which cannot become dated. It is the mainspring of the modern evangelical movement as it was of the sixteenth-century reformers. It will continue to demand attention as long as the Christian Church exists. My prayer is that some who read this commentary may discover the meaning of the gospel through studying its pages, and that others who have already imbibed its wisdom may themselves become wiser in the understanding of it.

LISTS OF ABBREVIATIONS

ABBREVIATIONS OF THE BOOKS OF THE BIBLE

OLD TESTAMENT (*OT*)

Gen.	Jg.	1 Chr.	Ps.	Lam.	Ob.	Hag.
Exod.	Ru.	2 Chr.	Prov.	Ezek.	Jon.	Zech.
Lev.	1 Sam.	Ezr.	Ec.	Dan.	Mic.	Mal.
Num.	2 Sam.	Neh.	Ca.	Hos.	Nah.	
Dt.	1 Kg.	Est.	Isa.	Jl	Hab.	
Jos.	2 Kg.	Job	Jer.	Am.	Zeph.	

APOCRYPHA (*Apoc.*)

1 Esd.	Tob.	Ad. Est.	Sir.	S 3 Ch.	Bel	1 Mac.
2 Esd.	Jdt.	Wis.	Bar.	Sus.	Man.	2 Mac.
			Ep. Jer.			

NEW TESTAMENT (*NT*)

Mt.	Ac.	Gal.	1 Th.	Tit.	1 Pet.	3 Jn
Mk	Rom.	Eph.	2 Th.	Phm.	2 Pet.	Jude
Lk.	1 C.	Phil.	1 Tim.	Heb.	1 Jn	Rev.
Jn	2 C.	Col.	2 Tim.	Jas	2 Jn	

ABBREVIATIONS REFERRING TO DEAD SEA SCROLLS

1QIs	First Isaiah Scroll
1QIs^b	Second Isaiah Scroll
1QLevi	Second Testament of Levi
1QpHab	Habakkuk Commentary
1QS	Rule of the Community (Manual of Discipline)
1QSa (= 1Q28a)	Rule of the Community (Appendix)
1QSb (= 1Q28b)	Collection of Benedictions
1QM	War of the Sons of Light against the Sons of Darkness
1QH	Hymns of Thanksgiving

4QFlor	Florilegium, Cave 4
4Qpatr	Patriarchal Blessing, Cave 4
CD	Fragments of a Zadokite work (Damascus Document)

ABBREVIATIONS OF JEWISH WRITINGS

BABYLONIAN TALMUD TRACTATES

Aboth	Aboth	Meg.	Megillah	Shek.	Shekalim
B.B.	Baba Bathra	Naz.	Nazir	Suk.	Sukkah
B.K.	Baba Kamma	Ned.	Nedarim	Ta.	Ta'anith
Ber.	Berakoth	Nid.	Niddah	Tamid	Tamid
Edu.	Eduyoth	Peah	Peah	Yeb.	Yebamoth
		Pes.	Pesahim		
Hag.	Hagigah	Sanh.	Sanhedrin	Yoma	Yoma
Kid.	Kiddushin	Shab.	Shabbath		

OTHERS

T Sota	Tosephta, Sota	Mek.	Mekilta
R.	Midrash Rabbah	Test.	Testaments of the Twelve Patriarchs
j	Jerusalem Talmud		
Jubil.	Jubilees		

BIBLIOGRAPHY

Alford	H. Alford, *The Greek Testament*, 1849.
Askwith	E. H. Askwith, *The Epistle to the Galatians, an essay on its destination and date*, 1899.
AV	Authorized Version.
Barclay	W. Barclay, *Galatians and Ephesians* (Daily Study Bible), ²1958. W. Barclay, *Flesh and Spirit*, 1962.
Bengel	J. A. Bengel, *Gnomon Novi Testamenti*, 1742.
Beyer	H. W. Beyer-P. Althaus, *Das Neue Testament Deutsch*, vol. 8, 1962.
Bonnard	P. Bonnard, *L'Epître aux Galatiens*, Commentaire du Nouveau Testament, 1952.
Bring	R. Bring, *Pauli Brev till Galaterna*, 1958, English translation *Commentary on Galatians*, by E. Wahlstrom, 1961.
Burton	E. de Witt Burton, *A critical and exegetical commentary on The Epistle to the Galatians*, International Critical Commentaries, 1921.
Calvin	John Calvin, *Commentarii in omnes epistolas Pauli Apost.*, 1539.
Cole	R. A. Cole, *The Epistle of Paul to the Galatians*, Tyndale New Testament Commentaries, 1965.
Duncan	G. S. Duncan, *The Epistle of Paul to the Galatians*, Moffatt Commentaries, 1934.
Ellicott	C. J. Ellicott, *A critical and grammatical commentary on St. Paul's Epistle to the Galatians*, 1854.
Emmet	G. Emmet, *St. Paul's Epistle to the Galatians*, Reader's Commentary, 1912.
Grayston	K. Grayston, *The Epistle to the Galatians and Philippians*, Epworth Preachers' Commentaries, 1958.
Lagrange	M.-J. Lagrange, *Saint Paul, Epître aux Galates, Etudes Bibliques*, ²1950.
Lietzmann	H. Lietzmann, *Der Brief des Apostels Paulus an die Galater*, Handbuch zum Neuen Testament, ³1932.
Lightfoot	J. B. Lightfoot, *Saint Paul's Epistle to the Galatians*, 1865.
Luther	M. Luther, *In Epistolam Pauli ad Galatas Commentarius*, 1519. M. Luther, *In Epistolam S. Pauli ad Galatas Commentarius ex Praelectione D. M. Lutheri Collectus*, 1535.
LXX	Septuagint.
Meyer	H. A. W. Meyer, *Kritisch-exegetisches Handbuch über den Brief an die Galater*, 1841.
Munck	J. Munck, *Paul and the Salvation of Mankind*, 1959.
NEB	New English Bible.
Oepke	A. Oepke, *Der Galaterbrief*, 1937.

Ramsay   Sir W. Ramsay, *A Historical Commentary on St. Paul's Epistle to the Galatians*, 1900.

Ridderbos   H. N. Ridderbos, *The Epistle to the Galatians*, New London Commentary, 1954

Ropes   J. H. Ropes, *The Singular Problem of the Epistle to the Galatians*, 1929.

Round   D. Round, *The Date of St. Paul's Epistle to the Galatians*, 1906.

RSV   Revised Standard Version.

RV   Revised Version.

Sanday   W. Sanday, *Galatians*, in Ellicott's Old Testament and New Testament Commentary for English Readers.

Schlier   H. Schlier, *Der Galaterbrief*, in the eleventh edition of Meyer's commentary, 1951.

Schoeps   H. J. Schoeps, *Paul*, E.T. 1961.

Tenney   M. C. Tenney, *Galatians: The Charter of Christian Liberty*, 1950.

Watkins   C. H. Watkins, *St. Paul's Fight for Galatia*, 1913.

Williams   A. L. Williams, *The Epistle to the Galatians*, in Cambridge Greek New Testament, 1910.

INTRODUCTION

1. THE AUTHOR

In the long period of critical studies in the New Testament there have been very few who have questioned the Pauline authorship of this epistle. The radical late nineteenth-century Dutch School of critics regarded it, like all the epistles of Paul, as pseudonymous, but the theories of these critics were short-lived, and had very little influence outside the immediate circle of their supporters. This epistle, perhaps more than any of the Pauline epistles, bears the deep marks of the author's personality and is wholly in harmony with what might be reasonably expected from the apostle Paul. Indeed, there never has been any dispute about this epistle, either in the early Church, or at the Reformation, or among the thorough-going Tübingen critics of the last century, or in fact in the recent computer attack on Paul's epistles. Galatians has remained a solid witness to many facets of the character of the great apostle to the Gentiles.

Using data drawn from this epistle alone it is possible to form a surprisingly full portrait of the apostle and to gather something of his movements and methods. It is worth doing this to show how personally revealing the letter is. With a few deft words Paul refers to his pre-Christian life. He uses great economy when speaking of this, partly because the readers already knew of it (see 1.13) and partly because it is of secondary importance to his main purpose. Paul could never forget his former life, but his deepest recollection is the profound change that Christ had brought. We learn from 1.13 that Paul was an ardent adherent of Judaism, that it was this ardour which caused his persecuting violence against the Christian Church. He sincerely believed at that time that he was earning merit with God. The quicker the church was destroyed, the better. Moreover, advancement in Judaism was his first priority. His ambition was unlimited. He himself claims (1.14) to have advanced in Judaism ahead of most of his contemporaries. He might have said ahead of any of them, but modesty restrained him. He was a true Jew, with the utmost enthusiasm to maintain tradition. The past was glorious.

The accrued wisdom of his fathers must be maintained at all costs. The man who now writes to Galatia was a one-time fanatic, convinced, moreover, that his fanaticism was God-honouring, always the most dangerous fanaticism when misguided so completely as Saul's. It is against this background that he tells of his liberation.

In many ways it is surprising that the apostle gives so little detail about his conversion. Yet what he says is highly significant. He selects rather the underlying principles than the actual details of the event. He passes by the sudden brilliant light, the heavenly voice which challenged him, the dramatic realization that he was blind, the dark vigil, the first real Christian prayer, the touch and tender voice of Ananias, his dramatic recovery of sight, and his baptism. He fastens on two revolutionary ideas which suddenly became clear to him— his separation and his calling (1.15, 16). The first happened long before he was conscious of it, i.e. before he was born. The truth had dawned on him that every aspect of his past life had been known to God. He does not enlarge on this, but it clearly cut the ground away from all his previous zealous and even violent attempts to earn merit. When Paul further speaks of his calling he is thinking of that moment in time when he became conscious that God's grace had transformed him. And the deepest impression it had on him was the commission to preach among the Gentiles. Indeed, what Paul says about his preaching in this epistle repays careful notice.

Throughout this letter the reader cannot fail to detect the words of a man who is essentially a preacher. He is no theoretical theologian. Here is a man used to pleading. It is thoroughly in keeping with this that he draws such specific attention to his divine commission to preach (1.16). Moreover, the gospel that he preached was not a gospel of man's making (1.11). There was an essentially divine character about the message as well as the commission. The apostle was a true ambassador. He had received his orders and was intent on carrying them out. Indeed, Paul boldly states that he received his gospel by revelation (1.12), by which he means not something visionary or ecstatic but a message received by direct contact with Jesus Christ and not mediated through others, not even through apostles. His calling was as highly individualistic as his character.

When recounting his visit to Jerusalem with Barnabas and Titus, Paul says he laid before them the gospel he preached (2.2), and this again shows his deep awareness of the supreme importance of the content of his preaching. He reminds the Galatians that he had placarded the crucified Christ before them (3.1), and recalls to their minds the physical difficulties which attended his first preaching among them (4.13).

In close association with his sense of call to preach the gospel was his call to the apostolic office (1.1). It was not without significance that he begins the epistle with an assertion of the divine origin of his apostolate, in view of the fact that he is clearly claiming equality with the Jerusalem apostles in the first part of the epistle. Not all preachers were apostles, but Paul is conscious of having received an appointment which could even rank alongside those who had companied with Jesus.

Some of the interesting details about Paul's movements are unique to this epistle. Almost directly after his conversion Paul spent some time in Arabia (see note on 1.17 for a discussion of this location). How long he was there he does not say. Moreover, he leaves us to conjecture the purpose of his visit. It may well have been to seek seclusion in order to have time to re-orientate his thoughts. But he does not say so. He refers to his return to Damascus (1.17) and again gives no hint of what he did there. It is unimportant for his present purpose. The Book of Acts fills in some of the gaps (cf. 9.19ff.). The Jerusalem visits to which he refers in 1.18 and 2.1 will require detailed examination under the discussion concerning the date. But there is no doubt of the importance of Jerusalem in Paul's mind, although his intention is to show his independence of the Jerusalem apostles. There is but a passing reference to the churches of Judea (1.22f.), although Paul disclaims any personal knowledge of them. He also mentions going into the regions of Syria and Cilicia, but gives no details of any activity there (cf. Ac. 15.41).

Paul's own Christian experience shines through his epistle. His call to the ministry is accompanied by a deep awareness of his new relationship to Christ. He uses the term 'bond-servant' (1.10), a characteristic description which occurs in many of his other letters.

He is not only an apostle, a position of honour, but also a slave, a position of humiliation. It is particularly significant that he should use the latter expression in an epistle in which he devotes such attention to Christian liberty. He is freed from bondage to law, but is still a bondman of Christ. Appeal to personal experience is often the most effective method of dealing with the problems of others. In this epistle the most notable example of this method is in 2.19, 20, where Paul appeals to his experience of death to the old life and to his new life in Christ. He knows what it means to be crucified with Christ. He has already experienced it.

The epistle reveals its author as an intensely human man. He feels deeply. He is astonished at the speedy defection of his readers from the true gospel (1.6). He is clearly disappointed with them, even fearful lest all his work among them should prove vain (4.11). He speaks of his perplexity about them (4.20). Yet in spite of this perplexity he is in no doubt about the issues at stake and uses great plainness of speech. For instance, when he thinks of men preaching some other gospel, he does not hesitate to declare an anathema against them (1.9). The same steadfast bluntness for truth's sake is seen in his own account of his public criticism of Peter (2.14). But the clearest instance of Paul's downright bluntness is seen in 5.12, where the somewhat crude expression which he uses testifies to the intensity of his feeling against those perverting the gospel. It is in the light of this that his concluding demand that no-one is to trouble him further is to be understood (6.17).

Perhaps the most salient feature of Paul's character seen in this epistle is a rugged independence. More than once he disavows either having been appointed an apostle or having received his gospel from men (1.1, 12, 16). Yet his strongly independent claims are not to be understood in any egotistical sense. He considered it to be a vital matter to establish that behind his ministry and the very gospel he preached was divine authority. Nevertheless, in spite of his own claims to equality with the Jerusalem apostles, he shows no antagonism to the latter and in fact mentions with evident favour that they extended to him the right hand of fellowship (2.9). In close association with an independent spirit goes a sense of freedom. It was Paul's

appreciation of this freedom (cf. 2.4; 5.1) whicn produced in him
such deep distress over the Galatians' apparent willingness to lose it.
His doctrinal argument is never purely intellectual but is an essential
part of his practical Christian approach. Let us call him a theologian
as we must, but let us not think of him as an armchair theologian.
He wrestled out his theology on his feet.

One other aspect of Paul's personal life demands to be mentioned,
i.e. his physical condition. He refers in 4.13 to a bodily ailment but
gives no details to enable us to identify it. It may have caused some
unpleasantness in his appearance since he commends the Galatians for
not despising him (4.14). Moreover, his reference to the fact that
they would have plucked out their eyes for him (4.15) has led some
to suppose that the ailment was ophthalmia (so Calvin, Emmet).
But Paul may simply be using a figure of speech. In the conclusion
of the epistle the apostle's allusion to the largeness of his handwriting may support the theory of eye-disease, but this is open to
other interpretations (see comment on 6.17).

Further illumination on the author may be obtained from an
examination of his style as a writer, and this will be more fully
developed in the next section.

2. THE STYLE OF THE EPISTLE

It is a general truth that the style reflects the man, although this must
not be too rigidly applied so as to exclude the possibility of a wide
variety of styles for the same author. In studying the particular style
of this epistle it is intended to examine the literary method which
the author chose in order to express most clearly the specific message
which he had to impart. What is characteristic in Paul's Epistle to the
Galatians need not necessarily be characteristic elsewhere.

The first feature which claims attention is the great number of
figures of speech. From many of them may be obtained some indication of Paul's background (see Tenney's discussion, 135ff.). An
author naturally takes the greatest number of his metaphors from
the sphere in which he himself moves. Those most characteristic of

the Epistle to the Galatians are the bewitching eye (3.1), the placard-
ing of news (3.1), the function of a guardian (3.24), the figure of
child-bearing (4.19), the yoke (5.1), the athletic course (5.7), the
leaven (5.9), the stumbling-block (5.11), the ferocity of wild animals
(5.15), the fruit harvest (5.22), the processes of sowing and reaping
(6.7), the household (6.10), and the process of branding (6.17). These
show the apostle's wide range of interests and his acute sense of the
value of metaphorical language in pressing home his points. Some
of these figures appear again in other Pauline Epistles, but some
(e.g. the first three mentioned) are peculiar to this epistle.

An even more marked feature of Paul's style here is the number
of rhetorical questions. These are not, however, evenly distributed
throughout, but are almost wholly concentrated in the central
doctrinal portion (i.e. chapters 3 and 4). The first example is in 1.10,
where Paul asks a double question, enquiring whether he is seeking
to please men or God. The answer is obvious, although Paul gives a
hint of the result which must follow if the reverse were true. In the
short passage 3.1–5, six rhetorical questions follow in quick suc-
cession. This quick-fire method of challenge was calculated to ensure
the maximum impact. For other examples, see 3.21; 4.15; 4.16.

There are some stylistic features which bring considerable warmth
to the epistle in spite of the strong line which the apostle feels obliged
to take. On several occasions he addresses his readers as 'brethren'
(1.11; 3.15; 4.12, 28; 5.11; 6.1, 18) and these must be set against his
ejaculatory 'O foolish Galatians!' of 3.1. The use of this style of
address occurs, as will be seen, in all sections of the epistle, which
suggests that Paul is determined, in spite of his criticisms of his
readers, to keep constantly in mind his relation to them in Christ.
He even calls those who are making false demands 'brethren' (2.4),
although he shows himself so definitely opposed to their so-called
'gospel'. The apostle is no self-opinionated heresy-hunter, but a
brother in Christ pleading with his fellows not to lose the precious
heritage of freedom which is rightly theirs. An even more tender
touch occurs in 4.19, where the apostle addresses them as 'my little
children'.

It is noticeable that not infrequently Paul uses the first person plural, thus identifying himself with his readers, although he uses the singular about seventy times. Sometimes the plural is used to include others (though unidentified) who are distinct from the readers, as, for instance, in 1.8, or else it is to be explained as the epistolary 'we'. In 1.9 Paul has both the plural and the singular, and in this case the plural may refer to Paul's companions. But when in 4.28, 31 he uses the plural there can be no doubt that he includes his readers among those who are children of promise, children of the free woman. In the practical exhortations of chapter 6 the plural is also used, because Paul is conscious of the need to apply to himself the same injunctions (cf. the sudden change from third to first person at the end of chapter 5).

Those who reflect carefully on the characteristics of style in this epistle will discover with increasing clarity an advocate who not only had a burning zeal for his cause, but also possessed considerable skill in pleading. Unfortunately, history has left us without knowledge of the sequel. Did the Galatians succumb to pressure or was Paul's powerful pleading an effective deterrent? Since this epistle was soon highly treasured within the Christian Church, it is a safe supposition that it was so treasured because of its effectiveness in combating Judaistic tendencies.

3. THE EPISTLE IN THE ANCIENT CHURCH

There is little need to discuss the authenticity of this epistle, for, as has been shown, it has been the least disputed of any of Paul's epistles. In the ancient Church no voice was raised against it, while in the modern Church only the protests of a few extremists, who have denied all the Pauline epistles, have been heard. Indeed at no time have any others of Paul's epistles been accepted and this rejected. If any standard epistle of the apostle's is to be chosen to act as a norm against which to judge the others there are few, if any, who would deny the right of this epistle to the strongest consideration.

Nevertheless a brief statement of the early patristic evidence for the Epistle to the Galatians will not be out of place. There are a few

possible allusions to the language of this epistle in the earliest patristic
writings. Barnabas 19.8 may be an echo of Gal. 6.6; and 1 Clem. 49.9
could be drawn from Gal. 1.4. The parallels in Polycarp are clearer
and more certainly indicate a knowledge of this epistle (Polycarp's
Philippians 3.3, cf. Gal. 4.26; Polycarp 5.1, cf. Gal. 6.7; Polycarp 9.2;
cf. Gal. 2.2). Justin is generally not the best witness in discussions on
canonicity since his quotations of New Testament books are very
l ose, a fact which makes the establishment of dependence more
difficult. But in the case of this epistle, it is significant that on two
occasions Justin applies the same Old Testament passage in a similar
way to Paul (cf. Justin's *Dialogue*, 95.1 and Gal. 3.10, 13, and Justin's
Apology 53 and Gal. 4.27). There is evidence that Marcion placed
this epistle first among all Paul's epistles, and the order must be
regarded as an indication of Marcion's evaluation of this epistle. Both
Tertullian (*Adv. Marc.* 5) and Epiphanius (*Haer.* 42) testify to this
order in Marcion's list.

The Muratorian Canon includes the Epistle to the Galatians as
fifth in order of the epistles of Paul addressed to churches, and there
is no doubt expressed concerning its genuineness. It is Irenaeus who
is first to quote the epistle as by Paul (*Haer.* 3.6.5; 3.10; and 4.4,. 5)
Similarly a clear statement by Clement of Alexandria in *Strom.* 3.18
cites Gal. 4.19 as words of Paul when writing to the Galatians. There
is no need to pursue the evidence further, since the canonicity of this
epistle was in all subsequent periods assumed without question.

4. OCCASION AND PURPOSE

This is one of the New Testament epistles of which it is possible to
be relatively certain of its occasion and purpose, for Paul has used
great plainness of speech about his intentions. It will be best to
summarize the occasion by considering in turn the relation that Paul
sustains to three different groups of people who are involved in the
situation.

The first consideration is the apostle's previous relations with the
readers. There is no doubt that a special relationship existed between

them, for they were his converts. He had preached the gospel to them
(1.8, 9; 4.13). Because of this and because of their response to the
preaching, they had formed a warm regard for the apostle, being
even prepared, had it been possible, to make sacrifices for his sake
(cf. 4.15). Clearly, also, Paul had from his side a warm feeling for
them, for the satisfaction was not one-sided. He remembered several
things about that first visit. He had not been well. He probably
looked the worse for wear. Travelling in those days was long and
wearisome, which could not have improved his physical condition.
And yet the Galatians gave him such a welcome that not even an
angel could have wished for more (4.14). The faith of these people
was strong enough to recognize in the ailing body of Paul an
indomitable spirit, which was none other than that of Christ himself.

It must be remembered that the Galatians had had no advantages
from a Jewish heritage. Paul reminds them of their former state when
they worshipped what he calls 'no gods' (4.8). The change from
paganism to Christianity was revolutionary. The apostolic mission
had preached to them about Christ, laying special stress on the
crucifixion. They in their turn had discovered a new liberty in Christ.
The heart of the great missionary apostle must have been greatly
thrilled as he saw the Spirit of God at work among these people.
Furthermore, he regarded them as the first fruits of a great harvest of
Gentile churches. And yet they have since caused him deep distress.
The reason will be fully discussed later, but for now it must be noted
that his present distress contrasts all the more vividly with his earlier
satisfaction. Many of the Galatians had been baptized (3.27), thus
openly testifying to their allegiance to Christ. Moreover, Paul's
preaching had been backed up by miracles (3.5), although he gives
no details about these. The Galatians had no excuse for any ignorance
regarding the content or the authority of Paul's gospel.

The second group with which he is concerned is the apostolic
group at Jerusalem. In the first two chapters he goes to considerable
trouble to explain his relationship with these, which could have been
necessary only because of some serious misunderstandings. It is clear
that the Galatians were being persuaded to heed other teachers at
Paul's expense, because he was said to compare unfavourably with

the original apostles in status, whereas they were claiming the support
of the leaders in Jerusalem. This latter factor would naturally have
carried some weight with the Galatians. In view of this, the epistle
is in the nature of an *apologia pro vita sua*. Paul's whole apostolic
authority is at stake. If his inferiority to the Jerusalem apostles is
allowed to pass unchallenged, his apostolic mission would be in
jeopardy. In the first part of the epistle, the Jerusalem apostles are in
the background. Paul in a general manner denies that either his
apostleship (1.1) or his gospel (1.12) is from man. If either had been
of human origin, it would have been *via* the Jerusalem leaders. Later
on (1.16) he refers to 'flesh and blood' and only then to 'those who
were apostles before me'. It is when he deals with his Jerusalem visits
that he becomes more specific, mentioning James, Cephas, and John
(2.9; cf. also 1.19). Of these three he says that they were reputed to
be 'pillars' (2.9), and his manner of reference suggests that he is
citing the language of his opponents. They were apparently drawing
a distinction between Paul and the 'pillars'. The 'pillars' were held
in repute (cf. 2.2, 6), but by implication Paul was not.

The most important aspect of the apostle's defence of his own
position is his express avowal that the Jerusalem leaders added
nothing to his gospel (2.6), that is, that both he and they adopted
precisely the same position and agreed amicably on their respective
spheres of mission activity. There had been one major clash with
Peter, but this concerned a matter of fellowship, not of doctrine. It
happened during a visit of Peter's to Antioch, during which he at
first shared meals with Gentiles but declined to do so when Jewish
Christians arrived from James. Paul refers to his public reprimand of
Peter because of his inconsistency in order to prove that his authority
was not less than Peter's. He does not tell us the outcome of the clash
because it is not essential to his argument. He leaves his readers to
assume that Peter heeded the rebuke. After 2.14, Paul says nothing
further about the other apostles.

The third group consisted of the conflicting teachers who appear
to be Judaizers. They are variously alluded to without any specific
classification being attached to them. The first reference is in 1.7,
where the phrase 'some who trouble you' occurs. These are said to

want to pervert the gospel. There is a vaguer reference in 1.9 to anyone preaching a contrary gospel. In 2.4, Paul refers to false brethren who had been secretly brought in at Jerusalem, suggesting some methods of which the apostle did not approve. It is noticeable, however, that he classes them as 'brethren', even although false. Moreover, their purpose is further defined as spying out the freedom of Paul and his companions. The apostle sees their movement as enslaving. In 2.11, 12 the description of 'certain men from James' and 'the circumcision party' suggests that they were of the same spiritual kith and kin as the Galatians' troublers. There is another vague allusion to these troublers in 3.1, where Paul asks the Galatians, 'who has bewitched you?' In 3.10 Paul makes a statement about 'all who rely on works of the law', which is in all probability a reference to the same people. The argument then proceeds without reference to the source of the trouble until 4.17, where there is a further vague reference: 'They make much of you . . . they want to shut you out.' Not until 5.2 is there any reference to circumcision, and yet there is no question that this is a major issue in Paul's controversy with his opponents. He addresses them directly, 'You are severed from Christ . . . you have fallen away from grace' (5.4). This is followed by a question in the singular, 'who hindered you?' (5.7), with a further reference in the singular in 5.10. In his rather harsh statement in 5.12 Paul alludes to 'those who unsettle you'. In the concluding chapter there is a parting reference to 'those who want to make a good showing in the flesh', and a further reference to circumcision (6.12). In this context there is an illuminating reference to them wanting to avoid persecution for the Cross of Christ. Paul closes with an appeal that no man should further trouble him (6.17).

From these incidental references it is possible to form a reasonably clear picture of the situation. How many people were involved it is impossible to say. There was certainly a group in spite of the few references to an individual. It is reasonable to suppose that in the latter cases the leader or leaders are mainly in mind. That they were regarded as part of the church is also evident, although they entered surreptitiously. The cause of all the trouble was their insistence on circumcision for Gentile believers and the securing of salvation through works. The apostle takes a serious view of this approach, for he sees it as an attack on the whole concept of Christian freedom. His strong reaction to this undermining movement provides the immediate occasion for the epistle, the details of which will be discussed in the next section.

5. THE IMPORTANCE OF THE ISSUE

Circumcision was integral to the Jewish system. It was the sign of the covenant and therefore involved initiation into a privileged position. It was, moreover, commanded in the Old Testament. The uncircumcised were essentially outcasts from the Commonwealth of Israel and became objects of contempt. The earliest Christians, in their pre-conversion days, had been conditioned to this kind of approach, and it was not surprising that they should bring something of it into the Christian Church. So long as all the believers were already circumcised there was no critical problem. It did not even dawn on them all at once that Christianity involved a totally different approach to the law. It was possible to continue under the old legal obligations with the addition of the acceptance of Jesus as Messiah. The radical nature of this Christian addition was not at first clear to their minds. It was not until the crisis had developed at Galatia that the serious character of the issue became clear. Paul had established Gentile churches and had himself not insisted on circumcision. It is important to recognize that the first and most important decision over the circumcision issue was taken, not in the Jerusalem church when the matter was discussed in Council (Ac. 15), but in the mind of Paul.

It is a tremendous tribute to the spiritual insight of this great missionary apostle that in spite of his strict upbringing as a Hebrew of the Hebrews, a privileged member of the chosen race, he does not entertain the thought that Gentiles must be circumcised to obtain the full benefits of the Gospel. So great had been the emancipation of Paul's Damascus experience that he seems soon to have recognized that an entirely new basis of approach to God had been inaugurated

by Christ. This was in vivid contrast to the ultra-conservative
approach of the Judaizers, who were convinced that the Jewish
Christian position was right and that Gentiles must therefore submit
to it. It was no easy matter for a pious Jew to conceive of the possibility of dispensing with circumcision, and this must not be overlooked in assessing the situation. There is nothing to suggest that
these Judaizers desired anything less than the best for the Galatians.
They were sincere, dangerously sincere, for they were clearly active
in the propagation of their opinions. But Paul at once sees the danger.
If the Judaizers were right, Christianity would be little more than a
sect of Judaism. At first, Paul seems to have been alone in recognizing
the importance of the issue. It is clear from the epistle that he assumes
that the Galatians had previously understood their Christian standing
apart from circumcision. In all probability Paul had positively
informed them that circumcision was not required, for otherwise he
would not have marvelled at their present readiness to lose their
freedom. The apostle writes as if they were blameworthy for their
action (or intended action), which could be true only if they were
already aware of the position.

An interesting aspect of the Galatian position is the attitude of the
Jerusalem apostles towards the Judaizers. Did they look with
approval on the mission to circumcise Gentiles, or was this mission
carried out by some extremists irrespective of their leaders? The
epistle itself certainly gives no indication, although there is a passing
reference to 'certain men . . . from James' (2.12) who did not favour
eating with Gentiles. It seems reasonable to suppose that the 'pillar'
apostles were more inclined to favour the circumcision party,
although Peter was apparently not so convinced about it as James.
According to Ac. 15.5, the advocates of circumcision for all are
described as 'believers who belonged to the party of the Pharisees',
who are obviously distinct from the apostles themselves. The best
supposition is that there was no clash between the Pharisaic Christians
and the apostles until Paul's Gentile mission precipitated a crisis, thus
forcing the apostles to face the issue. As far as the Galatian situation
is concerned, there can be no doubt that the Judaizers were claiming
apostolic authority, whether rightly or wrongly, for Paul goes to

considerable trouble to demonstrate that the Jerusalem apostles were in essential agreement with him.

It is important to have a clear picture of the way that Paul deals with the issue, and the following summary will assist to this end.

(1) First, there is *the historical approach*. Paul is determined to scotch the rumour that his opinion can be ignored in favour of the point of view purporting to have the support of the 'pillar' apostles. This section (1.1–2.14) is a necessary preliminary to the more important doctrinal approach. Unless he can establish his apostolic claims and the falseness of the Judaizer's assertions that there was a vital difference between his position and the 'pillar' apostles, his doctrinal section would carry little weight. The historical situation gives no occasion for the view that Paul's opinions are of secondary importance.

(2) The doctrinal approach consists of several steps, the first of which is an argument drawn from *personal testimony* (2.15–21). Paul testifies to the fact that, although he was born a Jew, he had not found justification through the law. Indeed, the Cross had become the centre of his life.

(3) The next stage is an appeal to *the Galatians' own experience* (3.1–5). They had known the aid of the Spirit and had seen miracles. On the basis of this, Paul challenges them with a series of questions. They know very well that they had not received the Spirit through allegiance to the law. What logical reason, therefore, was there for trying to continue in dependence on the law?

(4) This is followed by an appeal to the *Old Testament* (3.6–18). Abraham had a special interest for all Jews, and served admirably as an example to prove Paul's point that promise was superior to law. First Paul appeals to Abraham's faith, then adds an interlude on the curse of the law before returning to the promise made to Abraham as being prior to the law. Paul's use of the Old Testament is authoritative. Therefore he feels free to use an argument based on grammatical considerations (3.16).

(5) Next, Paul discusses the relationship between law and promise, bringing out particularly *the temporary function of the law* and the permanent function of faith in God's word (3.19–29). In the same

vein, he likens those still under law to bondservants as compared with the privileged position shared by sons (4.1-7).

(6) A further stage in the argument is a *warning* against returning to a condition of bondage, and an exhortation based on Paul's previous experience among them (4.8-20).

(7) The final stage in the doctrinal argument is an appeal to an *allegory* (4.21-31). This returns to the story of Abraham and makes use of historical incidents to illustrate spiritual truths. However strange such a method of argument appears in a scientifically dominated age, it would have had considerable relevance in an age when the allegorical interpretation of Scripture was receiving widespread attention, as is clear from Philo's expositions.

The result of this process of doctrinal argument is succinctly stated in 5.1 ('For freedom Christ has set us free'), on the basis of which the Galatians are exhorted not to allow themselves to be enslaved again. The focal point of Paul's approach to the Galatian problem is his firm conviction about Christian freedom. Anything which threatened this was a matter of such urgency that Paul sees it as a threat to the whole future of Christianity. It is for this reason that he uses such energy to refute the aims of the Judaizers.

6. THE DESTINATION OF THE EPISTLE

There has been much discussion over this problem, and it cannot be said that any indisputable conclusion has yet been reached. It will be necessary therefore to set out the evidence on this issue fairly fully in order to allow as fair an estimate of it as possible.

THE HISTORY OF GALATIA

At the time of the apostle Paul there was a provincial district under the organization of the Roman empire which was called Galatia, but this province had at that time only a short history. It was established as a province in 25 B.C. on the death of King Amyntas, who had reigned over the territories of Pisidia, Isauria, part of Pamphylia,

West Cilicia, Lycaonia, and Galatia, the latter being the geographical district of that name to the north of Lycaonia. The newly formed province consisted of the whole of this area except Pamphylia, which became a new province on its own. The province of Galatia, there-fore, took its name from one of its geographical districts. Henceforth the term Galatia could describe either the geographical district in the north of the province or the whole province. It is this ambiguity which has given rise to the two different theories for the destination of this epistle, the North and South Galatian theories, the former restricting the term Galatia to the geographical area and the latter interpreting it in the provincial sense in order to embrace the area in the south.

Long before the districts mentioned became a Roman province, groups of Celts had settled in the geographical region in the north, being confined there by the victories of the Pergamene kings in the third century B.C. Groups of the same tribes migrated farther into France and settled in Gaul. In the geographical region of Galatia the majority of the inhabitants were Phrygians, although the Galatians were the dominant group.

For a full discussion of the historical and geographical back-ground, cf. Lightfoot, 1–17, and especially Ramsay, 1–234.

The Traditional Interpretation of Galatia

Until the nineteenth century no commentator seems to have disputed that the Galatians were those of the northern geographical district. There were three main cities in this district, Ancyra, Pessinus, and Tavium, of which the first became the capital of the Roman province. In view of this interpretation it was maintained that Paul must have visited and established churches in these three cities on his second missionary journey in accordance with Ac. 16.6. It will be best to enumerate the various arguments for this North Galatian theory and then to set down the support for the South Galatian theory, remem-bering that the latter is the challenger of the older tradition.

Arguments for the North Galatian Theory

ARGUMENTS BASED ON THE USE OF THE TERM 'GALATIA'

It is valuable to enquire whether there are any parallels which enable the literary use of the term to be established. Lukyn Williams (pp. xiv–xv) cited three from the Greek Bible, 1 Mac. 8.1, 2; 2 Mac. 8.20; and 2 Tim. 4.10, and thought that the first favours a reference to Gaul but the other two to Galatia in Asia Minor. In the case of 2 Tim. 4.10, however, it cannot be determined whether the geographical or provincial district is meant. In addition there are various extra-Biblical allusions which suggest that the term was not restricted to those of Gallic descent, but also included Phrygians who resided in the northern area. Lukyn Williams thought that the term 'Galatians' was widely used to describe slaves, perhaps because the Roman Consul Manlius (189 B.C.) sold thousands of Galatians into slavery. It was used in the provincial sense subsequent to 25 B.C. by writers such as the elder Pliny and Tacitus when writing officially, and this is readily understandable, but it is disputed that Paul would have used it in this sense. At the same time there was no uniformity of usage, for many other writers use it in the geographical sense (e.g. Strabo, Memnon, Dio Cassius). It would seem that from the popular viewpoint Galatia would generally represent the geographical district.

ARGUMENT BASED ON LUKE'S USE OF NAMES IN ACTS

It may justifiably be claimed that Luke's usual practice in describing the location of places on the journeys of the apostle Paul is to cite the geographical district and not the provincial one. Hence he refers to Pamphylia (Ac. 13.13), Pisidia (13.14), and Lycaonia (14.6), but gives no indication of the provincial district to which they belonged. Moreover, the towns of South Galatia which Paul visited on his first missionary journey (Antioch, Lystra, Derbe) are listed by geographical, not provincial, districts. Had the latter usage been adopted, Luke would have referred to these as Galatian towns. Since he did not do this, it may reasonably be supposed that he treated 'Galatia' as a geographical district. This will throw light on the next matter to be discussed.

PAUL'S VISITS TO GALATIA ACCORDING TO AC. 16.6 AND 18.23

If the preceding deductions from Luke's practice are correct, the two occasions when Paul is said to have visited Galatia (Ac. 16.6 and 18.23) must refer to the geographical district and not to the province. The first occurrence reads as follows: 'And they went through the region of Phrygia and Galatia, having been forbidden by the Holy Spirit to speak the word in Asia.' If this is a correct interpretation of the text of Acts, two regions are referred to which are presumably mutually exclusive, in which case Galatia cannot be the province because that included part of Phrygia. This interpretation has been challenged by supporters of the South Galatian theory (see below for arguments), but it must be admitted that the above seems a natural interpretation of Luke's words. In Ac. 18.23, the statement reads: 'After spending some time there he departed and went from place to place through the region of Galatia and Phrygia, strengthening all the disciples.' The same remark as above applies here, and therefore a second visit to the geographical region of Galatia seems to be involved.

It is naturally essential to the North Galatian theory to establish that Paul visited the northern regions, for had he not done so he could not have addressed an epistle to the churches which he founded there. On the other hand, it should be noted that in neither reference in Acts does it state that Paul established churches, although this would be a reasonable inference from 18.23.

ARGUMENT BASED ON ETHNICAL CONSIDERATIONS

Lightfoot (13ff.) attempted to support the North Galatian theory by an appeal to the known characteristics of the Gallic people. They were, according to him, fickle. This would then account for the fact that the Galatians were so quickly turning away from their faith and were showing tendencies towards sins of temper (cf. Gal. 5.19, 20). But the argument here does not present solid ground for the theory, although it might be appealed to as corroborating evidence if the

theory were proved on other grounds. The Gallic people were not
the only people in the ancient world who were fickle, and little
importance may therefore be attached to this consideration. It should
also be noted that the majority of the inhabitants of Galatia were
Phrygians and not of Gallic descent.

AN ARGUMENT BASED ON GRAMMAR

In both of the Acts passages already mentioned (16.6 and 18.23) the
same verb is used of the journey of Paul in the Galatian area (i.e. to
pass through—*diēlthon*). According to Moffatt, this means more than
simply movement through, and involves a preaching ministry. This
argument is slight, but that based on the participle (having been
forbidden—*kōluthentes*, Ac. 16.6) is more weighty. It is contended
that the prohibition on Paul not to preach in Asia *after* visiting the
churches in the South Galatian cities would leave him with no
alternative but to turn northwards. It may, therefore, be contended
that the grammar of Ac. 16.6 requires the assumption that the Galatia
visited after Asia was closed to Paul must have been the geographical
district of that name. This grammatical argument has been disputed,
as will be mentioned below, but if it stands it is fair evidence of Paul's
missionary activity in North Galatia on the second journey.

In support of this theory, cf. especially Lightfoot 1–35, Oepke
4ff., Schlier 5ff., Bonnard 9ff., Moffatt, *Introduction to the Literature
of the New Testament* ([3]1918), 90ff.

ARGUMENTS FOR THE SOUTH GALATIAN THEORY

The arguments for this theory are of two kinds. The first type consists of reassessment of the arguments used to support the North
Galatian theory, and the second type consists of appeal to additional
considerations. They will be dealt with in that order.

A REASSESSMENT OF THE EVIDENCE FROM AC. 16.6 AND 18.23

Sir William Ramsay, the most notable advocate of the South Galatian
theory, recognized that these two Acts references were fundamental
to the traditional theory. It could not be shown that Paul was

addressing the North Galatians unless it could be proved that he had
visited the northern area. But Ramsay was not convinced that either
Ac. 16.6 or 18.23 were referring to Phrygia *and* Galatia. He maintained that both words should be regarded as adjectives, in which
case they would refer to the Phrygic-Galatic region (401ff). He understood by this the part of the province of Galatia which was known
geographically as Phrygia and was inhabited by Phrygians. In 18.23,
where the order of reference is reversed and where the construction
is slightly changed, the meaning would be the Galatian province and
Phrygia, i.e. that part of Phrygia in the province of Asia. Moreover,
this interpretation would suggest that by the Phrygic-Galatic region
Luke means to imply that Paul was not breaking new ground but
going again over old ground. This would mean that he not only
visited Derbe and Lystra, as mentioned in Ac. 16.1–5, but also other
places in this region, including Antioch in Pisidia and Iconium. If
this interpretation is correct the course of events on the second
missionary journey, after Paul's passing through Syria and Cilicia,
was as follows. He revisited Derbe and Lystra, specially mentioned
because of Timothy joining him there. From this point he had
intended to preach in Asia, but was by some means forbidden to do
so by the Holy Spirit, and so proceeded *via* Iconium to Antioch and
then passed up the Phrygic-Galatic district running northwards along
the Asiatic border until he reached that part of the border opposite
to Mysia. Being again prevented by the Spirit from preaching in
Bithynia, he evidently proceeded along the Asiatic-Bithynic border,
then through Mysia until he came to Troas. It must be admitted that
this is a more logical interpretation of Paul's movements in Ac. 16
than is possible under the North Galatian theory, in which a very
considerable and difficult detour is involved. It is no different in
18.22, 23, which describes in few words the commencement of the
third missionary journey up to the time of Paul's arrival at Ephesus.
The most natural reading of this brief statement would suggest that
Paul took the opportunity of strengthening the churches which lay
on the route from Palestine to Ephesus, and it is certainly difficult to
imagine that he would have chosen a route through North Galatia.
It may, therefore, be said that although it is not impossible, it is

improbable that Paul visited North Galatia on either the second or third journeys. But if he did not do so, the North Galatian theory must collapse.

PAUL'S USE OF PROVINCIAL TITLES

The first consideration has dealt with Acts, but supposing that the evidence did support the idea of visits by Paul to North Galatia it would still not be proof that Paul is addressing these churches, unless it can be shown that when Paul uses the terms 'Galatia' and 'Galatians' he meant the same as Luke did. There would, of course, be some expectation that both Luke and Paul are reflecting popular usage, which would in turn support the contention that Paul must mean the same as Luke. And yet further investigation shows that, unlike Luke, Paul often prefers provincial titles, especially when referring to the location of churches. It will be most valuable first to consider the regions named in this epistle apart from Galatia. These are Arabia (1.17), Syria and Cilicia (9.21), and Judea (1.22). Churches are specifically mentioned only in the case of Judea. A parallel phrase occurs in 1 Th. 2.14, but in that case there is a reference to Jewish persecutors (cf. also Rom. 15.31), which might suggest that the region described was essentially Jewish. In this case, it would not seem that the province was in mind since it included both Judea and Samaria. At the same time it is difficult to believe that Paul was restricting his reference to the churches in the specific geographical region of Judea. Was Galilee excluded? Of the other districts mentioned Arabia was in all probability the province (see comment on 1.17), although in 4.25 it may be used in a more restricted geographical sense. Syria and Cilicia are mentioned together in Ac. 15.23, 41. In the former of the two references they are included in the address of James's letter and in the latter they represent the districts containing churches which Paul and Silas visited on the second journey. Thus Paul's usage agrees with Luke's. But this would not seem to support the contention that Paul used provincial titles since both these districts were probably in Paul's time united to form one province in the Roman administration. In this case therefore no certainty can be achieved, but it is worth noting that Paul is describing his movements, not giving information about churches, and it may be that on this occasion his mind dwells on the geographical regions through which he passed (but see comment on 1.21). There would appear to be some intended contrast between the 'regions' of Syria and Cilicia and the 'churches' in Judea mentioned in the same verse.

In other epistles there are several instances where churches referred to are grouped under provincial titles. In 1 C. 16.19 Paul includes a greeting from the 'churches of Asia', and it would seem almost certain that he means the churches in the province of Asia in accordance with current usage. The only consideration which might appear to militate against this is the fact that in the early church the churches of Phrygia were sometimes separated from the churches of Asia, although Phrygia was part of provincial Asia (Tertullian. *Contra Prax.* 1, Letter of Churches of Vienne and Lyons (Euseb, *Ch. Hist.* 5.1.3)). Several times Paul refers to the believers in Macedonia and also on other occasions mentions his travels to and from Macedonia (e.g. Rom. 15.26; 2 C. 8.1; 9.2, 4; 11.9; 1 Th. 1.7; 4.10; note also 2 C. 1.16; Phil. 4.15). In these cases the province of Macedonia is almost certainly meant. The same goes for Achaia (Rom. 15.26; 16.5; 1 C. 16.15; 2 C. 1.1; 9.2; 11.10; 1 Th. 1.7, 8). An objection has been raised to this interpretation of 2 C. 1.1, since this appears to refer to all the believers including those at Athens, which was independent of the province of Achaia (so Williams, xix). Nevertheless an objection of this nature cannot invalidate the clear usage of Paul in referring to groups of churches in any district by the provincial name. This must have an important bearing on Paul's use of the term 'Galatians'. Although in theory it could be either geographical or provincial, it would accord with Paul's normal practice more closely if it were the latter.

A DIFFERENT INTERPRETATION OF THE GRAMMAR IN AC. 16.6
It has been seen that advocates of the North Galatian theory assume that the participle (having been forbidden) must be retrospective and must give the reason why Paul proceeded to Phrygia and Galatia. But this is not in harmony with Luke's grammatical usage. Askwith (7ff.) makes out a strong case for the view that the participle cannot be

retrospective. His understanding of it is that Paul and his companions proceeded towards Mysia, having gone through Phrygia and Galatia and having been forbidden to preach in Asia. This would slightly modify the suggested sequence of developments mentioned above. It would mean that the prohibition did not come until Paul was at Antioch on the borders of Asia. This certainly seems a reasonable interpretation and would at the same time exclude the North Galatian theory by making the prohibition subsequent to the Galatian journey.

THE ACCOUNT IN ACTS OF THE ESTABLISHMENT OF THE SOUTH GALATIAN CHURCHES AND THE LACK OF INFORMATION ABOUT NORTH GALATIAN CHURCHES

From the amount of space devoted to the incidents which occurred on the first missionary journey when the South Galatian churches were established it is obvious that Luke had special interest in these churches. The first happenings in any piece of work are of great importance to the historian because they illustrate the principles on which the work is based. Luke is clearly concerned to show that it was first of all in these churches that the circumcision problem arose, and that this led to the important conference at Jerusalem. If Paul in this epistle is addressing the South Galatians the details would fit quite naturally into the Acts account. But the North Galatian theory is here at a serious disadvantage, for Acts tells us nothing about any churches in North Galatia. Admittedly this consideration may seem to be weakened by the fact that Acts says nothing about the church at Colossae, which Paul also addresses. Yet it would be strange indeed if there was the same unresolved circumcision problem in both the Southern and Northern Galatian church, and Paul addressed only the latter by letter. It is not impossible, but nevertheless strange. It would seem preferable to suppose that this epistle was addressed to those churches of which we know much rather than to those of which we know nothing, not even for certain whether they existed.

THE APPROPRIATENESS OF THE NAME 'GALATIANS' FOR THE SOUTH
GALATIAN PEOPLES

It was Ramsay's contention that no other name was available to
describe comprehensively the people of all the towns in the South
Galatian area. They could not be called by the geographical area to
which they belonged since more than one geographical term would
be involved. However, this claim has not gone without challenge. It
has been considered that the Southerners would have been insulted
by the title 'Galatians', because it would have gone against their
national feelings (cf. Bonnard). But it may be argued that they may
have regarded it with favour because of the advantages that Roman
occupation had brought with it. Whatever objections the Southerners
may have had, if Ramsay is right that no other all-inclusive term was
available it would be a strong argument for the South Galatian
theory.

AN ARGUMENT DRAWN FROM PAUL'S PHYSICAL CONDITION

Whatever the precise nature of the ailment referred to in 4.13 (see
Commentary), it is clear that Paul came to these people on the first
visit in a poor state of health and actually states that this provided
the occasion of his visit. From this somewhat enigmatic statement it
may be deduced that through illness Paul was obliged to change his
sphere of service to a district healthier than that in which he had been
working. Under the North Galatian theory, Paul would have been
involved in a tortuous mountainous journey, which is not easy to
imagine for an ill man. It will not do to maintain that the illness did
not develop until after the journey, for this would not be supported
by Paul's own statement. Some advocates of the North Galatian
theory connect this illness with the prohibition mentioned in Ac.
16.6, but this is most unlikely. It would not be a normal method of
prohibition by the Spirit (cf. Askwith, 29ff.). It seems better to
interpret them separately, in which case the prohibition not to preach
in Asia had no connection with the initial preaching at Galatia. On
the South Galatian theory the first journey of Paul to Galatia was
from the low-lying district around Perga in Pamphylia to Pisidian

Antioch, a none too easy but much shorter journey than that involved in the other theory.

AN ARGUMENT FROM THE COLLECTION DELEGATES

According to Ac. 20.4, several companions accompanied Paul from Macedonia to Jerusalem. It is generally assumed that these were delegates from various churches who had been appointed to represent them in Jerusalem. Luke connects most of them with their home churches, and this may seem to support the theory of delegates. If so, it is to be noted that Gaius of Derbe (unless the Western reading 'Doberus' is preferred, in which case Gaius was a Macedonian) is mentioned and he is linked with Timothy. Both of these were from South Galatia. No-one is mentioned, however, from North Galatia. But there are some weaknesses in the argument, since no delegates are mentioned from Corinth, which certainly participated in the scheme. That the Galatian churches contributed is equally clear from 1 C. 16.1, and it would seem probable therefore that if Galatia contributed it would be represented. Nevertheless, since Acts makes no mention of delegates and since there is no guarantee that every church would have been able to send a delegate, this argument must be treated as conjectural. It may even be that the North Galatian churches (if existent) declined to join in the scheme.

THE REFERENCE TO BARNABAS

In the course of his explanation of his own position Paul refers to his companion Barnabas three times (2.1, 9, 13). If we may deduce from this that Barnabas was known personally to the Galatians, it would be a strong basis for maintaining the South Galatian theory, since, according to Acts, Barnabas accompanied Paul only on the first missionary journey. It must be conceded that the references would have had much more point if the readers could recall their own contacts with Barnabas, for they would know that he was a reliable corroborating witness of the truth of what Paul is here stating. This seems particularly so when the Apostle in verse 13 says that 'even Barnabas' defected. This implies that the Galatians will be as surprised as Paul himself that such a man as Barnabas would be carried away.

Nevertheless, too much weight must not be placed on this argument, since Paul refers to Barnabas when writing to the church at Corinth (1 C. 9.6) where, as far as is known from Acts, Barnabas had never visited and where he had certainly not accompanied Paul. Nevertheless, Paul assumes that the Corinthians will be well acquainted with the fact that he and Barnabas had at one stage been prepared to labour for Christ while supporting themselves by the work of their own hands. In spite of this argument, however, it would seem reasonable to regard these allusions to Barnabas in Galatians as possible support for a South Galatian destination.

THE OPPOSITION

It is not possible to define with any precision the origin of the Judaistic party apart from the fact that they appear to have had contact with the Jerusalem party. According to Ac. 15.1, the circumcision question had been brought up by Judean Jews, and if these were responsible for the trouble in Galatia they must have had access to the churches there. Yet the very existence of active Judaizers in the Galatians' churches would favour the South Galatian theory rather more than the North theory, since it is not easy to suppose that Paul and his companions had been pursued into the more inaccessible regions of the North. At the same time it cannot be pronounced impossible. (Compare Munck's contention (87ff.) that the Judaizers were Gentiles who were misrepresenting the opinion of both Paul and the Jerusalem apostles.)

INCIDENTAL INFERENCES

In Paul's defence of his position in chapter 2, he maintains that he did not yield to the false brethren during his Jerusalem visit so that the truth of the gospel might continue 'for you' (i.e. the Galatians). This would seem to imply that the truth had been declared to them before the Jerusalem visit, and if so this must have happened on the first missionary journey, in which case South Galatia would be specifically in mind. It is, of course, possible to interpret the 'you' more generally of Gentile Christians as a whole (cf. Askwith, 81), but this would not suit the context so well.

Other allusions which have been claimed to support a South Galatian destination are found in 4.14 and 6.17. The former, referring to Paul's reception among the Galatians as 'an angel of God', has been supposed to be an indirect reference to the incident at Lystra where Paul was called Hermes, but the connection of thought here is highly dubious (cf. Askwith, 77). It is more likely that 6.17 ('the marks of the Lord Jesus') could bear some reference to Ac. 14.19, where Paul is said to have suffered from the stoning by Jews at Lystra. Yet the apostle had suffered many more 'marks' than these, and there is no necessity to connect his reference with any specific occurrence known to the readers. Nevertheless since some of the South Galatians had certainly been witnesses of the infliction of scars, Paul's reference to them would be invested with added meaning if the South Galatians were the addressees.

These incidental inferences carry weight only in so far as they corroborate a position based on firmer grounds.

In support of this theory, cf. Ramsay, Duncan, xviiiff., Burton, xxiff., Ridderbos, 22ff.

CONCLUSION

In the foregoing discussion, it will have become evident that there is much to be said for both these theories. Indeed, it is not possible to be dogmatic in conclusion for this reason. Both theories can still claim the support of eminent names, and whichever view is favoured it must be held with some caution. On the whole it would seem preferable to hold the South Galatian theory, since this involves only churches of whose origin we know from Acts. But the exegesis of the epistle will not be greatly influenced by our decision regarding destination. The major factor affected is the date, although this is equally difficult to decide, as will be seen from the following discussion.

7. THE DATE OF THE EPISTLE

It is impossible to discuss the date of the Epistle to the Galatians without taking into account the divergent views regarding destination, although destination does not necessarily determine date. In the case of those who adhere to the North Galatian destination the dating of the epistle must be confined within narrow limits, for the hypothesis requires that it should have been sent while Paul was on the third missionary journey. But the South Galatian theory makes room for a much wider range of possibilities, as the following discussion will show.

DATES ACCORDING TO THE NORTH GALATIAN THEORY

If the apostle has visited the readers twice (see 4.13 in the Commentary) and if the North Galatian theory is maintained, the date must be after the events of Ac. 18.23. While this interpretation of Gal. 4.13 is not necessarily correct, the setting of the epistle during the course of, or soon after, the Ephesian ministry is generally conceded under this theory. In view of Gal. 1.6 it is considered unlikely that much time has elapsed since Paul's last visit, and this would support an Ephesian origin, although the adverb ('quickly') need not relate to the last visit but to the readers' conversion.

There is little other data to enable us to affix a date with any greater precision. It has been maintained that the contents of this epistle are an indication of a rather earlier date than the Epistle to the Romans, since the latter was clearly not produced under the same emotional tension as Galatians, although both deal with the same general theme. This was the contention of Lightfoot, who further maintained that since the Jewish controversy is absent from the Corinthian epistles, the Galatian epistle must have been subsequent to these. This led him to place the epistle in the course of Paul's visit to Corinth after his withdrawal from Ephesus. But this last argument is by no means satisfactory unless it can reasonably be assumed that the Jewish controversy developed simultaneously in all churches, but, in addition to lacking proof, such an assumption is highly improbable. Even without this supporting argument, Lightfoot's arrangement of the order of the epistles (Corinthians, Galatians, and Romans) has much to commend it, and may be correct (48, 49).

There is much more to discuss under the South Galatian theory, especially the problem which arises from Paul's visits to Jerusalem.

Dates According to South Galatian Theory

The dividing line between an early and a later dating of the epistle under the South Galatian theory is the important occasion of the Jerusalem Council in Ac. 15. Some date it before this Council and others after, the latter dating often coinciding with that according to the Northern theory. The data on which the matter must be decided may be summarized as follows.

THE THEORY THAT AC. 15 AND GAL. 2 REFER TO THE SAME VISIT

This is stated first because it is the traditional view. It is, of course, required by the North Galatian theory which *ex hypothesi* places the epistle after the Council of Jerusalem, but it may also be strongly maintained under the South Galatian theory. There are certainly some similarities between Ac. 15 and Gal. 2. In both passages Paul is accompanied by Barnabas, although an interesting difference is that Titus accompanies them in Gal. 2, but no mention is made of him in Ac. 15 (see later comment on this). In both passages Paul goes up to Jerusalem. It is also clear from both passages that Paul has to contend with Judaizers who are requiring Gentiles to be circumcised. In both accounts, moreover, Peter and James are named among the leading Jerusalem apostles. On the surface it would appear a reasonable proposition that Gal. 2 is to be equated with Ac. 15. There are two further, quite incidental, coincidences which add corroboration to the idea. Acts 15 tells us who 'the false brethren' are who Paul says had been brought in unawares. They were believers who still belonged to the sect of the Pharisees (Ac. 15.5), which would well explain why Paul deals at such length with the issue of circumcision. It should further be noted that in both accounts Paul and Barnabas are said to have laid before the Jerusalem leaders a report of their preaching (cf. Ac. 15.12; Gal. 2.2). Nevertheless, the theory is not without its difficulties.

The first difficulty arises from the word 'again' (*palin*) in Gal. 2.1.

It is reasonable to suppose that after referring to his first visit to Jerusalem Paul meant by 'again' his next visit. But according to Ac. 11.30 he had visited Jerusalem between his first visit (Ac. 9 (= Gal. 1.18)) and the Council visit, i.e. what is generally known as the famine visit. The significance of this will be considered later, when the theory that Gal. 2 = Ac. 11 is considered. But the present theory needs an adequate explanation of the *palin* in 2.1. The usual explanation is that, on the occasion of the famine visit, Paul had no communication with the Jerusalem apostles. Acts 11.30 states that Barnabas and Saul delivered the contributions of the Antioch church to the *elders* at Jerusalem. This is a reasonable explanation, although not altogether convincing, as the discussion which follows will show.

A way out of this difficulty which has been favoured by some scholars is to dispute the historicity of Ac. 11.30, or else to regard it as a duplicate of Ac. 15. But there is no supporting evidence for either of these views, and they can therefore carry no weight as a solution to the present problem. To make Ac. 11.30 to refer to the same visit as Ac. 15 requires no little ingenuity, to say the least, and the most natural and obvious interpretation is to take Acts as it stands and to assume two quite distinct visits. (Cf. A. C. McGiffert, *A History of Christianity in the Apostolic Age* (1897), 171.)

The second difficulty arises from differences between the accounts in Gal. 2 and Ac. 15. In the latter passage Paul and Barnabas meet the assembled company of apostles and elders, whereas Gal. 2 gives a very different impression. There the idea seems to be of conversations with a few of those who were held in repute, a kind of committee of leaders. The difference must at once be admitted, but are the two accounts incompatible? Behind every public conference there are committees which plan procedure and policies, and it would not be strange, therefore, to discover that the same thing happened at this official gathering of the Jerusalem church. In this way it is certainly possible to reconcile Gal. 2 and Ac. 15, but some explanation still needs to be given for Paul's omission to mention the official decisions of the full Council. The best that can be done is to claim that Paul's main interest is not in authoritative pronouncements of church councils, but in his relationship with the leading apostles individually. This is not an altogether satisfactory explanation, and the difficulty of Paul's silence must remain (see further discussion below).

In close connection with this is another omission on the part of the apostle, i.e. his failure to mention the so-called Council decrees, the prohibitions decided on as the sole requirements for Gentile Christians (cf. Ac. 15.20). Paul refers on the other hand to the leaders' request to Paul and Barnabas to remember the poor (Gal. 2.10), while he explicitly states that they 'added nothing to me' (2.6). Again the recourse of adherents of the theory that Ac. 15=Gal. 2 must be to an argument based on Paul's independence, which explains his preference for theological reasoning rather than an appeal to decrees. This must be conceded as a possibility, but does not greatly diminish the surprise occasioned by Paul's omission.

Another problem of a personal kind is that Paul makes perfectly clear that when he went up to Jerusalem he went up 'by revelation' (Gal. 2.2), whereas Acts make equally clear that he went up as representative of the Antioch church. Again it is not impossible to regard these statements as different aspects of the same event. From the historian's point of view the official position as delegate from Antioch was the most obvious aspect to record, but Paul himself, conscious as he was that all his affairs were under divine control, fastens upon his own reactions. He recognized the momentous character of his mission. To him it was not a parochial dispute between Antioch and Jerusalem. It was a matter of life and death for the church as a whole. He realized that he was being sent by God. There is, therefore, no fundamental discrepancy between Gal. 2 and Ac. 15 on this account (cf. a similar change of emphasis when Ac. 9.29, 30 is compared with Ac. 22.17ff.). It should, of course, be noted that the same difference would obtain if Gal. 2 refers to the visit of Ac. 11.30.

Another problem is the account of Paul's dispute with Peter at Antioch in Gal. 2.11ff. As Paul records it, the dissension would appear to have followed his discussion with the Jerusalem apostles, in which case some adequate explanation would need to be given of Peter's inconsistency. It constitutes a difficulty that Peter acts so blatantly against the decisions of the Council to which he himself had been a party. It may, of course, be maintained that the Council did not deal with the issue of Jewish-Gentile fellowship, although it is difficult to imagine how the question of Gentile membership could be discussed without reference to the problem of social intercourse, which must have arisen as soon as Gentiles were admitted on equal terms. There seems no real alternative but to regard Peter's action as inconsistent, as if he himself had not thoroughly thought through the principles of his own behaviour or its social implications.

To avoid having to adopt such a poor view of Peter some interpreters have claimed that the passage Gal. 2.11ff. actually preceded the narrative of Gal. 2.1–10 in chronological sequence. If this could be maintained it would certainly lessen the charge of inconsistency against Peter. But Gal. 2.11 does not lead one to suppose that Paul is recalling an earlier incident, and such a view tends to violate Paul's grammar (cf. Duncan's discussion of this, xxv).

THE THEORY THAT AC. 11.30 AND GAL. 2.1–10 REFER TO THE SAME VISIT
This represents the only alternative to the view just discussed. It certainly avoids some of the difficulties of the other view, but is not without difficulties of its own.

Its first advantage is that the *palin* of Gal. 2.1 may be taken literally as the *next* visit. This means that Paul need have no fear that any accuser will be able to confront him with another visit to Jerusalem which he has failed to mention. While this is an advantage, too much stress should not be laid upon it since Ac. 11.30 states quite explicitly that Barnabas and Paul delivered to the 'elders' the alms which the Antiochene church had collected. If 'elders' are distinct from 'apostles', it would have to be maintained that Paul and Barnabas saw both groups. Certainly Ac. 15.6 draws a distinction between apostles and elders, and it is therefore almost certain that the same distinction must be made in Ac. 11.30.

It will at once be apparent that it is easier to fit the informal character of Gal. 2 into the narrative of Ac. 11.30 than into Ac. 15, and this is a point in favour of the theory under discussion. The major problem, however, is the extent to which Paul and Barnabas would have had opportunity to discuss with any of the apostles. It was during a time of political agitation against the apostles, James of Zebedee being killed by Herod and Peter imprisoned. It may seem improbable that such a time would have been favourable for the discussion of so momentous a matter as Gal. 2 supposes. There is also the added difficulty of understanding the subsequent Council if the matter had already been agreed by the apostles, unless, of course, the apostles had not carried with them the narrower Jewish Christian party which was causing the trouble.

Another advantage of this theory is that it completely accounts for Paul's omission of the Council decrees by providing the opportunity of dating the epistle before the Council. It would undoubtedly be a more natural explanation of the omission than an appeal to Paul's independence, especially in view of the fact that he is anxious to prove in Gal. 2 the substantial agreement of the Jerusalem leaders with his position.

If the identification under discussion is correct it would be simpler to explain Peter's action at Antioch, for it would mean that it occurred before any official apostolic policy had been agreed. At the same time it does not absolve Peter from inconsistency, for he had already had social fellowship with Gentiles at Cornelius's house before the visit of Paul to Jerusalem in Ac. 11.30. Indeed he had already defended his action before the other apostles and elders at Jerusalem against the circumcision party. There is, in fact, no way of saving Peter from the charge of inconsistency. All that can be said is that it is lessened if the incident happened before the Council.

It is possible under this theory to make a reasonable reconstruction of the course of events, drawing upon both the Epistle to the Galatians and Acts. (1) When the Antioch church heard of the distress among the churches of Judea they decided to send a contribution in the hands of Paul, Barnabas, and Titus. (2) The latter, although a Gentile, was not obliged to be circumcised (Gal. 2.3). (3) The apostles recognized Paul's ministry to be among the uncircumcised, and requested him and Barnabas to continue to remember the poor, which, as Paul himself says, was the very thing that he was eager to do. (4) As a result of this visit Jewish–Gentile fellowship was permitted at Antioch and was assented to by none other than Peter himself when he visited them. But both Peter and also Paul's own associate Barnabas declined to have fellowship with Gentiles after their action had been criticized by some who claimed to represent James. (5) Following this incident, Barnabas and Paul were commended by the Antiochene church to their first missionary journey, in the course of which many Christian communities were established, mainly in South Galatia. These were Gentile churches and the members were therefore uncircumcised. But when Paul and Barnabas arrived back at Antioch and informed the church about the position, opposition again arose from the Judean Christians. It may be surmised that a considerable group in Jerusalem were alarmed at the idea of Gentiles joining the church without circumcision, and so dispatched representatives not only to Antioch but also to the South Galatian churches. (6) The church at Antioch recognized the need for an opportunity to discuss the question and sent Barnabas and Paul to Jerusalem for the purpose. At some time just before or during the journey the Epistle to the Galatians may have been written (cf. Duncan's reconstruction, xxviff.).

If this reconstruction were correct it would make this epistle the earliest of Paul's epistles. But the theory is not without difficulties. It has already been mentioned that Ac. 11.30 refers to elders but not apostles, and this is a not inconsiderable difficulty. It has been suggested that the matter of the contributions would no doubt come under the jurisdiction of the elders rather than the apostles, but the fact remains that according to Gal. 2 the leading apostles were by no means unconcerned about the relief of the poor. Another difficulty is the omission from Ac. 11.30 of any companions of Barnabas and Paul, thus making it difficult to reconcile with Gal. 2.1, where Paul states distinctly that they took Titus with them. It is just possible, of course, that the Acts' account concentrates on the official Antioch representatives and omits the travelling companion Titus. On the other hand, Acts generally mentions Paul's companions. It must not be overlooked that Ac. 15.2 mentions 'some of the others' who were

appointed to go with Paul and Barnabas, and Titus could well have
been included in the party. It should be noted, of course, that Titus
is never mentioned in Acts, although the references to him in
Paul's Second Epistle to the Corinthians show that he was not only
a most active associate of Paul but was one of his most reliable. The
silence of Acts about him is mysterious.

Perhaps the most serious obstacle to the preceding reconstruction
is that it presupposes that James's men were at first concerned about
Gentile-Jewish fellowship before the more fundamental problem of
Gentile circumcision arose. But it is most improbable that the food
restrictions could have been dealt with independent of the circumcision issue. Another difficulty which has some weight is that Paul
makes clear that he has already worked among the Gentiles. In
Gal. 2.2 he says that he had laid before the leaders the gospel which
he had preached among the Gentiles, while in Gal. 2.7 he says that
the leaders saw that he had been entrusted with the gospel for the
uncircumcised and were prepared to confirm him in it. It is difficult
to see how this could have happened prior to his first missionary
journey, as would be required if Gal. 2 refers to the same visit as
Ac. 11.30. The only recourse would be to suppose that he was
referring to his work at Antioch, a possible interpretation but not
the most natural.

When all these considerations are taken into account it will be seen
that both theories have their difficulties and it is not easy therefore
to choose between them. One consideration which has so far not
been taken into account is chronology, to which some attention
should be given. Paul himself supplies two dates in this epistle. The
first Jerusalem visit is said to be 'after three years' and the next 'after
fourteen years'. It would seem most natural to take these calculations
from the date of Paul's conversion, although Paul's language could
be construed to mean three years after his return to Damascus from
Arabia. However, taking his conversion as the crisis from which he
would tend to date his future movements, it still remains to decide
whether the fourteen years were also from his conversion. If so, the
three years would be included in the fourteen years. If not, a period
of seventeen years would be involved between his conversion and

the visit of Gal. 2.1ff. On the whole, the former of these seems the most probable in view of the importance of the conversion event in Paul's thinking, but the alternative is certainly possible and may be supported by the contention that Paul is giving here a sequence of events.

But is it possible to fix the date of Paul's conversion? Unfortunately not with any precision. It is bound up with the probable date of the crucifixion, which is itself a complex problem which cannot be conclusively settled. A date of A.D. 29-30 seems most favoured. The events in the history of the primitive church up to the conversion of Paul may easily have occupied a year or so, but even here it is impossible to be certain.

If it be assumed first of all that the visit of Gal. 2 was the visit of Ac. 15, an interval of at least fourteen years separated the Council of Jerusalem from Paul's conversion. Since the Council may with reason be dated in A.D. 49, it follows that Paul's conversion could not have been subsequent to A.D. 35. If the period was seventeen years, the conversion date would need to be placed at least as early as A.D. 32, which is a possible date in relation to the most probable date of the crucifixion. But do these dates leave any possibility of an earlier dating of the epistle (i.e. assuming Gal. 2 may correspond to Ac. 11.30)? The problem is to assess the time required for the first missionary journey, which took place between Ac. 11.30 and Ac. 15. There would not appear to be any necessity to assume a period of more than two years, which would date Paul's famine visit to Jerusalem about A.D. 47 and his conversion A.D. 33. Under this theory, however, it would be difficult to reconstruct the sequence of events if a period of seventeen years separated Paul's conversion from the famine, for this would push the conversion into too great a proximity to the Crucifixion. On the whole it must be admitted that from a chronological point of view the former view presents less difficulties.

Another matter worth mentioning is the doctrinal affinities of the epistle, although considerable caution is necessary in using doctrinal development as a datum for chronology, since this is so often a matter of opinion rather than of fact. When a comparison is made between this epistle and the First and Second Epistles of Paul to the Thessalonians, to which period it would belong if it were dated early, there are some marked differences in doctrinal emphasis. The Thessalonian epistles are mainly eschatological, while the Epistle to the Galatians contains few hints of such doctrine. There was, of course, no necessity for Paul to include eschatology in every epistle, even although his mind was being exercised about it. The more important consideration is whether the doctrine in the Epistle to the Galatians is too mature to be placed at the earliest stage of Paul's epistles. It has already been seen that J. B. Lightfoot maintained that doctrinal considerations would place this epistle between the Corinthian Epistles and the Epistle to the Romans, but this assumption is based on a particular theory of doctrinal development. It is not to be ruled out that Paul's first epistle may have shown theological maturity in view of the fact that so many years had already elapsed since his conversion. It is often forgotten that as many years passed before he wrote any epistle as actually spanned the period of his extant letters, and it is impossible to suppose that a mind as active as that of Paul would not have reached considerable maturity after such a period of extensive thought on the major themes of Christianity. Since all the data for any theory of doctrinal development are drawn from Paul's epistles themselves, it is unsatisfactory to use such evidence to determine dating.

To conclude, it may be said that although the evidence is not wholly satisfactory for either view, the earlier dating is slightly preferable for the South Galatian theory, while the later dating is unavoidable for the North Galatian theory. But uncertainty concerning the dating has little effect on the interpretation of the epistle.

For a fuller treatment of the problems surrounding the date of the epistle, cf. Round, Askwith, Duncan, xxiff., Lightfoot, 36ff., Watkins, 243–260.

8. THE MODERN RELEVANCE OF THE EPISTLE
TO THE GALATIANS

It may at first be thought difficult to find much modern relevance in an epistle which was addressed to a specific situation in a first-century group of Christian churches threatened with a danger which belonged essentially to the world of that time, the danger of Christianity becoming stultified as a branch of Judaism. However direct and powerful Paul's historic plea for Christian freedom from Jewish circumcision might be, the circumcision issue is now a back-number. In few, if any, of Paul's other epistles is the argument so closely tied to an historically out-dated issue as in this epistle. Yet in spite of its local historical setting its presentation of timeless Christian principles has generally been recognized. This was doubtless the motive for its preservation and for its unquestioned inclusion in the Christian canon. Before discussing the relevance of the epistle to the twentieth century, it will be valuable to consider three notable historical instances of the application of the epistle to changed circumstances to illustrate the continuous search for relevance from various points of view.

It was in the first half of the second century that Marcion launched his considerable challenge to the Christian church by the setting up of a rival organization, which nevertheless claimed to be nearer to the true apostolic position. This is not the place to discuss the nature of the Marcion heresy, but it is worthy of note that he placed the Epistle to the Galatians at the head of his list of Pauline epistles because it formed the basis of his anti-Jewish approach. Marcion, therefore, regarded the circumcision issue as typical of a general antagonism to Judaism. In spite of the fact that Marcion's exegesis was faulty, his high regard for this epistle is a significant witness to the need felt, not only by the orthodox, but also by the heretical, for an understanding of the epistle which finds a general or contemporary application.

Of much greater significance is the part played by this epistle in the Reformation, particularly in the thinking and writing of Martin

Luther. His commentary on the epistle is a notable exposition of Reformed doctrine, while in many of his other works the influence of this epistle is undeniable. In his great struggle with the papist doctrines he saw in this epistle an illustration of the position in which he himself was placed. He saw the Judaizers as examples of legalists in religion, and therefore as examples of any religious system in which approach to God was based on legal requirements. Luther knew by experience that the monastic system was as much bondage as the situation facing the Galatians. Justification by faith was Paul's answer to their situation and it became equally the answer to Luther's. It is no wonder that this became the main theme of his preaching. Luther's treatment of this epistle, while strongly conditioned by his own contemporary problems, points the way to the modern relevance of the epistle. Legalistic Christianity has shown itself in many forms since Luther's day, but the modern exegete can find no more effective way of dealing with it. It is still as true now as it was then that any form of legalism leads to bondage and that any form of bondage is alien to Christianity as Paul understood it. The modern student of the Epistle to the Galatians should be deeply grateful to Martin Luther for discovering its true relevance.

Our third example belongs to the age of modern criticism. The Tübingen critic, F. C. Baur, like Marcion, found this epistle much to his liking, to such an extent that it furnished him with an effective standard, as he thought, by which to measure the authenticity of the other Pauline letters. His fundamental premiss of an antithesis between Pauline and Petrine Christianity, once it was adopted, was illustrated basically from this epistle. But this approach was far removed from the traditional interpretation, and may be cited as representative of the radical criticism of the nineteenth century which still has some after-effects upon our own. Baur's theory of antithesis is now largely discounted, but there have been few throughout the period of modern criticism who have disagreed with his high opinion of Paul's Galatian letter. It is worth noting that a recent approach to Paul's epistles which is closely akin to Baur's type of criticism also claims Galatians to be the norm for measuring authenticity. A. Q. Morton begins his study of Paul's letters (cf. *Christianity and the Computer* (1964) 24ff.) by asserting that the Epistle to the Galatians is too individualistic to be a forgery, and therefore provides an admirable example for the statistical study of Paul's style, as a result of which he declares all but five Pauline epistles to be unauthentic. His method and conclusions may be challenged, but his high opinion of this epistle will not be disputed.

These illustrations of the adaptation of our epistle from totally different points of view remind us of the abiding interest in it, and supply in some cases a warning against using wrong presuppositions in its exegesis.

It is appropriate to consider whether this epistle has any special relevance for the mid-twentieth century and whether it may still be regarded as one of the major anchorages of the Christian faith. This study will lead us into a consideration of the modern applicability of the main principles which Paul enunciates in the epistle.

(a) A serious warning against legalism. There is no doubt that the Judaizers in Galatia were sincere people who honestly believed that the best possible procedure for Gentiles was for them to be circumcised so as to become *bona fide* members of the Covenant people and loyal adherents of the Jewish legal system. This was all the more confirmed in their mind by the fact that the Gentile Christians acknowledged the Jewish Scriptures as their own and by the constant appeal to those Scriptures in the exegesis of the primitive Church. To the sincere Jewish Christians it seemed quite natural that Gentiles should therefore come within the orbit of Judaism. They were so conditioned to a legalistic approach that they were oblivious to its dangers and indeed to the fatal threat that it contained to the very existence of Christianity itself.

The modern legalists are no less sincere and yet no less wrong. This epistle should be regarded as a challenge to all within the professing Christian Church to examine their basic principles. No-one would deny that in its past history the Church has been seriously weakened by formalism and there is no reason to doubt that religious formalism is still a basic threat to the prosperity of the Church. Any approach to Christianity which rests upon rigid observance of external rules as a means of salvation is no better off than that which the Galatians were in danger of adopting. The rapid decline in church attendance in Britain during the twentieth century has been partially due to the increasing dissatisfaction with a merely formalistic approach. If Christianity consists of no more than formal attendance at the place of worship, its inadequacy in the complex world of the mid-twentieth century becomes immediately apparent. The decline in church attendance is often more a condemnation of the Church than of the present generation. What message would the apostle Paul have given in a situation like this? Since there is a close connection between the circumcision issue and religious formalism in any age, it may safely be assumed that he would have given the same answer. In his mind salvation could come only as a result of personal faith, which made Christianity a living and powerful factor. Wherever the doctrine of justification by faith has not only been proclaimed but believed and acted on, Christianity has become a dynamic influence in human affairs, both individually and corporately.

But the legalistic method has its attractions. If the path to righteousness consists of well-defined duties which can be verified, it is a simpler matter for the individual to apply himself wholeheartedly to such a fixed procedure than if he has to exercise the discipline of a personal faith. Moreover, confusion is bound to arise if too much is left to the individual conscience. The Judaizers at Galatia could point to the law as their standard and expect conformity to it. Paul displaces this with the fruits of the Spirit, no longer appealing to a legal code but to a living organism. To the apostle there was a strong antithesis between them, but in the modern Church strong antitheses tend to be weakened in the attempt to find a common basis for church unity. Paul could not conceive how a formalistic approach could belong to a personal faith. It may well be that one of the most urgent tasks of the modern Church is to consider the relevance of the Pauline doctrine of justification by faith as a basis for church unity.

Of particular importance is a study of this epistle in view of the increasing modern tendency to discount the work of the Reformers. If the doctrine of the Reformers is to find no place in modern theology, this epistle will have correspondingly less significance. The whole of its doctrinal argument is so integral to the doctrine of the

Reformers that it is impossible to retain the epistle while rejecting the doctrine. There is no doubt that any attempt to bridge the gap between the Protestant Churches and the Church of Rome must inevitably begin with the minimizing of the work of the Reformation. It would be difficult enough to achieve this with integrity from a historical point of view, but it is impossible to do so if the abiding relevance of this epistle is to be maintained. Unless justification has ceased to be wholly by faith and Paul proved to be wrong, there can be no essential unity between those groups of Christians who believe that acceptance with God is mediated by faith in Christ and those who impose such a demand as priestly absolution.

(b) Another trend of our modern times is the growth of libertinism. The idea of an ethical code to which members of society may reasonably be expected to conform is at a discount. The individual's liberty has become more important than the well-being of society as a whole. To what extent does this epistle carry a message for an age which is being increasingly dominated by the new morality? At first sight, Paul's references to the freedom which we have obtained in Christ might seem to support the claim to individual liberty. But Paul in this epistle is not on the side of the new moralists. He makes perfectly plain that freedom must not be used as an opportunity for the flesh (5.13). Indeed, Paul's teaching about the flesh is a sufficient answer to those who would abolish time-honoured moral restraints. Much may have altered in the standard of man's intellectual and cultural achievements, but the 'flesh', as Paul understood it, is still unchanged. The concept of true freedom for the space age is no different from the concept which met the need of Paul's time. For this reason the moral relevance of this epistle cannot be overstressed.

Rather than a slackening of standards the apostle is in favour of the reverse. The type of Christianity which he advocated makes rigorous demands upon a man in spite of its anti-legalism. The major demand is for love. It is the primary fruit of the Spirit (5.22). It is the antidote to the works of the flesh (5.19ff.). It is the safeguard against a wrong use of Christian freedom, since it considers service to others of greater esteem than self-indulgence (5.13f.). It is prepared to bear the burdens of others (6.2) and to engage in well-doing for the benefit of others

(6.9f.). And apart from this it is accompanied by other fruits of the Spirit (5.22). The utter negation of the flesh is expressed vividly by Paul in his statement, 'I am crucified with Christ' (2.20). Here then is no immature ethical standard out of which modern man has been able to grow so that he no longer needs such exhortations. Rather is it the reverse. Paul's challenge to his age is even more a challenge to our own. If less of free self-expression and more of the tremendous demands and responsibilities of the Christian life as portrayed in this epistle were taught to teenagers the problems confronting our society would be drastically reduced. The lack of moral discipline cannot fail to produce an increasing crop of what the apostle calls 'works of the flesh'. There is no other answer to the increasing delinquency of our times than the answer that Paul found—the crucifying of the flesh with its desires and passions (5.24).

(c) A relevant enquiry is the extent to which Paul's handling of the Galatian situation was dictatorial and whether or not his action can provide any pattern for the twentieth century. As to the first, there is no denying that Paul took a strong line. Here was no matter for complacency or compromise. Paul sees it as a matter of life and death, and does not hesitate to use the plainest speech. There was no doubt in his mind that peaceful co-existence within the Gentile Church of a party which demanded circumcision and one that did not was impossible. He saw clearly that the former group did not represent pure Christianity at all and therefore must be vigorously excluded. The modern movement towards Church unity would do well to ponder, before being too generous in its attitude towards groups of different outlook, whether or not there is any danger of compromising the true Christian position as understood by the apostolic Church. The apostle Paul believed in adopting a firm line whether in matters of doctrine or discipline, for only in this way could a strong Church be built. There is, of course, a difference between Paul's generation and our own in respect of authority. He could claim apostolic authority which no modern leader can. Yet the only safe basis for theological and moral leadership in the twentieth-century Church is a reassertion of the authority of the apostolic testimony.

(d) Another factor of considerable interest is Paul's use of the Old Testament in this epistle and its relevance to modern approaches. Paul's use may be summarized under three categories. The first is direct citation. He does this rather less often in the Epistle to the Galatians than in some of his other epistles, but when he does it is evident that he cites it with authority. When discussing the position of Abraham, Paul personifies the Scripture (3.8), considering that it possessed power of foresight. This transference of foreknowledge from God to the Scripture is highly significant as revealing Paul's conception that when Scripture speaks it speaks with the voice of God. There is something of this authority behind the formula, 'It is written' (or 'it stands written', after Luther's translation). It is used in 3.10 for a citation from Dt. 27.26, referring to the curse of the law. Another passage from the same book (Dt. 21.23) is introduced almost immediately after by means of the same formula (3.13). It occurs again in 4.21 and 4.27 in the course of the exposition of the allegory about Hagar and Sarah, on the latter occasion for a citation from Isa. 54.1. In the same context appeal is made to what the Scripture says (4.20) in a citation from Gen. 21.10–12. In the practical part of the epistle there is only one direct citation (5.14 from Lev. 19.18). Sometimes Scripture is directly cited without any introductory formula, as for instance in 3.6, 11.

The second use of the Old Testament is seen in the indirect allusions. Sometimes it is no more than a possible echo of Old Testament language as in 1.15, where the language is reminiscent of Isa. 49.1 and Jer. 1.5; or 2.16 where the words are an echo from Ps. 143.2. In the deductions made from the use of the singular rather than the plural in 3.15f., Paul assumes that his readers will be acquainted with the Old Testament promise to Abraham and his offspring (singular). In Gal. 6.16 there seems to be an allusion to the language of Ps. 125.5. These instances are evidence of the high regard in which Paul held the language of Scripture and of the way in which it influenced his own.

The third use of Scripture is that of allegory, of which the Sarah and Hagar incident is an example. Paul's method of deducing spiritual principles from Old Testament incidents by treating them as allegorical in fact finds its most striking example here. Indeed, there are few examples of it elsewhere in his epistles, which should lead to caution before the conclusion is reached that the method was normal in Paul's teaching. Nevertheless the fact that he uses it at all is evidence enough that he considered it valid. It is important, however, to mark a clear distinction between Paul's use of allegory and that of Philo, for, unlike the latter, he treats the characters in this allegory as historical. In fact, the discussion hangs more on the historical relationship between Sarah and Hagar and Isaac and Ishmael than on the allegorical meaning deduced.

The problem arises as to how far Paul's use of the Old Testament is to be regarded as normative for modern exegesis. There is a tendency to dismiss allegory as an unscientific method, while appeal ot the Old Testament as authoritative is as firmly rejected. But is Paul's method so out of date? If there is any real continuity between Christianity and the old order—and there is no denying that Christ and his apostles believed that there was—then the modern exegete must be as clear as Paul over what method of interpretation to follow. From Paul's treatment of the Sarah-Hagar incident it is evident that he considered that Scripture conveyed both a literal and an allegorical interpretation. In a sense the spiritual significance of the historical event is to be found in a re-enactment of similar circumstances, also in history, but with a different set of characters. There is no difficulty in seeing the relationship between Isaac and Ishmael as representative of the relationship between the spirit of freedom seen in Paul's approach and the spirit of bondage seen in the Judaizers. This method is far removed from the highly imaginative allegorization of those early fathers who came under the influence of Greek ways of thinking. In the epistle of Barnabas, for instance, the number of Abraham's servants becomes symbolic in a manner completely alien to the historical context.

CONCLUSION

If the modern Church is to bear any relationship with the apostolic Church it goes without saying that this epistle has a modern relevance as important as its contribution to the first-century Church. It has rightly been described as the charter of Christian freedom, and so long as its teaching is heeded it will never happen that Christianity becomes enslaved in bondage of any kind.

9. ANALYSIS OF CONTENTS

Introduction (1.1-5)
The apostasy of the Galatians (1.6-10)
Paul's apologia (1.11-2.21)
The doctrinal argument (3.1-4.31)
  1. The Galatians' own experience (3.1-5)
  2. The case of Abraham (3.6-9)
  3. The different results from faith and works (3.10-14)
  4. Promise and Law (3.15-29)
  5. Emerging into sonship (4.1-7)
  6. Returning to beggarliness (4.8-11)
  7. A personal appeal (4.12-20)
  8. An allegorical approach (4.21-31)
Ethical exhortations (5.1-6.10)
  1. Christian life as a life of freedom (5.1-15)
  2. Christian life as life in the Spirit (5.16-26)
  3. Christian life in its responsibility to others (6.1-10)
Conclusion (6.11-18)

10. THE ARGUMENT OF THE EPISTLE

INTRODUCTION (1.1-5)

The opening to the epistle is abrupt. It lacks the usual commendations. It asserts Paul's apostolic authority and then asserts his central belief in the victory of Christ over the present evil age. This section ends with a doxology.

The Apostasy of the Galatians (1.6–10)

The apostle substitutes threats in place of thanksgiving. Without hesitation he launches an attack upon the Judaizers, whose gospel is so fundamentally contrary to his own as to constitute another gospel. He cannot refrain from pronouncing an anathema upon them.

Paul's Apologia (1.11–2.21)

Not only his gospel, but his own authority is under attack. Paul proceeds to defend his position in the following manner.

1. He makes clear the origin of his teaching (1.11, 12). It was received from God. A man with a divinely given gospel carries with it a divinely given authority.

2. He records how God called him from a successful career in Judaism to become a preacher of the gospel (1.13–17). Paul lays special emphasis upon his former zeal in order to prove that the commission to preach required a radical transformation of his whole position.

3. It is important for him next to describe his personal contacts with the Jerusalem apostles in order to make clear two facts (1.18–2.10). He needs to show that these apostles did not tell him what to preach, nor however did they disagree with him. He is both independent of them and yet in harmony with them. This double aspect is regarded by Paul as confirmatory of the position he is adopting. His commission to preach to the Gentiles is fully recognized by the 'pillar apostles', Peter, James, and John.

4. An incident is next mentioned which happened at Antioch in which Paul found it necessary to challenge Peter before the whole company (2.11–14). He refers to it in this context to show that his apostolic claims extended beyond mere words into action.

5. This leads Paul to assert that the principle of justification through works of the law is futile, while justification through faith in Christ is completely adequate (2.15–21). This is really the transition stage in the argument, for it prepares the way for the doctrinal section which follows. It is a good example of the way in which Paul turns almost imperceptibly from historical demonstration to theological discussion.

THE DOCTRINAL ARGUMENT (3.1–4.31)

In this section Paul develops his argument that justification by faith is superior to salvation by works, and in the course of it he makes reference to a wide variety of aspects of the Christian position, all of which strengthen his concluding assertion that faith leads to freedom.

1. THE GALATIANS' OWN EXPERIENCE (3.1–5)

There are two things which stand out in this experience: their initial life in the Spirit and their present folly in exchanging it for works of the law. Such an exchange could only have been made, as Paul thinks it over, by the readers being bewitched. No-one in their right minds would be so foolish.

2. THE CASE OF ABRAHAM (3.6–9)

Jewish and Gentile Christians alike acknowledged Abraham, and for this reason the method of Abraham's justification was relevant. Paul proceeds to point out that faith played the key role in Abraham's experience, and then shows that the same method of justification may be valid for all men of faith.

3. DIFFERENT RESULTS FROM WORKS AND FAITH (3.10–14)

These results may be summed up in the two words 'curse' and 'blessing'. Paul shows from the law that a curse rests on all who do not keep the whole law, and then proceeds to show how Christ turned the curse into a blessing by becoming a curse for us.

4. PROMISE AND LAW (3.15–29)

Since Paul has appealed to Abraham, it is necessary for him next to discuss the relationship of Abraham to the law. The fact that Abraham lived 430 years before the law does not affect the issue, since what God has previously promised must be maintained. But if the promise must be kept, what was the purpose of the law? In answer to this question Paul shows that until Christ came the law

functioned as a custodian. But now in Christ the promise has been
fulfilled.

5. EMERGING INTO SONSHIP (4.1–7)

If promise is superior to law so is full sonship superior to the period
of restriction and discipline under tutelage. The apostle develops this
theme by drawing attention to the Father-son relationship of the
believer in Christ, so strongly contrasted with the position of a slave.

6. RETURNING TO BEGGARLINESS (4.8–11)

In view of the privileges inherited by the Galatians, Paul now makes
another direct appeal to them not to return to a bondage no better
than that from which they had been delivered.

7. A PERSONAL APPEAL (4.12–20)

When Paul thinks back over the affectionate relations that he previously sustained with the readers he is perplexed over their present
attitude. They are not now acting as they once did when they were
prepared to do anything for him. He tries a tenderer appeal to them,
moved by his strong desires on their behalf.

8. AN ALLEGORICAL APPROACH (4.21–31)

He turns from appeal to argument again, maintaining that those who
wish to be under law should be prepared to heed the teaching of the
law. He therefore proceeds to illustrate his point by reference to an
Old Testament incident (Sarah and Hagar), which he then allegorizes.
Sarah symbolizes freedom and Hagar symbolizes bondage. The
sequel of the story shows that the son of the free woman and not the
son of the bond-woman inherited the promise. By this means Paul
transfers the thought from Isaac by treating him as symbolic of
Christian believers.

ETHICAL EXHORTATIONS

1. CHRISTIAN LIFE AS A LIFE OF FREEDOM (5.1–15)

If Christians are called to a life of freedom, bondage to the law is thereby excluded. Those who were attempting to lead the Gentile Christians into Judaism must therefore be strongly condemned. Yet a distinction must be made between liberty and libertinism. If love rules, the former will never degenerate into the latter.

2. CHRISTIAN LIFE AS LIFE IN THE SPIRIT (5.16–26)

Here Paul contrasts results of life lived under the opposing principles of flesh and Spirit. By means of an enumeration of examples he shows the immeasurable superiority of life in the Spirit. But he reminds his readers that such a life entails responsibilities as well as privileges.

3. CHRISTIAN LIFE AS A LIFE OF RESPONSIBILITY TO OTHERS (6.1–10)

There will be sympathy towards those carrying burdens and a readiness to share in the burdens. Moreover the believer must be prepared also to share with his instructors and must concentrate on doing good towards others, particularly towards other Christian believers.

CONCLUSION (6.11–18)

Taking the pen in his own hand, Paul adds a concluding appeal by reference to the Cross, which he has determined to place in the centre of his own life as the sole occasion for boasting. He assumes that his readers will see clearly how very different are the motives of the circumcision party. He is confident that he has satisfactorily dealt with the matter and hopes that he will no more be troubled with it.

11. COMMENTATORS AND COMMENTARIES

Since the literature on this epistle has been vast, it will be necessary to be selective in this bibliography. Some of the older commentators, whose work made a significant contribution, will be mentioned, but the major focus of attention will be on more recent books. Some Continental works will be mentioned, but most stress will be placed on English-speaking commentators.

The commentaries of Martin Luther are worthy to head the list.

The first book, *In Epistolam Pauli ad Galatas Commentarius*, was published in 1519, while a German edition of the same book appeared in 1525. Later, in 1535, Luther published a larger work on the epistle, which was not a revision of the earlier work and which appeared under the title of *In Epistolam S.Pauli ad Galatas Commentarius ex Praelectione D. M. Lutheri Collectus*. Luther is famed more for his penetrating grasp of the real essence of Paul's theology than for his exegetical powers. His firm convictions regarding justification by faith made the epistle a special favourite to him. Another of the Reformers, John Calvin, published a commentary on this epistle, included in his *Commentarii in omnes epistolas Pauli Apost.*, 1539. Calvin possessed more lucid exegetical ability than Luther and was less affected in his commentating by his personal feelings.

The next notable exegete was Johann Albrecht Bengel, whose commentary on Galatians in his *Gnomon Novi Testamenti*, 1742, still repays attention. Bengel was a master of conciseness and his comments are frequently suggestive and illuminative.

The nineteenth century produced a spate of commentaries on this epistle. Most of the early ones were by Continental scholars. Of these the most notable was in the series edited by H. A. W. Meyer entitled *Kritisch-exegetischer Kommentar über das Neue Testament*. The volume on the Epistle to the Galatians, written by the editor himself, appeared in 1841 under the title *Kritisch-exegetisches Handbuch über den Brief an die Galater*. The commentary is an example of the careful, but rather too philogical, treatment of the epistle which was typical of German commentating during the last century. An English edition was prepared by Venables and Dickson, 1873. Meyer's commentaries have been re-edited more than once since the original edition, the most recent being by Herman Schlier (eleventh edition, 1951), which continues the same tradition. It is noteworthy that Schlier supports the North Galatian theory.

The most important of the nineteenth-century British commentators were Alford, Ellicott, Sanday, and Lightfoot. Henry Alford's *The Greek Testament* (published in various editions from 1849) contains critical exegetical comments on all the books of the New Testament. Alford was a careful exegete whose observations are still useful. A similar kind of approach is found in Charles John Ellicott's *A Critical and Grammatical Commentary on St. Paul's Epistle to the Galatians*, 1854, which also passed through subsequent editions. This, like Alford's, was based on the Greek text. But Ellicott also edited an *Old Testament and New Testament Commentary for English Readers*, in which the author on Galatians was William Sanday, well known for his commentary with A. C. Headlam on Romans in the I.C.C. Sanday's comments are valuable for bringing out the meaning of Paul's thought and there is a useful excursus on Paul's visits to Jerusalem. But it was the careful exegetical work of Joseph Barber Lightfoot, *Saint Paul's Epistle to the Galatians* (first published in 1865), which was the most notable contribution of nineteenth-century British scholarship. Lightfoot was steeped in the classics, which provided the background to his lexical comments. His exegesis may generally be relied upon to present a sober interpretation, although some of his lexical comments need some modification in the light of more recent studies in Koiné Greek, facilitated by considerable papyrological discoveries.

At the close of the century appeared Sir William Ramsay's *A Historical Commentary on St. Paul's Epistle to the Galatians*, 1900. This work is notable because of its emphasis upon the historical background. It is also the first commentary to be published which was fully committed to the South Galatian theory.

During the twentieth century many valuable contributions to the study of this epistle have been made. A. Lukyn Williams' commentary in the *Cambridge Greek Testament* is valuable for its careful Greek exegesis and for the author's knowledge of the Jewish background. This commentary was published in 1910.

Two years later was published Cyril Emmet's commentary in the *Reader's Commentary*. It is concise, to the point, and suggestive. It was not until 1921 that the commentary on this epistle in the series of *International Critical Commentaries* was published by Ernest de Witt Burton. This author decided to concentrate on lexical considerations, as a result of which his commentary is a mine of information on the key words occurring in the epistle. In fact, in addition to his valuable lexical exegesis, Burton included an appendix which consisted of twenty-one notes on important terms, which is valuable not only for a study of this epistle, but also for Paul's epistles generally. Hans Lietzmann's commentary in his own series of *Handbuch zum Neuen Testament* has been published in several editions, the third being in 1932. It is valuable for background material.

The next important British work was George S. Duncan's commentary in the *Moffatt Commentaries*, which was published in 1934. It is written by an advocate of the South Galatian position, is clear and suggestive, and makes easy reading. While written from a historical point of view, this commentary aims to bring out the essential meaning. Another German advocate of the North Galatian position is A. Oepke, whose commentary, *Der Galaterbrief*, was published in 1937.

Since 1950 several works have appeared. In that year a second edition of Marie-Joseph Lagrange's *Saint Paul, Epître aux Galates*, appeared in the well-known series *Études Bibliques*. This is the best known commentary written from a Roman Catholic point of view. Another French commentator from a very different school of thought is P. Bonnard, whose commentary, *L'Epître aux Galatiens*, 1952, was published in the *Commentaire du Nouveau Testament*. Soon after this a commentary published in English by a Dutch commentator appeared in the series of *New London Commentaries*. This was Hermann N. Ridderbos's *The Epistle to the Galatians*, 1954, which is useful, but on some important passages suffers from over-conciseness.

Of special interest for preachers is the Epworth Preachers commentary by Kenneth Grayston, *The Epistle to the Galatians and Philippians*, 1958. A more popular treatment of the epistle may also be found in William Barclay's *Daily Study Bible* commentary on this epistle (second edition 1958). A fully theological commentary is that of the Swedish scholar Ragnar Bring, *Pauli Brev till Galaterna*, 1958, which has been translated into English by Eric Wahlstrom and published in 1961 in the United States under the title of *Commentary on Galatians*. Bring concentrates on the theological implications of Paul's statements and provides many valuable insights along that line. In 1962 appeared the most recent edition of *Das Neue Testament Deutsch*, volume 8, which includes a commentary on Galatians, originally written by Herman W. Beyer and now edited by Paul Althaus.

The most recent commentary is that of R. Alan Cole (1965) in the *Tyndale New Testament Commentaries*, which provides a concise and well-reasoned guide to the epistle. Cole's exegesis is balanced between good lexical comments and discussions of a more theological nature.

In addition to these books devoted to commentating on the text, there have been other works of a more general nature which deserve to be mentioned. In 1899 E. H. Askwith published an essay entitled *The Epistle to the Galatians, an essay on its Destination and Date*, in which he maintained a South Galatian theory for the destination. Another monograph on the date is D. Round's *The Date of St. Paul's Epistle to the Galatians*, published in 1906. A general treatment of the ideas of the epistle is found in C. H. Watkins' *St. Paul's Fight for Galatia*, 1913. In 1929 J. H. Ropes published his book on *The Singular Problem of the Epistle to the Galatians*. More recently Johannes Munck in his *Paul and the Salvation of Mankind*, 1959, also pays attention to the Galatian problem, as does H. J. Schoeps in his *Paul* (E.T. 1961).

A useful little book of word studies in Gal. 5.19-23 is William Barclay's *Flesh and Spirit*, 1962, while for a general discussion of various approaches to the epistle for study purposes reference may be made to Merrill C. Tenney's *Galatians: The Charter of Christian Liberty*, 1950.

THE EPISTLE TO THE
GALATIANS

GALATIANS

INTRODUCTION 1.1-5

Whereas all the salutations at the commencement of Paul's epistles have certain features in common, each has its own characteristics, and this epistle has one feature which marks it out distinctively from all the rest. It is more abrupt and omits the usual feature of commendation of the readers. It at once reflects the mood of the writer. He is not intent on emphasizing any feeling of affection for this group of Christians, for a more urgent purpose lies before him. He must have felt strongly about the failure of these people to measure up to his expectations, for in all other epistles he uses encouragement at the outset even where he later proceeds to criticism.

Another feature of this salutation is the extended description of the writer. It was not enough to give the name. Even the office was insufficient of itself. It needed authentication, and Paul gives this explicitly. Moreover, the formula used in the greeting is expanded into a theological statement and concludes with a doxology. The Epistle to the Romans can furnish a parallel example of a theological expansion, but lacks a comparable doxology. All this is undoubtedly designed to impress the readers with the fact that this epistle is not sent out as the mere expression of the opinion of an ordinary man. It conveys at once the impression of authority, which underlies the subsequent argument throughout the epistle.

1. **Paul an apostle:** there has been much discussion about the significance of the word 'apostle' in the New Testament. Its Greek derivation shows that the main idea is of a man who is sent, but in New Testament usage it carries a much fuller implication than this. There are some similarities with the Jewish office of *Shaliach*, which carried with it a legal status. The *Shaliach* could speak and act with the same authority as his commissioning agent (Bring). He was not an independent person. His importance was clearly conditioned by the status of the one who sent him. This was certainly true in the case of Paul. He wishes to remind the readers at once that the epistle has an official stamp upon it. He was representing another, i.e. God.

In using this title Paul also identifies himself at once with the circle of apostles appointed by Jesus, and there was obvious point in him doing so when writing to communities which were inclined to draw a distinction between the Jerusalem apostles and other Christian teachers. It was of paramount importance, therefore, for Paul to prove his claims. He was like an ambassador presenting his credentials. His office bore the stamp of its divine origin. This Paul proceeds to clarify in the next statement.

not from men nor through man: there must be significance in the change of preposition and in the change of number. Paul was generally careful in his choice of words, and it may reasonably be supposed that he intended to convey a difference of meaning. The preposition 'from' (*apo*) appears to draw attention to the source of Paul's apostleship, and the preposition 'through' (*dia*) to the agency through which it was bestowed. It was of utmost importance for him to make clear that he was not an apostle because he had been elected to that office by those who had been personally chosen by Jesus. The apostolate was certainly not a democratic institution. The casting of lots for Matthias in Ac. 1.26 was not in itself evidence of the democratic basis of the new Christian society, for it is clear that the assembled company definitely prayed that God would indicate by this means his own choice. But Paul's opponents probably placed him in an inferior category to Matthias, for the latter had apparently been a personal follower of Jesus (cf. Ac. 1.21f.) and had also been a witness of the resurrection. But Paul was outside the stipulation laid down by the Jerusalem church. In answer, he claims his authority to be independent of human appointment. It was true that he had never companied with Jesus and was not a witness to the resurrection, and so would not even have been nominated as a candidate for Judas' vacancy had he been present. In short, Paul had no human sponsors. The whole operation was in an entirely different category. It happened because God had appointed him. This epistle was therefore God-sponsored.

Some have supposed that the singular 'man' may refer to a particular agent in Paul's early Christian experience, such as Ananias (cf. Sanday). If so Paul is definitely repudiating any suggestion that such an intermediary had anything to do with his apostolic office. While this interpretation of the singular cannot be ruled out, it is more likely that Paul is using it almost in a general adjectival sense, equivalent to 'human'.

through Jesus Christ: having stated the negative side of the agency through whom he received his commission by denying human agency, Paul now comes to the positive side. He is thinking of a specific occasion when he became an apostle and it is most natural to connect this up with his encounter with Christ on the Damascus road. That event dominated Paul's later service for Christ for he could never forget the commissioning he received from Christ through the lips of Ananias (cf. Ac. 22.15). It was specially the living Christ to whom he traced his apostleship, for which reason he dwells on the reality of the resurrection.

God the Father: it is significant that Paul not only (a) links the Father with Christ in his commissioning, because he regards God as the ultimate source of all authority, but also (b) links them under the same preposition (*dia*), which suggests that for Paul no distinction could be made between the function of the Father and of the Son in his appointment to the apostolate. It might have been expected that Paul would have referred to the Father first, but it is possible that the existing order was prompted by the contrast with the previous phrase ('not through man'). Jesus

Christ was more than a man, and Paul assumes without question that the Galatian Christians will at once recognize this.

who raised him from the dead: Paul is not here simply calling attention to the miraculous element in the resurrection, although he would not have denied that the event itself was the most stupendous miracle connected with Jesus. It was the significance of the event which struck him forcibly. It was an act of God. It was, therefore, the divine seal upon Jesus as the Messiah. The resurrection banished all doubts about the authenticity of the claims of Jesus, and since Paul's status was bound up inextricably with Christ's, the resurrection became of vital importance to him whenever he thought of his apostolic office. Moreover, if the resurrection of Christ were not a fact the experience on the Damascus road must have been no more than an hallucination. Nothing would ever convince Paul that it was that. He knew Christ was risen and he knew that God had raised him.

2. all the brethren who are with me: it is worth noting that Paul does not name any associates in this epistle as he does, for instance, in his letters to Corinth and Thessalonica. There is good reason for this, for Paul does not wish to give the readers any grounds for supposing that he could not defend himself against the charges brought against him. He therefore refers only to the 'brethren' with him. Two interpretations are possible: (a) He may be referring to a church group in the area where he is at present working, but this is unlikely because it was his usual practice to define the location of church groups; (b) He is probably therefore referring to a small group of his fellow-workers or travelling companions. They cannot be further defined. The word *adelphos* used of membership of a religious community is not new with Christianity, but when used of Christian brotherhood it conveyed a deeper meaning than previously known (Cole). The gospel which Paul preaches is shared by others of the household of faith. It is just possible that the preposition which Paul uses (*sun*, with) may lend support to this view, since it may convey a more intimate association than *meta*.

churches of Galatia: the plural shows that this letter was intended to be shared by a number of communities. It must, therefore, be placed in the category of a circular. And yet it must not be forgotten that all the communities addressed were affected by the same threat to their liberty in Christ. The separate congregations must have formed a fairly closely knit society. The precise location of these churches has been fully discussed in the Introduction.

3. Grace . . . and peace: in the modern world greetings are inclined to be formal and meaningless. But in the ancient world they were rather more significant, particularly among Christians. The Hebrew salutation *shalōm* (peace) implied an absence of hostility between two people on meeting. But for the Christian 'peace' involved also a right relation with God. Christians were at peace with each other because they were at peace with God. The Greek greeting (*chairein*) became adapted to the more meaningful 'grace' (*charis*), a change which is deeply significant. When Paul used the combined form he may have been repeating a formula in common use among Christians (cf. its use in the Old Testament in Num. 6.24–26), but for him the special significance of the combination must be gauged by the key position of both these concepts in his theology. Grace was nothing less than God's unmerited favour in Christ, and peace was one of the major fruits of the Spirit (see 5.22), as well as being the symbol of reconciliation. Reliance on any other method of coming to God, as for instance on circumcision, Paul represents as a defection from grace (5.4). There is no Pauline concept more expressively comprehensive of the essence of the gospel.

from God the Father: there is some textual uncertainty as to whether the true reading is 'God the Father and *our* Lord Jesus Christ', or 'God our Father'. There is MS support for both alternatives and it is not easy to decide, but the latter seems to be the more natural and is paralleled in the salutation in all Paul's earlier epistles except 1 Thessalonians, which omits 'our' altogether. It should be noted that three times in his introduction Paul makes reference to the Fatherhood of God. The description does not occur elsewhere in the epistle except in the Spirit-promoted cry of the adopted son (4.6). There is no doubt, however, that the family idea occupied an important place in Paul's thought as he commenced his epistle.

and our Lord Jesus Christ: as in verse 1, Christ is closely linked with the Father. The grace and peace of Christ are indistinguishable from the grace and peace of God. It is interesting to note that the threefold name used here does not occur again in this epistle until the last verse, where it is also connected with the concept of grace. It is common in Paul's salutations and is frequently used in various other epistles. It may have been a familiar form among Christians in greetings and benedictions, although it was certainly more than a formal title. The combination of Lord (*Kurios*) with Christ (*Christos*=Messiah) is significant as expressing the fulfilment of the highest hopes of both Gentile and Jew. The full title had, therefore, deep theological meaning.

4. **who gave himself for our sins:** the first part of this statement recurs in Gal. 2.20 with the compound verb *paradontos* in place of *dontos*, as here. The idea involved is a delivering up of oneself for a specific purpose, and this conception of Christ's mission was not only fundamental to Paul's message, but was basic to his notion of apostleship. The one who had commissioned him was one who himself knew the meaning of sacrifice. There can be no doubt that Paul is thinking of the death of Christ as a voluntary sacrificial act. Particular significance attached to the phrase 'for our sins' in which the Greek preposition *huper* is used. The phrase is identical to that found in 1 C. 15.3, in which Paul sets out the most fundamental feature of the primitive Gospel as it had been delivered to him by others, i.e. that Christ died for our sins according to the Scripture. When used with such a word as 'sin', the normal meaning of *huper* (on behalf of) becomes modified into the ideas of deliverance and relationship (Burton). Hence Christ's work is inseparably connected with sin. The nature of the connection is not precisely defined, but the following phrase throws valuable light upon it.

to deliver us from the present evil age: the verb used (*exaireō*) is unexpected, for it does not occur elsewhere in Paul's epistles. It suggests deliverance out of the power of another (cf. Ac. 7.10; 12.11). The picture is of Christ as a victor who has conducted a successful rescue operation, an imagery which goes well with Paul's dominant theme of Christian liberty in this epistle. The apostle is not, of course, suggesting removal from an adverse environment, but triumph over it. The idea of the present age (i.e. the present period of time, as compared with a future period, the age to come) as evil is everywhere assumed in Paul's theology, as it is indeed in the teaching of our Lord. The whole world lay in the power of the evil one until Jesus triumphed over him. It is not always easy for modern man to accept this concept, largely because the concept of evil has been understood in a different way from Paul's understanding of it. For him it meant deviation from God's purposes, rebellion against God, transgression of righteous standards. It was not confined to action. It was tracked down to motive. As a consequence no man could claim exemption. This is the burden of argument in Rom. 1–3. Here Paul does not reason it out; he assumes it and expects his readers to assent.

It should be noted that a possible alternative interpretation of 'the present evil age' is 'the age of the evil one, which is now present' (cf. Lightfoot), drawing attention to the triumph of Christ over the agencies of evil. That Paul shared the contemporary belief that society was under the control of corrupt angelic powers cannot be disputed. There are frequent references to these powers in his epistles and there can be no doubt that in the present passage the evil age mentioned is closely linked with the widespread belief in principalities and powers (cf. the study on this aspect of Paul's theology in G. B. Caird's *Principalities and Powers*, 1956). It was one of the major aspects of Christ's work that the power of these evil agencies was overcome.

according to the will of our God and Father: the will of the Father in the redemptive acts of Christ is an important aspect of Paul's theology and is indeed integral to all Christian theology. It excludes any notion that what happened to Christ was an accident of circumstances. It was all part of a plan to overthrow evil and to deliver man from it. In several of his epistles Paul mentions that his apostleship was by the will of God, and this springs from his deep conviction that the will of God is behind every facet of the Christian gospel. In emphasizing it here the apostle is preparing his readers for the major theme of this epistle—the deliverance effected by Christ. It was never the divine purpose that men should be in bondage.

5. to whom be the glory: it is unusual for Paul to break into a doxology in the introduction to a letter, although Ephesians supplies an extended example. It is, moreover, unexpected in an epistle in which Paul finds nothing to recommend in his readers. Perhaps it was his disappointment over the lack of progress of these Christians which caused Paul to turn his thoughts towards God. The doxology appears to be spontaneous. It should be noted that the presence of the article concentrates attention on that glory which belongs particularly to God. The glory of God in Christian thought was conditioned by the Old Testament conception. **for ever and ever:** again this shows Old Testament influence. It literally means 'the ages of the ages', which expresses an undefinably extensive duration of time, an appropriate idiom in an ascription to God. The glory of God has an ever enduring quality which contrasts vividly with the fading splendour of man's greatest glory.

THE APOSTASY OF THE GALATIANS 1.6–10

6. I am astonished: in place of the usual thanksgiving the apostle gives vent to an unrestrained expression of amazement, which draws attention to a matter over which he clearly felt deeply.

so quickly: the reference would appear to be to the rapidity with which the Galatians were responding to a counterfeit gospel, in which case the event to which this relates must be the commencement of the false teaching. It is possible, of course, to identify the event as the time of their conversion, and the cause of Paul's astonishment would then be the rapidity with which they had forsaken the true gospel. It is also possible to relate this to the apostle's last visit. But the first of these interpretations would fit better into the context.

deserting: the verb is a colourful one, used both of military revolt and of a change of attitude. The apostle thinks of the readers as having changed sides. It was a serious case of defection. Another gospel was claiming an allegiance which should have been exclusive to the true gospel. Paul's astonishment that this should have happened is readily intelligible.

him who called you: there is little doubt that this phrase refers to God the Father. The opposing faction among the Galatians would certainly have been surprised to learn that their defection was in fact from God himself. Their enthusiasm was for the law of God. How then could they be said to be deserting God? Paul would well understand this for he had himself imagined that he was doing God service while persecuting the Church. This kind of delusion is one of the most difficult to deal with, for there is a strong element of pious conviction. But as soon as the realization comes that religious enthusiasm for God's law may turn out to be a desertion of God himself, there is hope that the true nature of the gospel will be discerned.

in the grace of Christ: some manuscripts omit 'of Christ', but the major evidence supports it. In any case the word 'grace' implies a connection with Christ. Paul's choice of the word 'grace' is probably intended to offset the emphasis on 'law' among the defectors. They must learn that when God called them it was through grace and not law. Failure to grasp this had been their fundamental mistake. The preposition (*en*) may be understood as instrumental (=by means of), although this does not exhaust the meaning here. It may also suggest the sphere in which the calling becomes effective or even refer to entrance into a new condition. In the latter case *en* would represent *eis*, but this is less natural than the other possibilities. Since the apostle is thinking of the Galatians' shift of position, some local significance in *en* would best fit the context. The implication is that by their different gospel the Galatians were stepping out of the grace into which they had been called.

to a different gospel: the adjective expresses a difference in kind and therefore differentiates the gospel of the false teachers from the gospel which Paul has preached. But in what sense is their gospel different? There is no evidence that there was any dispute about the facts of the gospel. The difference consisted in variant applications of those facts. No doubt the false teachers firmly believed that their position was a true representation of the gospel, but Paul's point is that their application of it made it, in fact, an essentially different gospel.

7. not that there is another gospel: Paul appears here to be correcting himself, as if he suddenly realizes that what he has just said might give the impression that he is prepared to assign the word 'gospel' to any other form of teaching. In fact, there cannot be any other gospel, if gospel is understood to describe God's way of salvation in Christ. What these other people are teaching is a perversion (Duncan). Paul has a clear idea of what he meant by 'gospel', but it must not be supposed that this was his own private notion. His words would in that case have carried no weight. There was presumably a generally accepted definition of what was basic to the concept. The modern Church has become less clear about the nature of the gospel, but it would do well to ponder the importance that Paul here attaches to distinctions between the true and false gospel.

some who trouble you: there are other occasions on which Paul refers to opponents without naming them (cf. Gal. 2.12; 1 C. 4.18; 2 C. 3.1; 10.2). The readers would know at once their identity. The word here used for 'trouble' (*tarassontes*) sometimes denotes physical agitation, sometimes mental disturbance, and sometimes seditious activity. Used in conjunction with the metaphor of desertion, the last of these three is to be preferred.

pervert: this word (*metastrephō*) means to transfer to a different opinion, hence to change the essential character of a thing. The word need not imply deterioration, but where that which is changed is good, the change must involve the idea of perversion as here. The idea is not merely a twisting of the gospel, but of giving it an emphasis which virtually transformed it into something else. In this way Paul shows his masterly understanding of the principles behind the policy of the false teachers. A salvation depending on circumcision, and by implication on legal observances, was no true gospel at all. It was a perversion. It is worth noting that Paul lays the responsibility for the perversion on the false teachers by showing that they themselves want (*thelontes*) to pervert.

the gospel of Christ: since in the Greek the article is used with the name of Christ, the genitive should be regarded as defining the gospel in a particular sense. It was the gospel belonging to the Messiah, and yet those who were perverting it were professing to be zealous for his messianic claims by insisting on an essentially Judaistic application. The genitive could also be understood as describing the gospel which Christ proclaimed (i.e. a subjective genitive, so Williams), but the former interpretation is more in keeping with the context.

8. But even if we or an angel from heaven: Paul is here anticipating an objection. The false teachers might claim that what he has just described as the gospel of Christ is really the gospel of Paul. They may well have put to the Galatians that there was no more reason why Paul's gospel should be the right one than their own, especially if they were claiming it to be the same gospel. But the apostle asserts with strong emphasis that the only authentic gospel is that originally preached by him. Neither Paul himself nor an angel could change it. It was not Paul's gospel, it was Christ's. This made it immutable.

contrary to: this is not the only interpretation of the Greek words (*par'ho*), although it is almost certainly the correct one here. Paul is thinking of what the false teachers are saying as being actually in opposition to the truth of the gospel. This is even more strongly expressed than the reference to perversion in the previous verse. The words could mean 'besides' or 'beyond', in which case the anathema would be against additions to the pure gospel, as for instance in the traditions of men. Some of the early Protestants so interpreted it in their denunciation of the Roman Catholic appeal to ecclesiastical tradition as being of equal value to the Bible. There is a sense in which Paul was probably thinking of the circumcision requirement of these teachers as an addition to the gospel originally preached to them, but the strong denunciation suggests that Paul views their actions as the direct antithesis of the true gospel.

accursed: the word *anathema* is related to the Hebrew *herem*, used of what was devoted to God, usually for destruction. Some have supposed that it was used among the Jews to express excommunication (so Williams). In New Testament usage it is a strong expression of separation from God. It implies the disapproval of God. Indeed, 'anathema' is the strongest possible contrast to God's grace. Its use here as an asseveration upon those perverting the gospel reflects Paul's assessment of the serious character of their outlook. Here was no outburst of personal anger because men were forsaking what Paul had preached. It was not an issue of personal prestige. The essence of the gospel itself was at stake. If the false teachers were directly contradicting the gospel of the grace of Christ, they could not possibly avoid incurring the strong displeasure of Christ. In some ways it is strange that Paul should express himself so violently before he has even outlined the nature of the perversion, but it shows the intensity of the apostle's apprehensions about the situation. In the early Church there was a fuller appreciation of the sacred character of the gospel than has often been the case in subsequent Church history. In modern times there has been too much inclination to confuse personalities with the content of the gospel, but Paul's inclusion of himself or even an angel in the possibility of an anathema makes indisputably clear the superiority of the message over the messenger. For a similar use of an anathema, cf. 1 C. 12.3; Rom. 9.3.

9. As we have said before . . . : this verse is almost an exact repetition of verse 8. But why does Paul repeat himself? It could not fail to impress the readers with a sense of solemnity when the anathema is pronounced twice. The only change is the substitution of 'which you received' for 'which we preached to you'. The focus shifts, therefore, from the messengers to the recipients. The two together reflect the co-operative aspect of the origin of every new community of believers. Paul not only himself declared the gospel, but it was fully acknowledged as the gospel by the recipients. The word *proeirēkamen* (we have said before) could refer to what Paul had said on his last visit to the Galatian churches (so Duncan), rather than to the statement in the previous verse. The latter interpretation is said to be excluded by the use of *arti* (now) in the next phrase (**now I say again**), since the statement of this verse would seem separated by an interval from what Paul had previously said (Lightfoot). If this is correct, the Galatians had no excuse. They knew that a contrary gospel would involve an anathema, and yet they had persisted in their seditious activity.

which you received: the verb used here expresses the communication of authorized Christian teaching. Paul himself had once been at the receiving end of this process as 1 C. 15.3ff. makes clear, in spite of what he says in verse 12 (see comment below). The gospel needs more than preaching; it needs receiving. The process of transmission is completed only when men acknowledge that the message preached is God's gospel, and once this has been done they have no excuse for deviating from it.

10. Am I now seeking the favour of men? The 'now' in this statement reinforces the 'now' in verse 9. It implies that Paul is answering a charge that his motives have changed since he first preached to them. His rhetorical question suggests that the charge of self-seeking was being brought against Paul, no doubt with the intention of discrediting him and therefore refuting his influence. The word used for seeking favour (*peithō*) means in this context 'to conciliate', and the idea seems to be that Paul, by relaxing the requirement of circumcision for Gentile converts, was making it easier for enquirers to become Christians. He was, in short, playing to the gallery.

or of God? It may seem strange that Paul should state as a second alternative the idea of seeking to win the favour of God, if the verb is to be understood in this sense. It is better to assume that this second part of the question means, Am I seeking God's approval? There seems to be a distinct assumption that man has a straight choice between pleasing other men or pleasing God and that those who do the first cannot also do the second. It was of utmost importance for Paul to demonstrate that he was in the latter category.

to please men? The first of the rhetorical questions is repeated for added emphasis, with a significant change of verb from 'conciliate' to 'please' (*areskein*). It is more than repetition that is involved. The former verb refers to making it easy for men to accept the gospel, whereas this verb suggests currying favour with a view to securing popularity.

If . . . I should not be a servant of Christ: the idea of Paul as a self-seeker can at once be challenged by an appeal to his experience. Was slavery to Christ likely to lead to popularity? The word used (*doulos*) suggests such servitude to Christ that any idea of popularity would be utterly alien. Paul uses the same description of his status in the salutation of his Epistle to the Romans (cf. also Tit. 1.1).

PAUL'S APOLOGIA 1.11-2.21

What has preceded has already prepared the way for Paul's defence. He now comes to a more detailed refutation.

11. **For I would have you know:** when Paul uses this method of expression he intends to draw particular attention to the subject about to be introduced, as is clear from 1 C. 12.3; 15.1; 2 C. 8.1. The origin of the gospel is of such vital importance that there must be no shadow of doubt about it. All his readers must know it. It is still as important as it was in Paul's day to be clear about this issue and his careful clarification of the matter has put Christians in all periods of history in his debt.

brethren: the apostle frequently addresses his fellow-Christians in this way, thus drawing attention to the concept of believers as a household of faith. It is significant that on eight other occasions in this epistle, Paul addresses the readers in the same way, which suggests that he was anxious to avoid any impression that his criticism of their doctrine and practice implied any lack of love towards them personally. **the gospel which was preached by me is not man's gospel:** Paul's first assertion about the gospel is a negative one. It is not of human origin. It has not been forged out by the human intellect. It is not a philosophic system, or a religious faith created by some religious genius. It was, furthermore, not a human development from the Jewish religion. It is something super-human, which cannot be reduced to human terms. The Greek phrase translated 'man's gospel' means strictly 'according to man' (*kata anthrōpon*). The thought is that the gospel does not conform to man's ideas of what a gospel was to be. It had another mould or pattern. Another kind of mind was behind it. This has always been part of the offence of the gospel in the eyes of those who bow completely to the authority of reason. The content of the gospel is often unacceptable to reason, when reason is not linked to faith. There is no substitute for a God-given gospel.

12. **For I did not receive it from man:** the conjunction (Greek *gar*) expresses the reason for the previous statement, although Paul is still concerned with the negative aspect. The apostle asserts that the method of transmission is a sufficient proof of its non-human origin. The same verb is used as in verse 9 of the handing-on of an authentic message. Although there was a sense in which Paul 'received' certain primitive Christian traditions (as 1 C. 15.3 shows), yet he did not regard the

human channels, through which the traditions came, as their original source. It would have been different if the gospel had consisted simply of a collection of facts. But since it also involved interpretation, its divine authentication was of utmost importance. The preposition *para* (from) is a general word to denote the idea of transmission, the notion being of passing the gospel on from hand to hand. It was not in this way that Paul received it. There is a strong contrast here with Jewish methods of transmission.

nor was I taught it: this statement almost amounts to a duplication of the last, but a subtle difference of meaning is implied. Paul wishes to exclude the idea of any private human interpretation. What human agencies there might have been are wholly subservient to the prime origin, i.e. God. In any case, as Paul proceeds to argue, he was independent of the Jerusalem apostles.

it came through a revelation of Jesus Christ: at last Paul reaches his positive assertion. The gospel was, in short, a revelation (*apokalupsis*) to him. This means that it was an opening-up of what was previously secret. Paul's Damascus experience is clearly in his mind. He had received a special disclosure. The revelation in this case was a personal experience which burst upon him, the miraculous origin of which he could not dispute. Paul's conversion colours his whole approach in this epistle. The precise meaning of the genitive ('of Jesus Christ') is not certain, for it can be taken in two ways, implying either that Jesus Christ was the agent through whom the revelation came (cf. Bring), or that Jesus Christ was the content of the revelation (Duncan). It is not Paul's most usual practice to speak of Christ as the Revealer; more usually it is God. At the same time in view of the Damascus experience the idea of a revelation by Christ himself would be intelligible. It is more probable, however, that Paul is thinking of the whole content of what had been revealed to him as being summed up in Christ. Some support for the former interpretation may be found in Rev. 1.1, but it is unparalleled in Paul's epistles.

13. For you have heard: the tense in the Greek points back to a specific occasion, but Paul does not state either the occasion or the means used to inform them. It is most natural to suppose that it was from Paul himself (so Burton). Probably he appealed not infrequently to his own experience when preaching, for he appears to have no doubt that his readers will be well acquainted with his experience before conversion. The conjunction 'for' shows that he appeals to his pre-Christian experience as evidence that he had no direct Christian influence upon him until his conversion experience.

my former life: the word used means 'manner of life' and involves more than behaviour, in the sense of outward activities. It refers to the whole way of life, ethical, mental, and religious. The same word is translated 'conduct' in 1 Pet. 1.15. Paul explains himself in the next phrase.

in Judaism: by this term the apostle describes not only his former religious ideas, but also his former ethical ideals. Judaism was not unmindful of the effect of faith on morals and there was undoubtedly much of good in it. Yet it was Judaism that had rejected Christ. As a religious system it was therefore in direct antithesis to Christianity. In the present context the use of the term, which occurs nowhere in Paul's epistles but in this verse and the next, is significant as demonstrating that Paul could never tolerate any presentation of Christianity which regarded it as a form of Judaism. Although Paul's readers were Gentiles they would no doubt have sufficient knowledge of the nature of Judaism to appreciate Paul's allusion, particularly as they were being led astray by teachers who were still under the strong influence of Judaism.

how I persecuted the church of God: in the Greek, the form of the verb suggests a period of persecuting activity, which applies similarly to the next two verbs. Paul's antagonism was not confined to a single occasion, but was marked by persistency. His reason for calling attention to his persecuting zeal is in order to demonstrate the divine origin of a gospel which could transform a violent enemy like him into a zealous missionary. By describing the church as 'the church of God', Paul is no doubt recalling that in persecuting the church he was in fact persecuting its divine originator (cf. 1 C. 15.9).

violently: the Greek phrase (*kath huperbolēn*) means literally 'beyond measure, excessively', and calls attention to the tremendous enthusiasm with which Paul pursued his persecuting purpose. Perhaps as he looks back he can see that even for a pious Jew he had gone much too far. It may also have happened that recollection of his excessive zeal before conversion contributed to his heroic labours as a Christian missionary, as he sought in some way to compensate for some of the havoc to the primitive church which his former zeal had effected. That this persecuting phase of Paul's life was often in his thoughts is clear from the references to it elsewhere (cf. 1 C. 15.9; Phil. 3.6; 1 Tim. 1.13).

tried to destroy it: the same word is used in Ac. 9.21. Later on in this chapter Paul recalls the report which circulated after his conversion, and the same verb is again used of his attempts to destroy the faith. There could hardly have been a more notable antagonist of the Christian Church. His transformation became not only an indisputable witness for the benefit of others to the power of God, but a never-ceasing cause of amazement to Paul himself.

14. I advanced in Judaism: what sense is here to be attached to the word 'advanced'? Does Paul mean that he had raced ahead of his Jewish contemporaries in religious achievement? Or does he mean that he had advanced more in his zeal to maintain the strictness of the Law as compared with some who were inclined towards slackness in their application of Judaism? The word literally implies a cutting of one's way in a forward direction, and if this root-meaning is present at all in this statement it would clearly favour the first view. That Saul of Tarsus was ambitious to further the cause of Judaism is not to be disputed. He was so intent upon it that he did not hesitate to cut down all opposition and in this respect he outstripped his contemporaries.

beyond many of my own age among my people: it is in no spirit of boasting that Paul says this. His purpose is to dispel any notion that he is not sufficiently acquainted with Judaism. Among his contemporary students of Jewish law and customs he felt that he had few equals. Rather than showing pride in this achievement, Paul marvels that the revelation of Jesus Christ should have come to so deep-dyed a Pharisaic enthusiast. In his pre-Christian career he appears to have found considerable favour among his superiors as a man of outstanding promise. It was all the more significant, therefore, that he turned his back on such brilliant prospects.

so extremely zealous: since a comparative adverb is used the idea of zeal beyond that of others must not be obscured. Paul is fond of emphatic words when describing faith and is equally inclined to use them of his former experience. Zeal is better than being lukewarm in the pursuance of one's convictions, but over-zealousness in a wrong cause can be very damaging, as Paul found out to his cost. At least none of his opponents could accuse him of half-heartedness over Jewish affairs. He was not at that time in a favourable frame of mind, from a natural point of view, to receive the gospel. He is implying that a more than human ingenuity would be required to dampen such zeal (cf. also Phil. 3.6).

the traditions of my fathers: it is usual for the word 'traditions' (*paradoseis*), when used in connection with Judaism, to refer to that body of oral teaching which was complementary to the written law and in fact possessed equal authority to the law. Saul as a Pharisaic student would have been well drilled in the minutiae of these oral traditions. The double use in this verse of the possessive 'my' is worth observing. The apostle is still deeply conscious that he belongs to the Jewish people. The Judaizers at Galatia should remember that. Some have interpreted the phrase 'my fathers' in a narrower sense of his own family connections (so Emmet), but that would seem to limit too much the traditions involved.

15. **he who had set me apart:** Paul here uses a word which occurs also in Rom. 1.1, where he makes plain that he was set apart for the gospel. The idea behind the expression is of a distinct delimiting of boundaries. No longer was he confined within the limits of Judaism, but he was still confined, nevertheless, to the purposes of God. He never conceived of his ministry as a voluntary process. He was called to it by God.

before I was born: literally, Paul dates the calling 'from my mother's womb'. His point is that this process of setting apart antedates the earliest years of discretion. The calling was in fact before he could think for himself, and this must prove that his gospel was not of his own making. It is one of the most characteristic features of Paul's theology that he was deeply conscious that divine influences had been operative in his life long before he had recognized them. It was part of his convictions about the sovereign purposes of God.

called me through his grace: this statement recalls the similar statement in 1.6, and shows Paul's deep consciousness of the effectiveness of God's grace. It will be noticed that Paul has changed the preposition from 'in' (*en*) to 'through' (*dia*), but here he wishes to emphasize the divine initiative.

16. **was pleased to reveal his Son to me:** again Paul draws attention to the fact that his knowledge of Christ came through revelation. The words 'to me' are literally 'in me', which may mean that Paul is thinking of himself as a channel through which revelation was being passed on (Lightfoot). But since the revelation had as its purpose to call Paul to be a preacher, it clearly had an intimate personal character which would suggest that the word *en* is intended to express the idea of inwardness. The revelation was in a sense localized in Paul. At the time of his conversion, others heard sounds but he alone received a direct message from God. Yet the inwardness of the revelation had an immediate reaching out for the apostle, as his next statement shows.

in order that: although Paul is not thinking specifically of the purpose of the remarkable character of his conversion, but rather of the fact of it, he cannot refrain from an incidental reference to its purpose. A revelation of such a character could never be intended merely for one man. It was intended to be shared. It was not an end in itself. All three accounts of Paul's conversion in Acts make this plain. **I might preach him among the Gentiles:** the commission was not simply to preach. Had it been so expressed, in all probability Paul would have confined himself to the Jews, ardent Hebrew of the Hebrews as he was. But the Gentile direction of his commission seems to have been borne in upon him from the time of his conversion. According to Ac. 9.15; 22.15; 26.16–18, the Gentile commission was given at that time, and this accords fully with Paul's own reflections upon that experience. The universality of the gospel message has been so abundantly illustrated in Christian history that it is not easy for the modern mind to think back to a time when for a Jew the very idea would have been revolutionary. When once this remarkable characteristic of the gospel had fully taken possession of the apostle it is small wonder that he felt so deeply the attempts of the Judaizers to insist on enslaving Gentiles in Jewish ritual requirements. Did he receive so clear-cut a commission for the purpose of proselytizing for a kind of modified Judaism? That was not the way that Paul had interpreted and pursued his mission. While this is really a passing reference, it nevertheless is all of a piece with his present purpose in writing to the Galatians. The gospel preached to them was preached by one who was *par excellence* the apostle to the Gentiles, not self-appointed but God-appointed. **I did not confer with flesh and blood:** in giving the immediate consequences of his conversion, Paul first expresses these negatively and then positively. The expression 'flesh and blood' is a common phrase to denote human beings generally, usually in distinction from God. In view of the more specific statement which follows, it is probable that Paul is here thinking mainly of the general rank and file of Christians. He did not begin researches into primitive Christianity. Had he done so, the Judaizers might well have had an opportunity to put a wrong construction upon it. No-one could assert that Paul's gospel was his own development from consultations with others. It is noteworthy that our Lord used the same expression as here in commenting on the origin of Peter's confession (Mt. 16.17). The verb *prosanatithēmi*, which occurs only in this epistle in the New Testament (here and in 2.6), means literally 'to lay on oneself in addition', and when used with a genitive suggests the gaining of information by communicating with others. Paul's revelation was not modified by additional information gained in this way.

17. nor did I go up to Jerusalem: since Paul in his pre-conversion days was based on Jerusalem in direct contact with the ecclesiastical authorities there, he was no doubt well acquainted with the arrangements within the Christian Church. He must have known that at the headquarters of the movement in Jerusalem the direction of affairs was under the apostles. He might therefore have been excused had he sought an interview with the leaders of the Jerusalem church. But he expressly denies having done that. He may well have known them sufficiently to suspect that he would not at first be made welcome, as turned out to be the case (according to Ac. 9.26) when he did eventually visit them. Whatever the motive behind his avoidance of such top-level discussion, he recognizes that he can appeal to it in support of his present argument. At the time of his conversion he was completely independent of the Jerusalem church.

those who were apostles before me: Paul has already in his salutation laid claim to the apostolic office and now he makes a fleeting allusion to what is in fact the crux of his apology. He admits the apostolicity of the Jerusalem leaders, but he will allow only a temporal distinction between his office and theirs. They were, of course, before him in point of time, but not in the importance of their office. He seems to imply that his apostolic commission was as good as theirs, and there was therefore no need for them to confirm his office, even although they preceded him in time. It must be remembered that Paul is in no way showing contempt for the original apostles, but is answering in a factual way the taunts of those who supposed his apostleship to be inferior or secondary (cf. Cole).

I went away into Arabia: this is Paul's positive action, but his fleeting reference to it raises several problems. Firstly, what does he mean by Arabia? The name was used of a very large area inhabited by Arabs, which in Paul's day was under the rule of Aretas. The area, in fact, seems to have included Damascus itself and to have stretched southwards in the direction of the Sinaitic peninsula. If by Arabia is here meant that part of the kingdom in the proximity of Damascus, it may readily be understood why the apostle chose to withdraw there. It was the nearest district to the scene of his conversion where he might find some temporary seclusion away from the immediate hostility of his former Jewish contemporaries. There is much to be said for this reconstruction of the events, especially in view of the fact that Paul himself says that he returned to Damascus. The major objection, however, is the use of the term Arabia in 4.25 of this epistle. There it is used to describe the geographic situation of Mount Sinai, and this has given rise to the theory that the apostle would have found a symbolic significance in visiting the same scenes as Moses had looked upon before launching his campaign (Lightfoot). The idea is suggestive but hardly practical or probable. The journey from Damascus to Sinai was difficult and is not likely to have been made in the spontaneous manner in which Paul's decision appears to have been effected. Moreover the return to Damascus suggests a closer proximity than this theory allows. It is furthermore improbable that Paul at this stage of his Christian experience had pondered on the symbolic comparison between the giving of the old covenant and the new. Such a comparison he would come to understand more fully as his Christian thought matured. It would seem unlikely, therefore, that Paul means the Sinaitic peninsula. In 4.25 his statement about Sinai would still be true, even if here the reference is to the wider connotation of the term 'Arabia'.

Secondly, what was the purpose of Paul's visit? He himself does not say, and it would probably be wiser to refrain from speculating. And yet the fact that he mentions the visit shows that it possessed some significance for him. Two suggestions have been made. Either he went there to meditate on the meaning of the tremendous experience through which he had just passed, or he went there to preach. Of these ideas the former is to be preferred (so Duncan), for if his motive was preaching it is strange that he should have chosen so sparsely populated an area to evangelize nomadic tribes while the populous district of Damascus lay close at hand. Moreover, the silence of Acts about this Arabian visit is more intelligible if Paul withdrew for meditation than if it were his first evangelistic campaign, since the latter would have had considerable interest for the historian. We would have liked more details of the spiritual and intellectual deliberations of those days, but the apostle leaves a veil over them. One lesson is relevant and important for all periods and personalities in Christian ministry. Movements of great activity must always be based on periods of seeming inactivity which allow time for reflection and for the clarification of ideas and motives.

Thirdly, what was the length of the visit? There is no certain answer. All that Paul states is that three years after his conversion he returned to Jerusalem (see comment on next verse). In that period must presumably be fitted his visit to Arabia and his preaching activity in Damascus. It is not known whether any other movements of Paul were included in this period, nor can it be determined how long Paul worked in Damascus before going to Jerusalem. Acts 9.19 states rather vaguely that 'for several days' he was in Damascus 'with the disciples', and after a reference to his preaching the plot to kill him is said to have been conceived 'when many days had passed' (Ac. 9.23). The Arabian visit might therefore have occupied no more than a few weeks, or could have covered many months. The matter is unimportant. What is vital for Paul's present argument is that no space can be found within the three years mentioned for consultation with the Jerusalem apostles.

Fourthly, does Paul's statement contradict Acts? There are two features to be considered—the absence of mention of Arabia and the impression given by Acts that Paul's preaching activity immediately followed his conversion. On the former, it may have been that Luke was not aware of Paul's Arabian visit, but

Christianity. It cannot be said, moreover, that Acts excludes the possibility of such a visit. On the second point, the real crux is the interpretation of 'immediately' (*eutheōs*) in Ac. 9.20, for the most natural interpretation of this is to suppose that no interval separated his conversion from his preaching. In this case, the Arabian visit would need to be placed after such a brief period of ministry. But since Paul confounded the Damascus Jews with his proofs that Jesus was the Christ, it is preferable to regard the Arabian visit as preceding this to allow time for the re-orientation of his thoughts. In this case, 'immediately' would need to be interpreted as immediately following his return to Damascus.

and again I returned to Damascus: since Paul has not before mentioned Damascus, the 'again' implies that his readers would know that his conversion took place near that city. No doubt they had heard about the details of that experience more than once from Paul's own lips. At least, he assumes that they are acquainted with this detail, even if they may be unaware of the Arabian visit. The fact that Paul himself makes clear that his Jerusalem visit was from Damascus is in complete agreement with Ac. 9.26. It was on this return visit that the apostle incurred the hostility both of the ethnarch Aretas and of the Jews (cf. 2 C. 1.32ff.; Ac. 9.24).

18. Then after three years: the word translated 'then' (*epeita*) draws particular attention to the next event in order of sequence (it is used also in verse 21 and in 2.1), and shows Paul's sensitiveness to the historical connection between the various events leading to his contacts with the Jerusalem leaders. The period of three years may represent in the Jewish method of calculation little more than a year if the first and third years represent only a part of a year, as is not improbable. It is impossible to be more precise, for the expression could equally well mean three full years. The shorter the period the better it would conform to the impression given by Acts. The period mentioned presumably dates from Paul's con-version, as that is the critical point in his experience.

I went up to Jerusalem to visit Cephas: the verb used is that regularly employed for travellers making acquaintance with places or people. Its choice here is in harmony with Paul's obvious desire to avoid any suggestion that he went to be instructed by Cephas, i.e. Peter. In spite of this, some have suggested that on this occasion Paul enquired from Peter the facts of our Lord's life (cf. Cole), but he must have been informed of these previously if he had been a Christian for some time. It should be noted that the name Cephas, the Aramaic form equivalent to the Greek Peter, is used in 2.9, 11, 14, but in 2.7, 8 the name Peter is used. In these former three references, many MSS read Peter for Cephas, no doubt because of its greater familiarity. In the First Epistle to the Corinthians, Paul refers to this apostle four times, but in each case under the Aramaic form (cf. also its use in Jn 1.42). In all probability both forms were current in Paul's time.

and remained with him fifteen days: why does Paul mention so specifically the period of his visit? It was evidently vividly impressed upon his mind, but his main reason for referring to it here is to emphasize its brevity. The period was not long enough to give any grounds for the charge that Paul had been dependent on Peter, and this is the special point that he is wishing to establish.

19. none of the other apostles except James the Lord's brother: the form of the Greek may be understood in two ways: either the exceptive phrase relates only to the verb, 'I saw', in which case Paul may not be describing James as an apostle (Emmet, Munck, 92); or the phrase may relate to the whole preceding statement, in which case James is numbered among the other apostles (cf. Burton). Since in 2.9 Paul links James with Cephas and John as reputed pillars of the church, it is most reasonable to suppose that he is here drawing no distinction between him and the others as far as apostolic status is concerned. This wider use of the term is probable here in view of Paul's own insistence on appropriating the term to describe his own position. It is part of his whole argument that apostleship is not confined to the Jerusalem leaders, let alone to the original Twelve. There are three different interpretations of the word 'brother' (*adelphos*) in this context. It may mean half-brother, full brother, or cousin. In the first case James would have been the son of Joseph by a previous wife; in the second case, he would have been a son of Joseph and Mary, born later than Jesus; in the third case a son of Mary's sister. It is certainly more natural to take the word as brother rather than cousin, but it is not easy to decide between the two interpretations of it. The second would avoid what is, after all, purely a hypothetical assumption, i.e. that Joseph had had a former wife. The balance of probability is therefore in support of the second. James' kinship with our Lord may well have been a dominant factor in his becoming leader of the Jerusalem church.

20. (In what I am writing to you, before God, I do not lie): although this is placed in parenthesis, it is no side-issue. It brings home the solemn seriousness of Paul's theme in that he feels the need for such an asseveration as this. No doubt this oath is to offset an adverse report which Paul's opponents had put out about him. Anything which conflicts with what he has just written may be disregarded as being false. For other instances of the use of similar strong asseverations, cf. Rom. 9.1; 2 C. 11.31; 1 Tim. 2.7.

21. Then I went into the regions of Syria and Cilicia: another stage in Paul's missionary movements is now mentioned, not because he is wishing to give his itinerary but because he wants to make clear that the sphere of his activity was far enough removed from that of the Jerusalem apostles to show his independence of them. The two regions specified formed one provincial district although there is evidence from Tacitus (*Annals* 2.78) that Cilicia had its own governor, at least in A.D. 67. Paul's home city of Tarsus was in Cilicia, while the chief city of Syria was Antioch, where by Paul's time the Christian community had already become a centre of missionary activity. This latter fact may account for the order in which the districts are mentioned. It should be noted in this connection that later on (in 2.11) the apostle specially mentions an incident which occurred at Antioch. It was also the church at Antioch and not the church at Jerusalem which had sponsored his missionary work. His time spent in Syria was, therefore, another link in his proof of independence of the Jerusalem apostles. Chronologically, according to Ac. 9.30, 11.25, the districts should be reversed. Another suggestion is that Paul is not referring to time spent in these districts, but only to the districts passed through on his way to Tarsus from Jerusalem. Too much emphasis should surely not be put on the order of mention since Paul's main purpose is to show how little he had had to do with Jerusalem (cf. Ridderbos).

22. And I was still not known by sight: the verb stresses the continuity of the state of not knowing. In this way, the apostle makes perfectly clear that until that time he had made no personal appearance in any of the churches of Judea. The Greek expression is vivid, meaning that Paul was unknown 'by face', although the Judean Christians must have known a good deal about him by repute, as verse 23 suggests.

the churches of Christ in Judea: the description of the churches here as *en Christō* ('in Christ' rather than 'of Christ') is a typically Pauline touch to distinguish the Christian from the purely Jewish communities in Judea. There has been much discussion over Paul's use of the term Judea, since Jerusalem was included in Judea and Paul had certainly paid a visit there. It has therefore been maintained that Judea could in fact be regarded as distinct from Jerusalem (so Lightfoot), as it is in Mt. 3.5. Whatever the decision regarding the precise meaning of Judea in general usage, there can be little doubt that in this case Paul intends it to be understood as exclusive of Jerusalem. If this is a correct interpretation, what would have been the point in Paul's mentioning the churches in Judea at all? The only reasonable answer seems to be that Judea would probably have been the sphere of Paul's missionary labours had he been working under the auspices of the Jerusalem church. Furthermore, would not the fact that he was unknown personally among the Judean churches have been to his disadvantage in the eyes of the Judaizing party to whom he is addressing himself? Would they not have had more respect for him if his work had been officially sponsored by these communities? But no! He is independent of Jewish Christian sponsoring. Indeed, the next verse adds further weight to this.

23. They only heard it said: again the tense is strongly frequentative and might be rendered, 'they kept on hearing'. Reports would come mainly from the Jerusalem church, but no doubt most Christian travellers would carry news of the remarkable transformation in Saul of Tarsus. He who once persecuted is now preaching. From persecuting to preaching was an astonishing change, but the active propagation of the very faith which he had so ardently wanted to stamp out was indisputable proof, even for those who had never met Paul personally, that a divine power had been at work. In similar ways in modern times Christian believers can be moved by reports of remarkable conversions.

the faith he once tried to destroy: Acts bears testimony to Paul's former zeal for persecuting Christians. But here Paul himself recognizes the underlying principle that it was not merely Christians he was harassing. His real target was 'the faith' itself. This word must be understood objectively of all that the gospel stood for, as it was this that was the content of Paul's preaching. But a subjective element cannot be excluded in view of the fact that Paul laid such emphasis on faith, as opposed to works, as the sole means whereby the gospel could be appropriated.

Many have since tried to destroy the faith in precisely the same way as Saul of Tarsus tried, but none has been any more successful than he. This fact alone is further evidence of the divine character of the gospel which Paul received and which he continued to preach. There is nothing man-made about a gospel that can effect a transformation like this.

24. And they glorified God because of me: again the tense of the verb is significant, for it means that the Judean churches kept on glorifying God on account of Paul. For the apostle to report that he himself was the cause of their praising God is no sign of boasting on his part, for he never ceased to marvel at what the grace of God had effected in his own life, and it was a source of gratitude to him when others also recognized it. But the real object of his mentioning it here is to demonstrate that even churches as Jewish Christian as the Judean churches could praise God for Paul, and yet the Judaizers at Galatia were critical of him. In the Greek the object, 'God', is placed last for emphasis and is clearly more important than 'because of me' (*en moi*).

2.1. Then after fourteen years: this is the third occasion on which Paul uses the particle of sequence (*epeita*). This suggests that the Jerusalem visit to which he is about to refer was the next important connection with the Christian leaders and by implication excludes any intervening contact; unless it is maintained, as by advocates of the North Galatian theory, that although he appears to exclude any other contact with the leaders this does not necessarily exclude contact with the Jerusalem church generally.

There is some question whether the fourteen years dates from the previous Jerusalem visit or from Paul's conversion (cf. Duncan). If the latter, it would shorten the period previous to his first missionary journey, and would make easier a chronological reconstruction of Paul's movements up to the Council of Jerusalem (see Introduction). Since the expression could be interpreted either way, the apostle clearly attaches little importance to the precise duration of the periods intervening his Jerusalem visits. Whether it was eleven years or fourteen years is immaterial to Paul's argument. The statement shows, under either interpretation, that a considerable interval elapsed without any official interchange between the apostle and the Jerusalem leaders.

I went up again: although the most natural interpretation of the word 'again' (*palin*) is that this was the next visit, it need not exclude an intervening visit (see previous comment). The main difficulty is that a comprehensive account of the

Jerusalem contacts seems required by Paul's arguments (see Introduction, p. 32 on this).

with Barnabas: during the apostle's earliest Christian life and missionary activity, Barnabas was his closest associate. Although at first Barnabas took the lead by reason of his seniority of Christian experience, it soon became evident that Paul was the dominant partner. The preposition 'with' (*meta*) means in this context 'accompanied by', which suggests that Paul was the leader. But, of course, Paul is listing his own activities here and his main attention is concentrated upon this. The partnership broke up subsequent to the Council of Jerusalem (Ac. 15.29), and so the visit mentioned here must obviously be placed before that. But why is Barnabas specifically mentioned? He was certainly well known in the South Galatian churches, who would be well aware that he came from a Jewish Christian background and would probably not have questioned his orthodoxy.

taking Titus along with me: why does Paul mention Titus? Of his earliest movements we know nothing, for it is strange that Acts contains no reference to him. This could hardly be because Luke did not know of him as a companion of Paul, even if he had not known him personally. In the absence of data, it is of little value to speculate. The suggestion that Titus was a brother of Luke is not impossible but is purely hypothetical. In the end no answer can be given to this puzzle. But one thing is clear from Paul's own references to him elsewhere, and that is the high regard in which he held him. Yet this would not account for Paul mentioning him in this context, unless there was some dispute about him among the Judaizers. The precise form of the expression here shows that Paul took full responsibility for his presence with him at Jerusalem. A particular aspect of that visit is mentioned in verse 3.

2. I went up by revelation: Paul does not tell us to whom the revelation was made. It may have been to the group of Christians at Antioch or it may have been to Paul himself or it may have come in some other undefined way. The feature which the apostle wishes to make clear is that it was not his own idea. He was not going with the intention of asking for the approbation of the Jerusalem leaders. He felt he had no option but to respond to the divine leading.

I laid before them . . . the gospel which I preach: the verb conveys the idea of consultation. It is to be noted that Paul does not define 'them'. It could be a reference to the Jerusalem Christians generally or to the leaders, most probably the former since the authorities are mentioned in the next clause placed in parenthesis. It is instructive to observe that Paul did not confine himself to reporting his missionary work among the Gentiles. He was most concerned that the Jerusalem Christians should know the content of his preaching. To the apostle this was of paramount importance. In modern times there has been a tendency for the procedure to be reversed and sometimes for all too little interest to be shown by congregations at missionary gatherings in the character of the gospel being preached.

The present tense is used in the reference to preaching, because although Paul is describing an event in the past he knows that the Gospel he preached then is the same as he preaches now.

(**but privately before those who were of repute**): while he had had opportunity to speak publicly to the Christians generally, he was able to speak with the leaders in private conference, and this had afforded a much better opportunity to avoid misunderstandings. It is a process worth copying. The phrase 'those who were of repute' may seem later on in the chapter to be used in a derogatory sense, but the word itself implies some position of honour. We have no grounds for supposing that the apostle had no esteem for the Jerusalem leaders, and we must therefore suppose that in this epistle he is bearing in mind his opponents' opinions. He may even be echoing their language. If the Judaizers were maintaining the reputable character of their teaching on the grounds that it came from a reputable source, the slightly derogatory tinge in Paul's references becomes more intelligible. It seems certain that those named in verse 9, James, Cephas, and John, are to be identified with those mentioned here.

lest somehow I should be running or had run in vain: it may at first seem that by this statement Paul is, in fact, conceding what he has all along been denying, i.e. that he needed his course of action to be authenticated by the Jerusalem leaders if he were to avoid making his work useless. But since he cannot mean that and remain consistent in his argument, some other interpretation must surely be possible. There is no suggestion here that Paul would have modified his gospel had it not met with the approval of the Jerusalem apostles, but the position would clearly be happier if there was seen to be general agreement between them and Paul. The athletic metaphor is used to describe a futile procedure, i.e. a race in which it is impossible to win. But what precisely was the goal that Paul has in mind? Would he have regarded disagreements between him and the others as leading to futility? Or is he thinking that failure to report his gospel to them would be a disqualification in the 'race'? This latter suggestion is possible. The progress of the Church as a whole and of Paul's work in particular would have become seriously impaired had there been any open rupture between two rival factions. The importance attached to the conference in Ac. 15 bears witness to this.

3. But even Titus: the statement which commences with this verse presents certain difficulties owing to the peculiarities of the Greek. Nevertheless the general drift of the passage is clear. The 'but' (*alla*) at the beginning does not express an opposing qualification, but serves to strengthen the more general statement just made. The approach of the authorities to Titus serves as a kind of test case, which illustrates without question their attitude towards the problem of circumcision.

was not compelled to be circumcised: there are two ways in which this can be understood. It can be interpreted either as an indication (a) that Titus was not circumcised (Lightfoot), or (b) that Titus's circumcision was not by compulsion but was voluntary (Duncan). The latter alternative assumes that the verb

is emphatic, but it is not placed in an emphatic position in the Greek text. Moreover, it is difficult to believe that Paul would have agreed to the circumcision of a
Greek like Titus, for this would have undermined his whole position (cf. Watkins,
178f.) He may be answering insinuations against him on the part of the Judaizers,
and if this could be substantiated, it might lend support to the second alternative.
On the whole it seems better to suppose that Paul is referring to the case of Titus
to show that he had no clash with the Jerusalem leaders over circumcision, for if it
were a requirement for salvation the leaders would clearly have insisted on Titus
being circumcised. But they did not insist (cf. Munck, 95ff.).

though he was a Greek: the term *Hellēn* is sometimes used of non-Jews generally,
but here it possibly conveys its more limited meaning of a Greek speaking non-
Jewish person. The main significance of the mention of Titus is as an example of
a Christian Gentile whose relationship to circumcision might be regarded as being
typical for all Gentiles.

4. But because of false brethren secretly brought in: the connection of
thought is not transparent, but Paul appears to be saying that it was the surrep-
titious entry of false brethren which brought the matter to a head, causing him to
take such a definite stand on this crucial issue. His description of them as false
brethren suggests that they were purporting to enter the church as Christian
believers, but that they were not true Christians at all. The fact that Paul refers to
them here shows that they were quite distinct from the Jerusalem leaders and the
rank and file of the Jerusalem church. The trouble evidently arose because these
intruders were attempting to force the apostle to submit to their own narrow
Jewish approach to the Gentile world. It is of small importance where the infiltra-
tion happened, but Antioch is as good a guess as any, since that church had much
to do with Paul and Barnabas. It is noticeable that the verb is passive, which implies
that some of the members of the church had invited them.

who slipped in to spy out (our freedom): here the main verb is active, placing
the responsibility squarely on the shoulders of the false brethren. They had come
with a specific purpose—to discover what attitude Gentile Christians were taking
towards the law. The analogy to spying is suggestive. They were acting like
intelligence-agents building up a case against slackness over Jewish ritual requirements. The word implies close scrutiny, which brings out the seriousness of the
intruders' intentions. The matter had not come to a head as a result of casual
observations. It was a planned campaign.

our freedom which we have in Christ Jesus: no phrase could sum up more
adequately the real theme of this epistle. Paul had known only too well the
bondage of Judaism. Indeed, the tremendous sense of liberty which he found in
Christ was the most notable feature of his conversion. Yet the policy of these false
teachers would have robbed him and his Gentile converts of this liberty. On the
words 'in Christ Jesus', see the comment on 1.22. Here the force of the words
shows that because of their identification with Christ they possess a special liberty.

The phrase means more than 'Christian' liberty. There is a mystic quality about this liberty which belongs to Paul's doctrine of the union of the believer with Christ (Ellicott). As a result legal requirements have become dispensable. Since Christ is free, no member of Christ's body can be bound.

that they might bring us into bondage: the apostle states this as their specific purpose. They aimed to make Paul and his converts slaves of the law. The words suggest that an alien objective was being introduced into a situation in which liberty was at present enjoyed. This was not the most primitive situation. It must not be supposed that in pursuing their purpose the intruders were conscious of any insincerity. They would probably have rejected Paul's description of their policy as 'bondage', but they would not have denied that to them an unquestioning adherence to the requirements of the law was an essential feature of their Christian faith. They had never known the glorious sense of freedom in Christ and had never realized the real bondage of legalism.

5. to them we did not yield submission even for a moment: there is a textual problem here which materially affects the interpretation of the passage. While most authorities support the text behind the RSV there is evidence that the Western text behind many of its representatives omits the word 'not' (*oude*). In this case the meaning would be, 'we did yield to them for an hour' (the Greek has *hōra* (hour) and the RSV 'moment' is therefore interpretative). This would require verse 3 to mean that Titus was circumcised for the expediency of that 'hour'. But apart from the fact that the weight of MS evidence would appear to favour the inclusion of the 'not', the omission would involve Paul in a glaring inconsistency.

A case has been made out for a concession by Paul on the occasion of the visit of Titus to Jerusalem, as otherwise he would have been unable to have fellowship with the Jewish Christians there (so Duncan). But this is based on the prior assumption that none of the Christians would have found the same liberty in Christ as, for instance, Paul had done. This may, of course, be a correct assumption, but at best it is only an assumption. Indeed, Paul's argument in this chapter suggests the reverse, for the leaders did not raise any objection. At the same time there was evidently some inconsistency, as Peter's action at Antioch referred to in verses 11ff. illustrates, but Paul would surely never have made any concession to this!

The passage yields the most satisfactory exegesis if it be supposed that Paul resolutely refused to concede anything to those whom he deliberately describes as 'false brethren'. The word 'submission' not only has an article but is in the dative case in the Greek text. The meaning is therefore 'we did not yield with respect to *the* submission', i.e. with regard to the matter under discussion, circumcision.

that the truth of the gospel might be preserved for you: the previous verse ended with a purpose clause and so does this. But the aims are opposite. One group was out to make slaves; the other to ensure the continuance of a free and pure gospel. The phrase 'the truth of the gospel' is intended to contrast with the perverted form of it which the false brethren were advocating. Paul's special mention of preserving the gospel 'for you', i.e. the Galatian Christians, is a pointed reminder that his firm stand was for their benefit, not so much for his own.

6. And from those who were reputed to be something: the construction here is broken. The apostle is so deeply involved in his subject that he does not finish what he begins to say. This statement has in fact a closer connection with verse 2 than with the previous verse. It is probably best therefore to treat the Titus incident as a parenthesis. Paul reverts to his associations with 'the men of repute' at Jerusalem. Yet the parenthesis supplied him with an opportunity to show that the attitude of the false brethren had not affected his own stand before the Jerusalem authorities. It must not be supposed that the present statement is derogatory. What Paul is opposing is an excessive estimate of the position of the Jerusalem leaders. He was opposed to authoritarianism of an ecclesiastical kind. It should be noted that the expression should strictly read, 'those who are reputed', referring to their present status, not simply to a past estimate of them.

what they were makes no difference to me: here the verb changes to the imperfect, and this is deeply significant for a true exegesis. 'What they were' would appear to refer to the previous status of those mentioned (i.e. in verse 9), and can hardly fail to be an allusion to their knowledge of Jesus in the flesh. It is a fair inference that Paul's opponents had appealed to the position of the Jerusalem apostles as being superior to Paul because he had not had personal contact with Jesus in the flesh. His reply is that their previous advantages make no difference now. This is in line with the apostle's contention in 2 C. 5.16, where he repudiates the necessity of having known Christ from a human point of view.

God shows no partiality: whenever the Greek word translated 'partiality' occurs in the New Testament, it always carries the sense of 'looking upon and being influenced by the outward appearance' (literally the 'face' or 'mask'). By making this assertion here Paul is maintaining that God does not base his judgments on external factors such as knowledge of Christ according to the flesh. He judges according to the condition of the spiritual life of each. By implication, any partiality on the part of the false brethren is at once seen to be inconsistent. That it was difficult for Jewish Christians to appreciate the impartiality of God is seen from the account of Peter's vision before he went to Cornelius, as recorded in Ac. 10. The Jewish background of intense nationalism led to the conviction that God must show special favour to Israel in contradistinction to Gentile peoples. But such a notion is alien to Christianity.

added nothing to me: Paul repeats his reference to those of repute to make more impressive the real crux of the matter. The 'authorities' had imposed nothing beyond what Paul had already proclaimed and practised. When they had heard what had happened among the Gentiles they made no modifications whatever. *Prosanatithēmi*, here rendered 'added', can mean 'confer', as in 1.16 (v. Lightfoot), in which case Paul would mean that the authorities took up no questions with him; or it can mean 'to set forth', as in 2.2 (so Burton), which would suggest that they did not present Paul with any demands. Whatever the precise meaning of the word, the apostle clearly intends to imply that he conceded nothing to the 'authorities' because there was nothing he was required to concede.

In the Greek text a conjunction (*gar*) joins this statement to the first statement in the verse, although this conjunction is omitted from the RSV. It seems to be used to explain the significance of the first mention of the authorities.

7. **but on the contrary:** up to this point Paul has given only the negative side. He now comes to the positive one. What the authorities were prepared to do was diametrically opposed to what the false brethren were alleging.

when they saw that I had been entrusted: the first positive action on their part was to perceive the nature of Paul's commission. They were able to discern at once from Paul's report to them of his preaching that he was evidently specially set apart for this particular work. The recognition in the case of both Paul and Peter that their ministry was a divinely given trust meant that there could be no question of either submitting to the other. An entrusted ministry was accountable only to God. It speaks highly of the spiritual perception of Peter and his fellow apostles that they at once recognized Paul's calling. It seems best to take the 'seeing' in the sense of mental and spiritual perception as above, although the word may be meant to convey also a literal meaning. Yet the only possible assumption in that case is that Titus was regarded as a living testimony to Paul's commission.

the gospel to the uncircumcised . . . the gospel to the circumcised: the same word is used in both phrases and it cannot be supposed that Paul means to suggest any difference of content. There is a distinction of the mode of presentation, but no more. The gospel to the circumcision was in no way superior to the gospel to the uncircumcision. Indeed, circumcision is not therefore a *sine qua non* of the gospel. The apostle could never conceive of two gospels adapted to different kinds of people. Both Jew and Gentile needed essentially the same good news. The genitives are not therefore descriptive but objective, as the RSV makes clear.

just as Peter: it is significant that Peter alone is mentioned here, whereas James and John are included in verse 9. The reason would appear to be that Peter's special commission was evangelistic work among the Jews and so formed a close parallel to Paul's work among the Gentiles.

8. **he who worked through Peter:** this verse strengthens the statement in verse 7 and gives the basis for it. As the entrusting of the different commissions are parallel, so the enabling was parallel. The verb used is a favourite one with Paul. Indeed, almost all the instances of its use in the New Testament are in Paul's epistles. It draws attention to the dynamic of the gospel. The translation 'through Peter' for the simple dative puts rather too much emphasis on the idea of agency. A better rendering would be 'in respect of' Peter, in the sense of 'on Peter's behalf' (so Lightfoot). The motive force was God's, but Peter's own activity was needed.

the mission to the circumcision: this time Paul uses the word 'apostleship' (*apostolē*), which the RSV translates as 'mission'. This word is found elsewhere in the New Testament only in Ac. 1.25, Rom. 1.5, and 1 C. 9.2. Paul is once again deeply conscious of the equality of his own apostleship with that of Peter. No doubt he changes the emphasis from the gospel to the apostolic office to draw more specific attention to the implication that a common apostleship must go hand in hand with a common gospel.

through me also: there is something rather pointed about Paul's frequent reference to himself in this chapter by means of the emphatic pronoun (*emoi*), cf. verses 3, 6, and 9 as well as here. Again the dative bears the same sense as in the statement above about Peter.

for the Gentiles: it is noticeable that in this comparison Paul substitutes 'Gentiles' for the 'uncircumcised' in the previous verse. A similar substitution is found in verse 9. The reason seems to be that here and in verse 9, Paul's thought turns away from the people to whom he and Peter were called to preach and concentrates more on the location. Paul thinks of his apostleship as relating to Gentile areas. This interpretation is supported by the Greek construction used (*eis ta ethnē*), which stresses more pointedly the objective of Paul's apostleship than the genitive in the parallel statement about Peter. God's operation through Paul had as its target the Gentiles.

9. when they perceived: this is really a repetition of the opening part of verse 7 but with a different verb. In the former verse the word used indicated 'seeing', but now Paul uses the word 'knowing'. As a result of what they saw, they came to the point of recognition. But the distinction cannot be pressed, for the two verbs are complementary.

the grace that was given to me: Paul is clearly here thinking of his commission to preach (as in verse 7). The fact that he uses the word 'grace' (*charis*) draws attention to the divine favour through which alone the commission was given. In a sense this 'grace' would not have been understood until after Paul had recounted his experiences. So manifestly had God endorsed the policy of Paul among the Gentiles that the Jerusalem authorities could not deny the evidences of Divine grace.

James and Cephas and John: the James mentioned here must be the Lord's brother, as in 1.9, of whom we are informed in Acts that he presided over the Jerusalem church. It is significant that he is here mentioned first, which suggests that he took precedence over the others in the negotiations with Paul. This detail accords well with the description of James' position at the Council of Jerusalem in Ac. 15. The other two apostles, Cephas and John, so closely associated together in the Gospels, were evidently still influential in the Jerusalem church. According to Acts, John appears to have played a less dominant part than Peter and is not referred to again after chapter 8.14.

who were reputed to be pillars: in all probability Paul is here borrowing the language of the false brethren. They might well have been in the habit of referring to the 'pillars'. The metaphor is not altogether inappropriate since the Church of God is sometimes likened to a building. The view that Paul is here really disputing the description, and implying that the three mentioned are not in fact 'pillars', but are only reputed to be, cannot be ignored. It is not impossible that there was some tension between Paul and the Jerusalem apostles, but it is hardly conceivable that Paul would have implied any opposition towards them, if his aim was to show that real fellowship existed between him and them. It is much more probable, therefore, that Paul is referring to the reputation of James, Cephas, and John in order to bring out more forcefully the significance of his agreement with them. It was as if Paul had said that even the acknowledged 'pillars' were prepared to have fellowship with him (cf. Luther).

gave to me and Barnabas the right hand of fellowship: in modern parlance this means that they all shook hands to signify agreement. Then as now refusal to shake hands would have been regarded as an open testimony to disunity. The characteristic word 'fellowship' (*koinōnia*) sums up the true sense of Christian oneness. Such fellowship would be completely denied by the policy which the false brethren were insisting upon. The word for fellowship contains the basic idea of sharing and implies some common ground. There was nothing to prevent Paul and the 'pillar' apostles from joining forces.

that we should go to the Gentiles and they to the circumcised: in the Greek there is no verb, but it is implied by the preposition (*eis*), which occurs in both phrases and which expresses the goal of the activity of each group.

10. only they would have us remember the poor: again the Greek construction is unusual, as the verb here is introduced in a subordinate clause (with *hina*) but without a main clause. Some such main verb as 'they requested that' might be understood, or else this present clause should be interpreted as an accompaniment of the similar clause in the previous verse and the meaning of the whole would be as follows: 'They extended the right hand of fellowship so as to make it plain that we went to the Gentiles and with the one proviso that we should not forget the poor.'

The condition of the Judean Christians was the cause of Paul's collection scheme. Their poverty called forth the sympathy of the Gentile churches (cf. Rom. 15.25ff.; 1 C. 16.1ff.; 2 C. 8.1ff.; 9.1ff.). Here it was the one condition laid upon Paul and his main reason for mentioning it was to exclude the possibility of any other conditions. It should be noted that the verb 'remember' is in the present tense and implies continual memory. Cf. Bring's discussion of the collection.

which very thing I was eager to do: Paul changes to the first person singular here, so excluding Barnabas. It was Paul who was perhaps the chief architect of the schemes for helping the poor. He is particularly concerned to emphasize his eagerness, even to the extent of anxiety as the Greek word implies, to do what the authorities suggested. It is strange that Paul uses a past tense (aorist) when referring to his eagerness, but this must be understood of his diligence subsequent to the

Jerusalem meeting, but before the writing of the letter. The readers may well have had evidence of Paul's deep interest in Gentile benevolence towards their afflicted Jewish brethren.

11. **But when Cephas came to Antioch:** for a full discussion of the timing of this incident, see Introduction, pp. 31 ff. The salient points to be noted here are as follows. (a) The introductory particle (Greek *de*) need not imply that this incident was next in sequence to the last. It is clearly intended rather to draw attention to the inconsistency of Peter's action in view of the agreement reached, as reported in the previous section. (b) The location of the incident was no doubt the Syrian Antioch, not Antioch of Pisidia. This is significant because of its importance in early Christian missionary activity, where the matter of Jewish-Gentile fellowship would at once have been an issue of critical decision. (c) It would seem that Cephas came into an existing situation and at first conformed to the practice which had already been adopted. In this respect Antioch was clearly more broadminded than Jerusalem, owing, no doubt, to the less exclusive character of Hellenistic Judaism.

I opposed him to his face: the sole reason for Paul's mentioning this personal confrontation with Peter is to add further support to his previous arguments that he was not called upon to submit his policies to the Jerusalem authorities. When he actually withstood Peter publicly before the Antioch church, there could not have been a clearer evidence of his own apostolic status. Peter's action called forth opposition, for it was by inference an attack on Paul's own policy, and also if the inference mentioned in the previous note is correct, it would have amounted to a criticism of current Antiochene practice. Paul would have gained a considerable amount of sympathy for his action.

because he stood condemned: by this brief phrase Paul gives the reason for his opposition. Since he does not say who condemned Peter and since it is highly unlikely that it was the church at Antioch, however much they may have questioned his actions, it seems best to suppose that Paul regarded Peter as self-condemned. His inconsistency was so apparent that there was no question of any communal decision about the matter. It was unnecessary.

12. **certain men came from James:** this expression may be compared with Ac. 15.1, where there is a reference to some men coming down from Judea. There can be no question that these belonged to the circumcision party, which believed that all Gentiles should be circumcised, and which was apparently appealing to the authority of James in support of their demands. If they had been commissioned by James personally, it would be extremely difficult to harmonize this with James' action reported in verse 9, unless some considerable interval separated the events. Since this is unlikely it is more probable that these men were doing some special mission under the direction of James and had not been specifically sent to spy out the position regarding Jewish-Gentile fellowship. They possibly protested when they saw what had happened and their protests may have been the occasion of Peter's inconsistency, since he wished to avoid a rift.

he ate with the Gentiles: the food laws of Judaism were stringent, based on
Levitical law. Segregation from Gentiles while eating was not because of any
personal animosity towards the individual Gentiles concerned, but because of the
fear of contamination by eating food forbidden under the law. It was, therefore,
an essentially protective measure. It is understandable that many Jewish Christians,
with their continued respect for the Old Testament teaching, would assume
without question that the old prohibitions still existed. But Christian liberty and
fellowship were never intended to be shackled by ancient taboos. Peter had been
large-hearted enough to recognize this, until the narrower Jewish Christian
brethren arrived. If the Gentile is freed from the necessity of circumcision, he
cannot be bound by the concommitant food taboos. Indeed, the Christian gospel
demanded a new approach to the whole subject of taboos.

he drew back and separated himself, fearing the circumcision party: separation among brethren is not only lamentable but always causes embarrassment to the
whole movement. We are left to imagine what the Gentile believers thought about
it when not only Peter and all the Jewish believers but also Barnabas withdrew.
These probably at once discussed the matter with Paul, whose keen perception saw
the wider implication of the matter. Peter's fear of the circumcision party seems to
have outweighed entirely any consideration he may have had for the Gentile
brethren. Paul's use of the imperfect tense in the verbs denoting withdrawal is
significant in that it suggests a process rather than a single action. Perhaps Peter
vaccillated in his mind before finally yielding to the circumcision party.

   13. with him the rest of the Jews: Peter's action was all the more blameworthy because it implicated many others. If the chief apostle is bound by Jewish
scruples, it is no wonder that all the Jews follow suit. This is a fitting reminder that
Christian leadership always involves responsibility towards others. Nothing could
make plainer than the action of these Jews that Peter's policy could not fail to
produce a distinct division within the church. Any action which was divisive
destroyed the essential ingredients of Christian fellowship.

acted insincerely: the word used is a colourful one. It means to play the hypocrite
together with others. The underlying Greek word was that used of actors hiding
their true selves behind the role they were playing. The implication is that neither
Peter nor the other Jews were acting true to character when they withdrew.
They were in fact going against their better judgment, and were giving a totally
wrong impression.

even Barnabas was carried away by their insincerity: Barnabas was well
known to the Galatians, and in all probability the readers had heard about his
implication in this affair, for the false brethren would not have allowed such
a notable support for their contentions to pass unnoticed. But it is important
to observe that Paul does not suggest that he played any active part in the dissi-
mulation, for not only does the verb appear in the passive but its very meaning
implies that Barnabas was swept off his balance. It is also noteworthy that Barna-

bas is not himself charged directly with insincerity, but is implicated in 'their insincerity'.

14. But when I saw: compare verse 7, where the same verb is used of the Jerusalem authorities' observance of Paul. Here it is the opposite. Paul conceives himself as a kind of watch-dog for the gospel. It is possible that he had been in Antioch all the time, and the perception to which he refers was the point at which the full implication of Peter's action dawned upon him. But more probably he was absent for a time and observed the situation when he returned.

they were not straightforward: literally the word means that they did not walk straight, suggesting a crookedness of action. Peter and his fellow-Jews were looking in one direction and walking in another. Onlookers would never know the truth about the gospel from their actions. Many times in the history of the Church inconsistency has marred the witness to the truth. Straightforwardness is as essential now as it was then. The major problem with all forms of inconsistency is the unawareness of it on the part of those involved. It often takes a spectator to see the position clearly.

I said to Cephas before them all: evidently a gathering of the whole is in mind, but whether it was called specifically for the purpose is not stated. Paul considered a public remonstrance was essential, because of the basic principle involved.

'If you, though a Jew . . .': Paul's statement must be understood in the context of the religious taboos under dispute. It was Peter's ostensible allegiance to Jewish religious demands, while at the same time living generally according to Gentile customs, which showed the inconsistency.

'how can you compel the Gentiles to live like Jews?' Whether Peter had been a party to the demand by some that Gentiles should be circumcised is not stated, but his separatist action implied that the only satisfactory solution would be for Gentiles to adopt Jewish customs. There seems to be no question here whether or not Peter was previously right when he was prepared to live like a Gentile. Paul takes it for granted that his previous policy was proper. His failure was an inability to recognize the implications of this. He probably thought that compromise was the best solution, both Jews and Gentiles keeping respectively to their own customs. But Paul saw with acute penetration that this was no solution at all.

15. With this verse Paul leaves his historical comments and passes on to a theological discussion of the main principles lying behind the incidents just mentioned, although he still mentally addresses Peter and his fellow Christian Jews.

We ourselves, who are Jews by birth: this refers primarily to Peter and Paul, but embraces all Jewish Christians. Every Jew was particularly conscious of the richness of his heritage, and this accounts for his pride in his birth-rights.

not Gentile sinners: the description here must be viewed from the standpoint of the law. According to this standard all Gentiles have fallen short. Here the apostle is thinking mainly of the fact that Gentiles were outside the old covenant. But the major point of his argument is not that Jewish privileges must be compared with Gentile guiltiness, but that the best of Jews with all their privileges must still come through faith, and not works.

16. yet who know: the Christian faith is an intelligent faith, and there are certain fundamental facets which must be known by all believers. The content of knowledge here is Paul's theme not only through most of this epistle but also in the Epistle to the Romans. Both Peter and Paul are convinced about the validity of the assertion that faith, not works, justifies a man. It is important to recognize that the starting-point of Paul's doctrinal argument is an appeal to a basic conviction.

not justified by works of the law: the verb used here (*dikaioō*) is so characteristic of Paul and so integral to his theology that a right understanding of it is imperative. In the RSV margin it is rendered 'reckoned righteous', i.e. regarded as righteous or approved in the sight of God. Burton rightly maintains the forensic aspect in this word (46of.). The issue at stake was the means by which a man might attain a right standing before God. Whatever marred God's highest purpose for man merits condemnation, and justification is inextricably linked with the divinely appointed means of obtaining release from this condemnation. Moreover, the ideas of reconciliation and restoration are not lacking. A man cannot be regarded as righteous in God's eyes if any sin remains unforgiven and if the man is still left in his old relationship. Justification is consequently more than merely legal acquittal. In Paul's vocabulary 'works of the law' always denote efforts to attain a stated goal by conformity to a legal pattern, and have a particular application to the Jewish doctrine of works (or merit). It should be noted that the Greek phrase contains no article and need not therefore be restricted to the law of Moses. There is no justification through the mere observance of any form of legal code.

through faith in Jesus Christ: the words could be construed to mean 'faith of Jesus Christ', but that would not be meaningful in this context. It clearly means that faith which is centred upon Jesus Christ. Faith is set over against law, but it is worth noting that Paul uses a different preposition. In the former phrase he uses *ek* (i.e. out of works of the law) but here he uses *dia* (through). The first draws attention to origin, the second to agency. Justification does not proceed from faith any more than works, but it is appropriated by faith (cf. the similar distinction in Rom. 3.30; Phil. 3.9). But see the further comment on *ek* in the note below.

even we have believed in Christ Jesus: the pronoun 'we' (*hēmeis*) is emphatic here and is clearly intended to reinforce the similar pronoun in the previous verse. The formula used is literally 'believed into Christ Jesus', and conveys a characteristic of Christian faith, i.e. the entrusting of oneself to Christ. The change from Jesus Christ to Christ Jesus has no significance, and shows the interchangable character of these forms.

in order to be justified by faith in Christ: the repetition of the word 'faith' here, where it is not strictly needed in view of the preceding statement, serves to emphasize its cardinal importance in Paul's theology. He loses no opportunity to place emphasis upon it. Again, faith in Christ is expressed by the genitive, which must again mean that kind of faith of which Christ is the object. In the phrase, 'by faith' the preposition used (*ek*) denotes source and not agency (cf. *dia* in the previous phrase). The reason for the change is not easy to determine. It may be that in this case Paul's mind is obsessed with the contrast between faith and works, and for this reason he brings out the parallel in the preposition (cf. Lightfoot).

not by works . . . no one be justified: there is more repetition here, but Paul repeats the impossibility of justification by mere works in order to cite an Old Testament passage in support, although he cites very freely. It is from Ps. 143.2. It is thereby claimed to be an authoritative Scriptural principle that no living person (Greek *sarx*, flesh) shall be justified, i.e. on his own merits.

17. **in our endeavour to be justified in Christ:** the apostle thinks of it as a quest requiring effort. Indeed, the expression is particularly appropriate for those who, in spite of being Christians, imagine their own efforts will contribute something to secure acceptance with God.

we ourselves: is Paul still thinking of Peter and the Jewish Christians? The whole verse only becomes intelligible if this assumption is made. The matter under discussion has point only for those who have been in the habit of thinking of justification in terms of law, as the following statement shows.

if . . . we . . . were found to be sinners: the connection of thought is not obvious. Is Paul thinking purely hypothetically or is he basing his argument on experience? The 'if' clause suggests that he is putting it in the form of a rhetorical question to draw attention to the obvious answer which must be given. In all probability, the Judaizers were maintaining that all who were ignoring the ceremonial requirements of the law were found to be sinners, just as they were in the habit of describing Gentiles (as Paul does in verse 15). If so, Paul nullifies the position by implying that all who seek justification in Christ, by that very quest, place themselves in the category of sinners. But the 'if' clause may be intended to suggest an impossible state of affairs. If what the Jewish teachers conceive to be justification in Christ leads to an increase of sin, clearly there must be something wrong with their conception of justification.

is Christ then an agent of sin? The thought is that if the process of justification leads men into sin, this would make Christ an agent for producing sin, which would clearly be opposed to the nature of Christ. Paul strongly repudiates such an idea.

Certainly not! This represents a characteristic Pauline repudiation of an unthinkable suggestion (Greek *mē genoito*). It is frequently used in the Epistle to the Romans. There is no doubt that Paul rejects the conclusion (that Christ is an agent of sin), but does he reject the supposition that turning from the law makes men sinners? He seems rather to be rejecting the notion that justification can leave sin untouched.

18. **But if I build up again:** it is clear from the Greek conjunction used here (*gar*) that there is a close connection between this and the preceding statements. The rebuilding relates therefore to the idea of seeking justification by works, and so Paul maintains that such an action would make him a transgressor. It is to be noted that Paul, for the sake of demonstrating his point, is applying to himself the procedure adopted by the false teachers. It was they who were attempting to rebuild the citadel of the law and it was they who were demonstrating that they were transgressors. But it was much more effective for Paul to describe the process in the first person, because by this means he tactfully avoided sounding officious.

those things which I tore down: the same verb as is used here (*kataluō*) is used metaphorically of annulling or abrogating. It was appropriate, therefore, in a context in which Paul is referring to the annulling of the statutes of the law. The tearing-down operations were strenuous enough, but it would be more than mere folly to begin to rebuild. It would be sinful to reimpose law as a method of salvation.

I prove myself a transgressor: the verb is much more forceful than the words 'were found to be sinners' in the previous verse, because the action is described as active rather than as passive. The responsibility would rest squarely on the shoulders of Paul himself if he acted so inconsistently, as the argument supposes. The change from 'sinners' (*hamartōloi*) to 'transgressor' (*parabatēs*) is noticeable, and draws more specific attention to contravention of that which is right. The word means 'one who steps aside', used in a metaphorical sense of one who deviates from a straight path. Paul uses it in this sense in Rom. 2.25, 27, apart from which it occurs only in Jas 2.9, 11 in the New Testament.

19. **For I through the law died to the law:** the drift of Paul's argument can be understood as follows. He thinks that the real transgressors of the law are the very people who are claiming to be its main supporters. But having transferred the argument to himself, he realizes at once that the conclusion just stated at the end of verse 18 is contrary to his own experience. He has died to the law, and any rebuilding on the basis of law is clearly impossible. But what does he mean by dying to the law? The answer seems to be that he ceased to live in that world in which law was dominant (i.e. in Judaism). This dying had in fact come about by his experience under the law (cf. especially Rom. 7 as a commentary on this statement). The expression really stands for the idea of the law dying as the controlling principle of Paul's life, but it is much more vivid when Paul speaks as if it was he himself who had died to the law. Moreover, it forms a better parallel with the following phrase.

that I might live to God: Paul could never leave any description of his experience on a negative note. Dying to the law immediately suggests living to God. The one results from the other. The expression 'live to God' is clearly intended to contrast with 'died to the law', and must therefore mean life under the control of God and for the honour of God, as contrasted with the mere observance of legal statutes. Legalism could not infuse life, a fact that Paul had had to learn the hard way and which the Judaizers had apparently not yet begun to learn.

20. **I have been crucified with Christ:** the transformation from death to life causes Paul to dwell on the means by which this had been achieved, and his mind turns instinctively to the cross of Christ. But he does not give a theological exposition. Instead he shows the part played by the cross in his own experience. The expression of it is mystical, and for that reason is difficult to fathom, but it is clear enough that Paul conceives that he had a part in Christ's experience on the cross. He may be thinking of the objective effects of Christ's death which every believer enjoys, or he may be meditating on the believer's fellowship with Christ in being called upon to endure a similar spiritual crucifixion to self. The tense of the verb (perfect) suggests that Paul is thinking of that specific completed event which marked his identification with Christ and which has had an enduring effect upon his life. The persecutor Saul would never have become the missionary Paul by his own efforts. Saul had to die with Christ.

it is no longer I who live, but Christ who lives in me: Paul's sequence of argument is clear. 'I died' is explained as being crucified with Christ; 'I live' as Christ living in me. In one sense the apostle has ceased to have his own independent experiences. He has become so identified with Christ that what Christ does, he does. Yet when in this context he speaks of living, he gives a slightly different slant to it. It is not merely that he lives with Christ, but that Christ takes up his abode with him. There is a touch here of Paul's mystical 'in Christ' train of thought, but rather less mystical, for Paul thinks of himself as having become so closely identified with Christ that Christ dominates his whole experience (cf. Duncan).

and the life I now live in the flesh: what Paul means is that if he now talks of life in the generally accepted sense of the word, he thinks no longer of carnal living pursuing the desires and impulses of the self, but a new kind of living, a faith-life. The 'now' in this phrase marks the transition from his old life. Flesh (*sarx*) is used to draw out the contrast between the physical and spiritual aspects of life.

I live by faith in the Son of God: the same preposition is used with the word 'faith' as is used with 'flesh' (Greek *en*), which suggests that Paul is here thinking of faith as the sphere in which he lives. But he is careful to define the faith, which is specifically centred in the Son of God. Some texts read 'of God and of Christ' instead of 'Son of God', but the latter is probably correct. Whichever is the true reading, it is noticeable that this statement draws attention to the divine character of the object of faith, and accordingly enhances the value of the life of faith itself.

who loved me and gave himself for me: the mention of faith in Christ as Son of God leads Paul to dwell on what he has done. This is a dominant idea which occurs elsewhere in Paul's letters (cf. Rom. 4.25; 8.32; Eph. 5.25), and in each instance the same verb is used (*paradidōmi*). The combination of the concepts of love and sacrifice shows that the apostle has no harsh legalistic interpretation of the death of Christ. To him Christ's self-giving upon the cross was a definite act on his behalf (*huper emou*). The main wonder for him is the love which prompted it. The motive of love behind the self-giving of Christ is not only a powerful aspect of Paul's doctrine of the Atonement, but it is strongly emphasized in other streams of New Testament teaching. Nothing but love would have been a sufficient motive for God to send his Son to the cross, nor for the Son voluntarily to accept it.

21. I do not nullify the grace of God: the sudden introduction of this statement may suggest that Paul is answering some criticism that he is in fact setting aside the grace of God, i.e. as it is seen operating in the law. In this case his statement amounts to an emphatic refutation. Yet there is no special emphasis in the Greek of this sentence. It is better, therefore, to regard it as a brief summary of Paul's present position. In identifying himself with the crucified Christ, he was not making of none effect God's grace, and the implication seems to be that by contrast the Judaizers are doing precisely this. For a comment on the word 'grace', see 1.15.

for if justification were through the law: here Paul summarizes the position of the Judaizers. 'Through the law' is in direct contrast to the phrase 'by faith'. This antithesis is constantly in Paul's mind in this epistle and in the Epistle to the Romans. He once again draws from personal experience. He had tried to gain justification through law and had utterly failed. As he ponders the hypothetical possibility, he at once sees the implication it would have for his understanding of the Atonement.

then Christ died to no purpose: the necessity for Christ's death rests on the utter failure of all human methods of being justified. If legal observance could have achieved it there would have been no need for the cross. But since the cross is a fact, it must imply in Paul's reasoning that there was a definite purpose behind it. This is a basic assumption of all early Christian Christology. To the apostle it was so utterly unthinkable that Christ died to no purpose that he does not even consider that there is any alternative but to reject justification through law.

THE DOCTRINAL ARGUMENT 3.1-4.31

THE GALATIANS' OWN EXPERIENCE 3.1-5

3.1. O foolish Galatians: the description given here, which is prompted by Paul's contemplation of the folly of seeking justification by the works of the law, suggests not so much inability to think as a failure to use one's mental powers. The suggestion is that anyone with spiritual perception ought to be able to see the impossibility of legal efforts to save a man. This idea Paul proceeds to develop.

The fact that he addresses his readers by name suggests strong feeling on his part, mostly of indignation that they should have allowed themselves to be misled.

Who has bewitched you: the verb is one that was sometimes used in magical spells, and while we cannot suppose that the apostle had any personal acquaintance with contemporary magic, the word is vividly appropriate. They had looked, but had not seen. It was as if some spell upon them completely distorted their vision. The apostle cannot imagine that any whose minds were not under some external influence would have been so foolish as these Galatians. He can only suggest somewhat ironically that they must be under some adverse magic.

Jesus Christ was publicly portrayed as crucified: Paul is here using a suggestive figure of speech. Items of news were normally announced in the ancient world by means of a placard in some prominent place where it would catch the public eye. When Paul had preached to the Galatians it was as if he had held up before them some such placard (Lightfoot). And yet their eyes had turned away from it.

The tense of the word 'crucified' should be noted, for the perfect participle means literally 'having been crucified', and suggests that more than the mere historic event is in mind. Paul is thinking in fact of the abiding significance of the event, hence the perfect tense. The cross occupied a large place in the thoughts of the apostle in this epistle, and is undoubtedly central to his theology of justification. His basic assumption here is that those who have looked upon the cross should be free of adverse influences. It was an anomaly that any who had understood the significance of that event should ever be bewitched.

2. Let me ask you only this: literally the words should read, 'this thing alone I am wanting to learn from you', although the verb (*manthanō*) should probably be understood here in the sense of 'ascertain'. Paul is clearly not asking for information, for he knows the answer. Why then does he use this particular verb? Is he wishing to imply that for a moment he has become a pupil to these senseless people? That is probably reading more into the verb than is warranted. Paul is rather like a teacher with a class of unresponsive children demanding an answer from them which will banish their inattention. Such a dialogue method of argument is used elsewhere to equally good effect by the apostle (cf., for example, Rom. 2).

Did you receive the Spirit by works of the law? The apostle appeals to the experience of his readers. How did they become Christians? They knew very well it was not by fulfilling the law. The coming of the Spirit upon them marked their initiation. They could not deny that law had had nothing to do with it. This is the first of many references in this epistle to the Holy Spirit. It is significant that Paul takes for granted here, what he specifically states in Rom. 8.9, that every believer possesses the Spirit of Christ.

or by hearing with faith? The Greek phrase so translated is exactly parallel in form to the antithetical 'by the works of the law', and could be rendered literally 'by hearing of faith'. Yet there is a difference, for 'works of the law' are works done in conformity with law, whereas the present phrase means the kind of hearing which leads to and is, therefore, accompanied by faith. The gift of the Spirit comes when faith gives its response to the preaching of the gospel.

3. Are you so foolish? He does not answer the first question. It must have seemed to him too obvious to need answering. So he asks another, calculated once again to bring them to their senses, almost as if he can hardly credit the extent of their folly.

Having begun with the Spirit, are you now ending with the flesh? The compound verb rendered 'begun' (*enarchomai*) is used in the New Testament only here and in Phil. 1.6, and in both cases Paul links it with the same verb (*epiteleō*, to complete). The question as Paul states it here is incongruous, for such an antithesis exists between Spirit and flesh that it is impossible to begin with spirit and end with flesh. What Paul means therefore is that abandonment of the Spirit excludes the possibility of ending. If they are trying to do so, this shows the extent of their folly. The order of the Greek words in this statement is not without importance, for the word Spirit (*Pneumati*) is brought into juxtaposition with flesh (*sarki*), no doubt to heighten the contrast.

4. Did you experience so many things in vain? The question may be rendered, 'Did you suffer?' Either interpretation is possible. If, of course, the Galatians had actually suffered for their faith, Paul's allusion to it here would be very much to the point. But if the other rendering is preferred, the reference would be to the general Christian experience of the readers (Lietzmann). The word is neutral, but all the other occurrences of it in the New Testament are in the sense of misfortunes. It would be expected that if the experiences did not involve suffering some qualifying word would have been inserted to indicate this. The second rendering would seem to have rather more in its favour. In either case, the apostle appeals to what they have already known. Could they possibly regard this as vanity? The phrase 'in vain' (*eikē*) can mean either 'ineffectively' or 'needlessly', the latter obviously being more appropriate if the verb is understood to mean suffering. They could have avoided suffering altogether if they had begun in the flesh.

if it really is in vain: it would seem that Paul is still hopeful that they will change their approach and so save the results of their previous experience. In other words, he wants to put out of his mind the possibility that his previous work among them was to no effect. The present statement seems intended to indicate that Paul is treating his argument as hypothetical.

5. he who supplies the Spirit to you: this is an indirect description of God, calling attention to the origin of the gifts of the Spirit. If the readers are turning away from the Spirit they are turning away from God. The verb used here is also used by Paul in 2 C. 9.10 and Col. 2.19, and the corresponding noun in Eph. 4.16 and Phil. 1.19, in all of which instances there is the idea of abundant supply. In Phil. 1.19, the notion is applied as here to the Spirit.

and works miracles among you: there is but one article in Greek to serve both the last phrase and this, which shows the close connection between the gift of the Spirit and miracles. The latter word focuses attention upon the divine power as the former does on the divine grace. It could also be understood that the latter is a description of the former, in which case it is the miraculous manifestation of the Spirit which is in mind. But it seems better to regard the gift of the Spirit more comprehensively as representing all spiritual gifts (so Burton).

Does he . . . do so by works . . . or by hearing? This is almost a reproduction of the question in verse 2, with the significant difference that the emphasis now shifts from the recipients to the giver. Neither the Galatians received nor did God give His Spirit according to legal measurements. It was an act of pure grace which faith alone was able to appropriate. The question here arises from Paul's doctrine of God. He could never conceive of God as being bound by law. The spiritual character of God demanded an altogether different motive. Since the Spirit was essentially a gift, it could not be earned. Works of the law were therefore an incongruous channel for the reception of a gift from such a source. If it be argued that law as much as Spirit originates with God, it must be acknowledged that the fundamental difference is that one must be obeyed by human effort, the other received by faith.

THE CASE OF ABRAHAM 3.6–9

6. Thus Abraham believed God: Paul's sudden appeal to Abraham appears somewhat unexpected, but he evidently assumes that his readers will recognize at once that the case of Abraham answers the question he has just posited. The apostle proceeds to cite Gen. 15.6 in such a way as to imply that Scripture supplies a conclusive answer. He assumes that these Gentile Galatians would be acquainted with the salient features of Abraham's life. That the statement cited must have been very well known is clear from the fact that it appears in Rom. 4.3 and Jas 2.23. But what interest would the Gentiles have had in Abraham? It is most probable that Gentile converts would soon learn the significance of Abraham for the history of salvation. In the case of the Galatians it is possible that the Judaizers had already appealed to Abraham in support of circumcision and that Paul found it necessary to show that Abraham is a witness for faith over against works. The passage cited was much debated among the Jews at this time, and the apostle had no doubt been involved with it before his conversion (cf. Lightfoot).

In what sense did Abraham 'believe'? He was prepared to take God at his word when he promised him a multitudinous inheritance, but what connection did this have with Christian faith? Paul makes a tremendous assumption here, i.e. that all true faith in God is a unity. Moreover, he further assumes that his readers will at once assent to this. They would readily recognize that there was nothing Abraham could himself do to implement the promised inheritance, in view of the barrenness of Sarah. All he could do was to believe in an attitude of utter dependence upon God, and it is this element which is common to all true faith. The principle underlying Abraham's faith was no different from the basic principle of Christian faith, although the latter was necessarily more comprehensive because of the revelation of Christ.

'**reckoned to him as righteousness**': the verb involves the idea of calculation. It is a metaphor drawn from the realm of accountancy, and yet the commercial illustration must not be pushed too far. The reckoning was a reckoning of divine grace, far removed from any idea of merit or of debt. The statement clearly means that Abraham was regarded as a righteous man on the basis of his preparedness to believe God. The apostle develops the same thought more fully in Rom. 4.

7. So you see: Paul proceeds to show the logical outcome of the Scriptural statement about Abraham. The verb is *ginōskō* (to know) and implies here mental perception. The readers should know the implication of Abraham's faith. The verb could be regarded as imperative (so Emmet), but this is less likely.

men of faith: it is significant that Paul does not define the object of faith, because to him Abraham's faith was the same kind as Christian faith. The Greek phrase means literally 'those who proceed from faith as their source', i.e. those in whom faith is basic.

sons of Abraham: this was no doubt an echo of a term that the Judaizers were using. To be sons of Abraham, they were maintaining, it was essential to be circumcised. This was considered so great a privilege for the Jew that it is not surprising that the idea of becoming one of the faithful was appealing to Gentiles. See the comment on 4.5 on the non-Jewish notion of adoption. The Jewish argument is understandable, since circumcision was, after all, the sign of the inheritors of the Abrahamic covenant, but Paul lifts the idea of 'sons of Abraham' from a physical to a spiritual level. A son must substantiate his claims by walking in the footsteps of the father, and in this case it was very evidently a matter of faith. Paul sees that the common link of faith is a much stronger basis for sonship than physical descent.

8. And the scripture: this verse is closely connected with the last and develops the idea of Abraham's family by again appealing to Scripture. Since Paul is dealing with Judaizers he is particularly anxious to answer their arguments from Scripture, which they would have regarded as authoritative in common with all the early Christians.

foreseeing that God would justify: Paul treats Scripture as a personal agency, no doubt because of his deep conviction that God speaks through it. By the verb 'foreseeing' (*proidousa*), Paul indicates something more than priority in time. It implies a view of the continuity of the new order with the old. What happened in Abraham's day was, in fact, a forecast for the future. The faith element in God's method of justification is therefore timeless.

the Gentiles by faith: the thought here is that the promise to Abraham must have embraced the Gentiles since the promise extended to all nations, and this inclusion had come not by circumcision but by faith.

preached the gospel beforehand to Abraham: the choice of this verb in relation to Abraham is significant, because it shows Paul's conviction that the promise to Abraham foreshadowed the gospel. It was fulfilled only in the gospel. With this thought may be connected the words of Jesus, 'Your father Abraham rejoiced that he was to see my day; he saw it and was glad' (Jn 8.56). Both our Lord and his apostle recognize that there is continuity between Abraham's faith and the Christian era. This is clearly more than exegesis of the Genesis passage. It is a reappraisal of the original promise in the light of the coming of Christ. It was only in retrospect that it was appreciated that the word to Abraham was to be fulfilled in the gospel.

'In thee shall all the nations be blessed': whereas the Jewish interpretation of this was that other nations should be blessed through Israel, Paul understands it more comprehensively of the coming of the gospel to the Gentiles. The statement here is based on Gen. 12.3 and Gen. 18.8. The Old Testament form of the verb is reflexive ('shall bless themselves'), but the change is clearly more appropriate for application to the gospel. Paul might well have claimed that by understanding the words of Genesis as referring to the inclusion of the Gentiles the promise gains much fuller significance. Contemporary Jewish nationalism could only conceive of an ideal world with Israel at the centre and with Gentiles subsidiary. That was as far as the blessing could reach. But Paul has a larger vision.

9. So then: this verse is presented as a sequel to the last. Paul is drawing out the consequences of the promise to Abraham for the present situation. In view of what is admittedly true about Abraham, Paul considers that it must be equally true for all genuine faith.

men of faith: this takes up the same phrase as in verse 7, but applies it differently. Here the emphasis is laid on the blessing, there on the status of sonship.

blessed with Abraham who had faith: more literally this would read 'with faithful Abraham' (as AV). Nevertheless, the adjective certainly has an active meaning here, which the RSV clearly brings out. The other rendering would suggest trustworthiness which does not fit the context. Abraham was a shining example of a 'man of faith' (*ho ek pisteōs*).

The Different Results from Faith and Works 3.10–14

10. For all who rely on works of the law: the same phrase is used in verses 2 and 5, with the addition of the word 'all' (*hosoi*), which makes it more comprehensive than Judaizers alone. Any who rely on legal efforts, whether Jew or Gentile, are included. Although Paul develops a new line of argument, he makes this connect up closely with the preceding argument, as is clear from the initial conjunction 'for' (*gar*).

under a curse: the idea is of separation from God and is the very antithesis of blessing.

'**Cursed be . . . and do them**': this quotation of Scripture is from Dt. 27.26, where it closes the list of curses pronounced at Mount Ebal. When Paul uses the formula 'It is written' (*gegraptai*) he is doing so in more than a merely formal way. It is an assertion of the authority of Scripture. To show that Scripture itself demonstrates the judgment due to all who do not abide by everything in the law would clearly be an effective argument in refuting those who were appealing to Scripture in support of a continued legal approach to righteousness. The point is not that justification by works of the law was impossible. But by insisting on the necessity of any part of the law (such as circumcision) the Judaizers were, argues Paul, incurring a curse if they failed in any other part of it. The fact was that law as a means of salvation could bring only a curse and was therefore ineffective (cf. Bring).

11. Now it is evident: the word used (*dēlon*) means 'clear to the mind', in a way that should be generally admitted.

justified before God: the addition of the words 'before God' (*para tō Theō*) focuses attention on justification as seen in the eyes of God, and is contrasted with any human interpretation of justification. An altogether different standard would have obtained if man could have decided his own means. He would certainly have chosen a course which would have ministered to his pride, which is precisely the effect of the emphasis among the Judaizers on works of the law.

by the law: it is important to note that throughout his argument Paul is not denying the function of law but only a legalistic interpretation of it.

'**He who through faith is righteous shall live**': here is a citation from Hab. 2.4, but without any introductory formula. It evidently had made a deep impression on the mind of Paul, for it is cited also in Rom. 1.17, and may be said to be the key to the understanding of that epistle. No doubt its main appeal lay in its combination of faith and righteousness in a sense close to its Christian meaning. The words undoubtedly had a deeper meaning for Paul than for Habakkuk, but the germinal ideas were there. Thus 'faith' becomes faith in Christ, 'righteous' means accounted righteous in God's sight, 'living' refers to the highest form of life, embracing eternal life.

The rendering could be, 'the righteous shall live by faith' (RSV *margin*), in which case the function of faith in the continuing life of the justified is in mind. But the former translation is preferable, especially as it has more relevance to Paul's argument here, although the former fits better the historical context of Habakkuk.

12. but the law does not rest on faith: there is no point of contact between law and faith. A man is not called upon to believe the law but to do it. In the Greek no verb is used, but the idea is expressed by the prepositional phrase (*ek pisteōs*) already used several times in this epistle, which in this case effectively denies that law proceeds from faith. The apostle is not, of course, asserting that no legalist can possess faith, but that law does not depend on faith for its basis (so Duncan).

'**He who does them shall live by them**': this is the essence of legalism. The law

lays down its commandments. Those who fail to fulfil them incur its condemnation, whatever their own attitude might be. Faith in this case is irrelevant. The
statement here is a free rendering of Lev. 18.5 and the same idea is echoed elsewhere
by Paul in Rom. 10.5. But does this Scriptural statement refute Paul's assertion in
the first part of the verse? Is it possible to live by legal observance? If so, faith can
be ruled out without loss. But the apostle would never make Scripture contradict
itself like this. No doubt he means to demonstrate that a pure and perfect legalism,
had it been possible, would have led to justification. But the mere fact that he
reverts in the next verse to dwell on the curse of the law shows that he assumes,
without the necessity to prove, that no-one is able to do, and therefore no-one is
able to live by, the law. Indeed, Christ is the only one who has ever been able fully
to do the law (cf. Bring's discussion).

13. **Christ redeemed us from the curse of the law:** without using any connecting particle Paul abruptly introduces an important doctrinal assertion. The
previous verses have made abundantly clear that those who seek for justification
by legalistic means are in a hopeless position. The only hope is an entirely new
departure, and this is where Paul brings in Christ. He has not been mentioned since
verse 1. The idea of redemption had originally a commercial significance involving
the payment of a price for the purchase of a slave. Since the slave was sometimes
bought to be set free, the word particularly signifies 'deliverance' when applied to
the work of Christ. Our Lord's own 'ransom' saying (Mk 10.45) must be understood in this sense.

But to whom is Paul referring by 'us'? Clearly those who are under the curse of
the law. But does this restrict it to those who have known the yoke of Judaism?
This is possible, and would appear to gain some support from the mention of
Gentiles in the next verse, since these seem to be a distinct group. But it is
questionable whether Paul would have so restricted the redemptive work of Christ.
It is reasonable to suppose that although he is thinking primarily of himself, of the
Judaizers and of all those who have tried to attain justification by means of law, he
would assume that if Jews were under the curse, so also were the Gentiles. There
was no denying that all needed deliverance.

having become a curse for us: this is the real crux of Paul's statement, for it
explains how Christ could redeem men from the curse of the law. And yet the
explanation needs explaining. How could Christ possibly become a curse for us?
Such a notion does not come easily to modern minds, with the result that some
expositors have maintained that Paul is not dealing here with an actuality but with
the wrong idea of the Judaizers (so Burton). But this would empty Paul's
argument of its main spearhead. Justification by means of law is impossible because
law brings only a curse on those disobeying it. But the fact remains that all have
disobeyed and therefore Christ must do something about the curse. This was no
imaginary situation, but an intensely real one. Paul had known the acute tension
of it in his own experience. And he had found deliverance only when he realized

that Christ had done something for him. He uses the preposition *huper* (which means 'on behalf of'), but the context implies that Christ took our place in becoming a curse. What should have come to us went to him. No-one will deny the mystery of this, but other Scriptures support the underlying principle. Our Lord's word of forsakenment on the cross, and Paul's declaration in 2 C. 5.21 that Christ was made sin are as unfathomable as this statement, but there is no justification for weakening them. Paul had caught more than a glimpse of the cost of our redemption. It should be noted that the apostle uses the word 'curse' (*katara*), not 'accursed' (*anathema*), since the latter would have been unthinkable. He does not state that Christ had become the curse of God. The curse is defined in relation to the law.

for it is written: the same formula as in verse 10. Paul is determined to prove his points from Scripture, not only because he knows that in this he shares common ground with the Judaizers, but more fundamentally because any truth supported by Scripture is, in his view, fully authenticated. The formula is repeated again in 4.22, 27. It is significant that in two of its occurrences the apostle is drawing attention to curses pronounced by the law, in one to rejoicing (4.27) and in the other to a historical narrative (4.22). Except in 4.22, the formula carries with it an authoritative tone.

'Cursed be every one who hangs on a tree': this is quoted from Dt. 21.23, which in its context refers to the practice of hanging on a tree the body of a criminal who had been put to death. It did not primarily therefore refer to crucifixion. But it would not have been inappropriate to apply it to the crucifixion of Christ, for his dead body had hung upon the cross before being removed by Joseph of Arimathea. Paul sees in this statement of Scripture an explanation of how Christ became a curse. The manner of his death had involved him in this. But the apostle sees an infinitely deeper significance in Christ's death than this, for the passage does not and could not illuminate the mystery of how Christ became a curse *for us*. Christ became implicated in the law's condemnation of those with whom he was identified. But some expositors interpret Paul's intentions differently. Since Christ hung upon a tree, from a legalistic point of view he must be cursed, but no Christian could admit this, hence the legalistic view must be false (cf. Burton). But this renders almost unintelligible the first part of the verse. Christ did not redeem us from something only imaginary or something valid only from a legalist point of view. The curse resting on the crucified Christ was the same curse resting on all men.

14. This verse states the results of Christ's death in a two-fold form: (a) that Abraham's blessing might become universal and (b) that all, Jew and Gentile alike, might receive the Spirit.

in Christ Jesus: whatever blessings have accrued they come only to those in Christ. The phrase here seems to refer to all Christians as forming a corporate fellowship with Christ. The idea of a common union in him is integral to Paul's theology. See further comment on the phrase in 1.22.

the blessing of Abraham: Paul returns here to the thought expressed in verse 9. The promise to Abraham was one of blessing, but the law had intervened with its curse. However, since Christ has removed the curse of the law by taking it on himself, a return to Abraham's blessing is possible. Indeed, Paul states this in a purpose clause (with *hina*), which makes clear that the removal of the curse was n order that the blessing might be shared.

upon the Gentiles: while it was a question of legalism, the Gentiles were excluded from the blessing. But if the promises come by faith instead of law, as they do in Christ, there is no longer a barrier. Gentiles are at no disadvantage compared with Jews.

that we might receive: this further consequence of Christ's death is similarly expressed in the form of a purpose clause (*hina*), and is probably to be taken as co-ordinate with the first clause. This would mean that the extension of the blessing to Gentiles and the gift of the Spirit are different aspects of the same operation, rather than being distinct from each other. By using the first person plural here Paul not only includes himself, but comprehensively includes all Christians, Jews and Gentiles alike.

the promise of the Spirit: in most cases where the word 'promise' (*epangelia*) occurs in the New Testament it refers to a divine promise in the sense of something given as a gracious act of God. To what does the promise in this passage relate? It is natural to link it up with the promise of the Spirit made by Jesus (Lk. 24.49; Ac. 1.4; Jn 14-16). There were also some Old Testament passages, such as Jl 2.28 and Ezek. 36.27 which pointed forward to the activity of the Spirit. It is highly unlikely that Paul was unacquainted with the remarkable outpouring of the Spirit at Pentecost. In any case the Galatians had experienced the presence of the Spirit. The promise had been realized. The phrase may therefore be understood to mean 'the promised Spirit' (Moffatt's rendering). The fact that Paul associates the gift of the Spirit with Abraham's blessing, although there is no mention of the Spirit in the original promise to Abraham, shows that he conceives the fulfilment of the blessing to be *par excellence* in the universal activity of the Spirit in men of faith.

through faith: already this has been strongly stressed, but the mention of promise prompts a further reference. Receiving a promise is an act of faith, not of merit.

PROMISE AND LAW 3.15-29

15ff. Having introduced the idea of promise, Paul at once realizes the necessity to discuss its relationship to law. The Judaizers, whom he has in mind all along, would have been as zealous as anyone to claim a share in Abraham's blessing and would in fact imagine that they were doing so in insisting on circumcision. In this next passage the apostle shows how law could not annul promise.

15. To give a human example: this is rather a free rendering of the Greek, which literally states, 'I speak according to a man' (*kata anthrōpon*), a phrase which occurs also in Rom. 3.5. In both cases the phrase means that Paul is attempting to express the matter in terms of human speech and analogy, with the suggestion that such terms are not entirely adequate to convey divine truths. Here he appeals to a common practice of his time, and seeks to show how even a human analogy is in harmony with the statements from Scripture just stated.

no one annuls even a man's will: the word translated 'will' may equally well be rendered 'covenant' (*diathēkē*), but this raises a difficulty. The two ideas are quite different, and it is important to decide which is correct. At first sight the former would appear more probable since it is the more normal meaning of the Greek word. Indeed, the latter meaning finds no support in classical usage, nor in the inscriptions, nor in the papyri. Yet in the LXX the word almost invariably means 'covenant'. When the apostle uses a word which for every Christian acquainted with the Scriptures would have overtones of meaning which were absent from contemporary usage, it is not easy to decide whether he intends the biblical or the everyday sense. Since Paul was deeply versed in Septuagint usage, having been steeped in it all his life, he could not have used the word here without thinking of the idea of a contract between God and man. Moreover, his mind has been dwelling on God's covenant with Abraham. At the same time the word 'covenant' is apt to suggest an idea which is not to the fore here. It was not a bargain struck between God and man. Even Abraham, with all his immense stature as a man of God, depended wholly on the divine initiative for the effectiveness of the covenant. It was a matter of grace, and therefore one-sided. Paul may be using the term here in a sense somewhat between the idea of a 'will', which is too restricted because no mention is made of the death of the testator, and the idea of a covenant. He means that once an agreement has been made for the disposal of property, nothing can alter this except the party or parties who have effected the agreement. It cannot be cancelled by anyone else.

or adds to it: the legal imagery is clear. A codicil which modified the original terms was always possible in a legal disposition. Paul imagines that some may regard the law as a kind of codicil to the promise which therefore cancels out the effect of the latter. But he cannot conceive that God would ever contradict himself like this, and no-one else had the power to do it, as is sufficiently illustrated by human dispositions, where only the parties concerned can change the terms.

ratified: when an agreement has been ratified it is actively in force. Paul is thinking of God's covenant, which has been operating in history since Abraham's time.

16. Now the promises were made to Abraham and to his offspring: here Paul identifies the covenant to which he has just alluded. It is no new thing but was made to Abraham. No-one has since been able to annul it or to modify it. In spite of its antiquity and in spite of all that has happened during the intervening period, it still stands ratified.

What significance is to be attached to the change from the singular 'promise' in

verse 14 to the plural 'promises' here? It is to be noted that in verse 17 Paul returns
to the singular, although the plural reappears in verse 21. In all probability there is
no significance in these changes at all, although the plural may conceivably allude
to the frequent repetition of the same promise to Abraham. This plurality only
serves to emphasize the real basis of Abraham's inheritance. Romans 9.4 furnishes
another example of Paul's choice of the plural when speaking of Israel's heritage.

The inclusion of Abraham's offspring (the Greek has *sperma* (seed)) is essential to
Paul's argument, for the covenant was not restricted to Abraham's own lifetime.
It spanned the centuries of his descendants. But this idea leads to another, for he
notes that the promise was directed to offspring in the singular and the resultant
comment, though slightly parenthetical, is fraught with deep spiritual meaning, for
it turns his thought once more to Christ. As Duncan points out, Paul is
spiritualizing, not allegorizing as in 4.22f.

It does not say, 'And to offsprings', referring to many: is Paul's argument
valid from a merely grammatical feature? At first it seems not only strange but
strangely unlike Paul to deduce so much from such a narrow basis. From a logical
point of view the singular could as easily denote plurality (considered collectively)
as the plural, just as the English word 'seed'. An argument of this kind may savour
of illegitimately fine distinctions. And yet Paul is not basing a truth on a small
point of grammar. He has a deep spiritual appraisal of the real nature of
Abraham's covenant. It was pointing to its fulfilment in Christ (Ridderbos).
Grammar was but indirectly supporting a truth which had already dawned on
the apostle as the real essence of the promise.

referring to one . . . which is Christ: there is no denying that there is a touch
of Rabbinical method in Paul's argument, but he seems to have at the back of his
mind, even although he does not enlarge upon it, a conviction that none of
Abraham's seed had inherited the promise until Christ. The real blessing which has
come upon Jew and Gentile alike has come only in Christ. He is the Seed of
Abraham *par excellence*, and all who are in him are equally Abraham's sons, as Paul
has already shown in verse 7. The Jewish Christians would not readily admit that
all who were in Christ were thus sons of Abraham, but this is clearly a deep
conviction with Paul, and because of this he can conceive of all men of faith as
summed up in Christ.

17. This is what I mean: the apostle now proceeds to a further development
of the argument begun in verse 15, and the present phrase draws attention to this.
four hundred and thirty years afterwards: the reason for the mention of the
number of years is to draw attention to the considerable priority of the promise to
the law. There are difficulties over this period of 430 years, for there seems to have
been difference of opinion whether it referred originally to the sojourn in
Egypt or, as here, to the period separating the patriarchs from the giving of the
law. Exodus 12.40 supports the former in the Hebrew text, but in the LXX the
wording would support the latter. Genesis 15.13 and Ac. 7.6 both mention round

figures of 400 years. There seems to be some confusion over the interpretation of
this period. Josephus makes contradictory statements concerning it. But the precise
explanation of the 430 years is unimportant for Paul's argument.

a covenant previously ratified by God: this is the crucial factor in the argument.
The promise was ratified long before the law was instituted, therefore on the basis
of the principle enunciated in verse 15, the law could not possibly annul it. Particularly is this the case since the covenant was ratified by God, which is clearly
intended to contrast vividly with any human covenant, as mentioned in verse 15.
This brings out very clearly the one-sided nature of God's covenant. So long as he
kept his promise the covenant would stand, for it did not depend on the merit of
the recipients.

so as to make the promise void: the verb used here occurs elsewhere in the
New Testament only in Mt. 15.6 and its parallel in Mk 7.13, where it expresses the
statement of Jesus about the effect of 'tradition' on the law (or word) of God. If
the law had made modifications to the promise, it would have emptied the promise
of its original meaning, which in Paul's view is unthinkable.

18. **the inheritance:** by this term Paul means to include all the spiritual
blessings promised to Abraham and his seed. The Jews were deeply conscious of
their share in Abraham's inheritance. This accounts for their jealous concern to
assert that they were Abraham's children (cf. Jn 8.33). When Jews became
Christians they would not lose this sense of privilege. But the criterion used by the
Judaizers to determine the heirs was different from that used by Paul. The former
said that the qualification was circumcision and legal observance; the latter that
faith alone was sufficient. There could be no compromise between these opposing
principles. Law cancels out promise.

but God gave it to Abraham by a promise: the verb here indicates that behind
the promise was God's free favour, which would be contradicted if inheritance
came by law. Paul makes this assertion as if there can be no question about it. The
emphatic position of Abraham in the Greek text suggests that Paul regards this
appeal to the historic covenant with Abraham as a conclusive test case. What is
true for Abraham must have a timeless validity. In Paul's mind, once a divine
promise has been made it could not possibly be nullified without necessitating a
change in the divine character, which for him was unthinkable. It is noteworthy
that Paul's argument throughout is soundly based in history.

19. **Why then the law?** If the promise to Abraham was entirely unaffected by
the law, what was the purpose of the law? Paul at once faces this perfectly fair
question which the Judaizers might ask. His argument thus far might seem to
suggest that the law could be completely ignored, and it was clearly essential for
him to deal with this problem, if he was to influence readers who were being taught
the absolute necessity to abide by every ordinance of the law.

it was added: the concept of the law as an addition or interpolation to the promise
would have been a revolutionary idea to pious Jews and scarcely less so to Jewish

Christians still devoted to the sanctity of the law. So great was the esteem for the Torah in Jewish thought that to think of it as an addition would have required a complete reappraisal of its real significance. But this is precisely what had happened in Paul's thought.

because of transgressions: Paul's choice of wording here must be noted. He speaks of transgressions (*parabaseis*), not 'sins', for he has in mind intentional faults, and the word used means a stepping aside from a right track. The law had laid down the right track and had made men conscious of deviations from it. It is in this sense that the apostle means that the law came 'because' of transgressions. The law had no power to check transgressions, which could be achieved only by the gospel.

till the offspring should come: the reason for Paul's parenthesis in verse 16 now becomes clear. 'The offspring' has already been identified as Christ. The apostle points to the fact that the coming of Christ marked a crisis in the function of the law (cf. Luther). He conceives of a sequence which may be summarized as follows: age of promise, age of law, age of Christ, the last being conceived as a fulfilment of the age of promise.

to whom the promise had been made: the verb used is in the perfect tense and indicates a past promise with a present effect. This idea transforms the ancient promise to Abraham and brings it into the first century A.D. The age of promise is still present, in spite of the interlude of the law.

ordained by angels: the idea of the part played by angels in the giving of the law occurs also in Ac. 7.53 and Heb. 2.2, but has no basis in the Old Testament except in the LXX text of Dt. 33.2. It was a common notion of later Rabbinical teachers. It was clearly a firm conviction of the early Christians. Paul's allusion to it here was to prove the secondary character of the law. The word translated 'ordained' (*diatageis*) is used in the sense of 'administered'. The rendering 'by' would be better translated as 'through', i.e. 'through the agency of', which would then distinguish the angels from the ultimate originator of the law, i.e. God himself.

It is a relevant question what Gentile Christians like the Galatians would make of Paul's reasoning here. He assumes that they would not only understand but be convinced by the force of the argument. It may well be that the Judaizers had instructed them about the superhuman origin of the law and had cited the widely held conviction that it was administered by angels to enhance its authority. If this is a true picture, Paul's appeal to the same conviction to prove the secondary character of the law would be exactly relevant. He had no fear that anyone would deny angelic participation in the giving of the law, nor did he anticipate that anyone would dispute that a promise by direct revelation would be superior to a law mediated by angels.

through an intermediary: literally this means, 'by the hand of an intermediary', thus introducing the human agent by whom the law was passed on, i.e. Moses. It is worth noting that although Paul says so much about the law in this epistle he does not once mention Moses by name. He is concentrating on principles and not personalities in the case of the law. He is certainly not wishing to set Abraham over against Moses. The word for 'intermediary' (*mesitēs*) occurs elsewhere in the New Testament only in Heb. 8.6, 9.15, 12.24 and in 1 Tim. 2.5, in all of which cases it refers to Christ as the mediator between God and man. Here, however, it cannot sustain that interpretation and must refer to Moses. It occurs in a similar sense in the *Assumption of Moses*, 1.14; 3.12.

20. **Now an intermediary implies more than one:** the obscurity of this verse is at once obvious, and it is not surprising that there have been a vast number of different interpretations. Many of them can immediately be ruled out because they do not conform to the sound exegetical principle that the writer must have intended his words to be intelligible to his immediate readers. The first half of this verse is evidently meant to be a development of the concluding section of verse 19, which has referred to the mediatorial work of Moses. It states a general principle about intermediaries as a class. Although a definite article is used in Greek, it seems highly probable that this is a generic usage since it states what is not confined to any particular mediator but is true of all. The principle itself is indeed a truism, for the root-idea of a mediator requires that there must be two opposing parties which need reconciliation. It must follow, therefore, that at least three parties are involved in mediatorship. In the special case of the law, apart from the agency of angels, the mediator acted as the representative of the people to God and as the representative of God to the people. The giving of the law was not therefore a direct divine communication to those who were to be the beneficiaries. This at once put the law in a different category from the promise which was a direct revelation to Abraham. This makes reasonably good sense, but there is one problem. Is Paul's assumption that there is a real distinction between primary and secondary revelation valid? He himself would not have denied the divine origin of the law. Was the means used then of any real significance? Although the ultimate result was not affected, to an oriental mind the means used would certainly tend to affect the esteem with which the revelation was held. There would be some difference if a king sent an ambassador to negotiate with an enemy or if he went himself. The peace would be the same, but the importance of the mission would be differently construed. The apostle by his own experience (see 1.12) had discovered the superior value of a direct personal intervention from God, and this colours his whole approach to the law. Paul's conversion experience certainly partook of the nature of promise and not law, which made him spiritually conditioned towards the position in which Abraham was placed.

but God is one: it is this part of the verse which contains the greatest obscurity. Two features, however, are clear. (1) There is an intended contrast between God and an intermediary. Clearly, God is superior to anyone who acts as a representative for him, or as an intercessor before him on behalf of others. (2) There is equally a contrast between 'one' and 'more than one', with the assumption that one is better than a plurality. Since the oneness applies to God it may be inferred that it concerns the perfect unity of his person, although Paul does not make this explicit. The unity of God was a dominant feature in the creed of every Jew and would not have been less so among the Christians, although in a different sense when they once appreciated the divine character of Christ and of the Holy Spirit. But theological unity is not to the forefront in this passage. It is probably better to confine the notion of oneness to numerical unity cited to support the superiority of promise to law. God consulted with no others when he made the promises to Abraham. They were his own supreme declarations. But the law was different, because this was essentially a contract which depended on the good faith of both parties concerned, and if one party failed a mediator would be necessary. But with a promise it is all in the hands of one person, i.e. the giver.

Because of the difficulty of the verse, some have treated it as a gloss (so Emmet), but this must be rejected, not only because of the lack of any manuscript support, but even more because it is inconceivable that a statement of such apparent difficulty would ever have found its way into the text if it did not originally belong.

21. Against the promises of God: a real problem arises over the relation of law to promise. If law is inferior to promise, is there any possibility that they conflict? Paul might have answered this by showing that since both had a divine origin there could be no contradiction in the divine mind. But he does not answer in this way, although his next statement implies it.

Certainly not: this is Paul's usual strong expression for the rejection of an idea (*mē genoito*), and here it is called forth by the implication of contradiction in God. The conviction of the essential consistency of God's character may be said to be a sheet-anchor of the apostle's theological position. If a man's conception of law creates a contradiction with promise, Paul can only conclude that that particular view of law must be wrong. This was a lesson that he had had to learn himself at considerable cost.

for if a law had been given which could make alive: here Paul gives a reason for his emphatic rejection, and in doing so introduces a new element into the discussion, i.e. life. It has previously occurred in verses 11 and 12, but only in the passages quoted and has been left in abeyance until now. Paul's method of reasoning appears to be as follows. Law is associated with curses, the very antithesis of life. Law in fact could only show that man did not qualify for life. It had no power to bring to life that which it had pronounced dead. That is because it is contrary to the nature of law to give life. Paul's if-clause is therefore positing the impossible but his purpose is to show that the reason for the superiority of promise over law is not due to any failure on the part of the latter to achieve what it was designed to do. It had brought no life because it had never been intended for that purpose. If law could have brought life, it would have no longer been inferior to promise.

then righteousness would indeed be by the law: in this then-clause, righteousness is shown to be the counterpart of 'life' in the if-clause, and this combination. has been carried over in Paul's mind from the Habakkuk quotation in verse 11. Here the apostle is probably using the word 'law' quite generally, since no article is found in the Greek. At the same time, there can be little doubt that he could not think of law generally without thinking of the supreme example of it in the Mosaic law. To impart life, law would need to pardon the condemned, i.e. to justify him or to give him a righteous standing. But this is beyond the province of law. Both law and promise therefore had their respective spheres, which neither overlapped nor conflicted. God could pardon those whom his own law condemned. But this was an act of grace as the promise was also an act of grace.

There is an alternative reading that would make the last phrase mean 'in the sphere of law' (*en nomoi*) rather than 'by law' (*ek nomou*), but the latter is more strongly supported in the manuscripts and is probably the correct reading.

22. But the scripture consigned all things to sin: the first word 'but' (*alla*) is significant here because it draws attention to a contrast with the hypothetical supposition of the preceding verse. What is the Scripture referred to here? That is problematic, for no individual passage of Scripture makes a statement of this character, although the general tenor of Scripture supports it. It seems best to suppose that by the singular (*graphē*) Paul is not conforming to general New Testament usage in referring to a specific passage. By personifying Scripture the apostle reveals his estimate of the activity of the Word, which derives its authority from the activity of God.

The imagery in Paul's mind is that of a gaol, with sin as the gaoler, Scripture as the magistrate, and 'all things' (understood primarily as 'all people') as the prisoners. In the Epistle to the Romans Paul uses a similar figure of speech in a semi-personification of sin (cf. Rom. 7).

The whole statement is an example of a compressed sentence, which depends on some unstated suppositions. What the apostle means is that Scripture shows the true state of mankind before God, with the result that no-one is clear of guilt. It therefore shuts up everyone to the consequences of sin. The verb used (*sunkleiō*) is vivid, for it means 'to shut in on all sides' with no possibility of escape (v. Duncan). The apostle thinks back to the sense of hopeless frustration through which he had himself passed before his conversion. In such a situation law had no help to offer. It could only assure the miserable prisoner that his present plight was indisputably just.

But why does Paul use the neuter 'all things' (*ta panta*)? While he thinks mostly of people, it is not impossible to suppose that he implies the involvement of the impersonal creation in the sinful consequences of man's action. Yet since his whole argument here is on the personal level it seems better to interpret the neuter in a personal way. A clear parallel to this personal use of the neuter to bring out the idea of comprehensiveness is found in Jn 6.37, 39 (cf. Ellicott, Lightfoot).

what was promised to faith: in the Greek text the phrase used *ek pisteōs* (pro-

ceeding from faith) is the same as used in verses 7 and 9 with the article to denote
'men of faith', men whose lives are based on faith. Here the similar idea is present
in the description of the promise, i.e. a promise grounded in a faith–relationship
with Jesus Christ. The primary reference to Abraham's faith is here extended to the
new covenant.

in Jesus Christ: this is a genitive construction and is to be distinguished from the
use of *en* or *eis* with a verb of believing. Here it could be understood either of the
faith which Jesus Christ possessed, or of the faith directed to Jesus Christ as its
object. Clearly the latter is more in harmony with the context.

might be given to those who believe: it is possible to connect the reference to
faith with the verb 'believe' rather than to the noun 'promise', although in this
case the idea of faith would be duplicated. Not only is the promise grounded in
faith; it is also dispensed only to those who believe. In no clearer way could Paul
bring out the inseparable connection between promise and faith. It would seem
that the giving to believers is here to distinguish it from the promise given to
Abraham's physical descendants. Wide as the original promise was its application
is immeasurably increased in Jesus Christ.

23. Now before faith came: in the Greek there is an article which should be
observed in English if the full meaning is to be brought out. Paul is thinking not
of faith in general, which had, after all, been seen in Abraham's experience, but in
the particular kind of faith to which reference has just been made in verse 22, i.e.
faith centred in Christ.

we were confined under the law, kept under restraint: of the two verbs used
here, one is the same as that used in the previous verse, but the other (*phroureō*) has
the idea of setting a guard to protect. The function of law was not, therefore,
entirely adverse. Yet it clearly imposed such a severe limitation that even its custodian function resulted in a sense of hopeless imprisonment. It should be noted
that the confinement is here related to law, not to sin, as in verse 22, although the
parallelism brings out the close connection between the two ideas. Being shut in
by the law would have an obvious relevance to the Judaizing Christians.

until faith should be revealed: the preposition translated 'until' (*eis*) could be
rendered 'with a view to', suggesting purpose (so Williams). The temporal idea
seems preferable, since the argument is concerned with historical sequences. The
coming of the Christian faith ended the custodian function of the Jewish law. The
preposition must, in fact, be understood in conjunction with the use of the same
preposition in the next verse.

The verb 'should be revealed' consists of two Greek verbs, the auxiliary one
(*mellō*) stressing the future anticipation of the revelation. Such anticipation was
strong in the pre-Christian era.

24. So that the law was our custodian: this statement is closely connected
with the last, and defines in general terms the function of law in the pre-Christian
period. The word 'custodian' does not quite capture all the meaning of the Greek

paidagōgos, which was a term used for the attendant of a Greek boy whose duties consisted of escorting the child, such as to and from school. But in addition to escort duties there were disciplinary duties of a moral kind. The educative idea (cf. AV 'schoolmaster') was not dominant, and was probably not present at all. By describing the law under this metaphor, Paul means to bring clearly to the fore the inferior function of the law as compared with Christ. Law was essentially a disciplinarian.

until Christ came: some exegetes have supposed, that the law as a *paidogōgos* led men to Christ as a superior teacher (cf. Cole, Williams). Law thus becomes an active agency for salvation. But this seems to introduce a thought somewhat alien to Paul's earlier argument. The law could hardly shut us up to sin and lead us to Christ at one and the same time. In the present phrase the preposition *eis* must mean 'up to', which therefore requires the interpretation that the law's function as a *paidagōgos* ended with the advent of Christ (as Duncan).

that we might be justified by faith: it is as if the law lands us in such a hopeless position that the only possibility is for a much stronger agency to take over and deal with the situation on the basis of an entirely new principle—faith. This is the essence of Paul's position. The only hope was not a super *paidagōgos* or instructor in some superior way of life, but a redeemer who could break open sin's prison-house and liberate its captives. To secure such liberty the sole requirement was faith. This statement which consists of a purpose clause implies that the disciplinary activity of law was indirectly designed to lead to justification by faith.

25. This verse states by way of conclusion the cessation of the custodian function of law and supports the interpretation of verse 24 favoured above. It should not be inferred from this that for Paul law has now ceased to have any function at all. He is dealing here only with law as a method of acquiring justification.

But now that faith has come: again 'faith' must be understood of that faith which has Jesus Christ as its object.

26. in Christ Jesus: this contrasts with the position of those under the custody of the law. For believers there is a remarkable change of sphere. This phrase may be understood either as relating to 'sons of God' or to 'faith'. The result is the same, although the emphasis is different. Sonship exists only in Christ Jesus, and this is no doubt part of Paul's thought here, understanding 'in Christ Jesus', (*en Christō Iēsou*) in Paul's mystical sense. But it is equally integral to Paul's theology that faith must be centred in Christ.

all sons of God: the difference of status is intended to stand out in bold relief when compared with the status of those who still need a *paidagōgos*. When the child grows to the age of maturity and responsibility he takes on the full privileges of sonship. The superiority of gospel over law could hardly be more succinctly stated. It would have been foolish in the extreme for a child to claim the privileges of sonship and still continue to rely on the protection and correction of the *paidagōgos*. In fact it was a sign of sonship that the services of the latter were no longer needed. This idea is more fully developed in the next chapter.

What is the significance of Paul's 'all'? The context would suggest that it is intended to cover both Jews and Gentiles and is designed, therefore, to contrast with the narrowness of the Jewish outlook. This 'all' is further illustrated in verse 28 as inclusive of all kinds of people.

It should be noted that the apostle transfers from 'we' in verse 25 to 'you' in this verse to bring out more clearly his appeal to these readers.

through faith: there is again an article in the Greek, which identifies the faith once more with that mentioned earlier, i.e. faith in Christ.

27. For as many: this verse gives the basis of the confident assertion in verse 26. **as were baptized into Christ:** the same thought in a more developed form occurs in Rom. 6.3–11. The early Christians attached great importance to the baptism of believers. It was the sign of an entry into a new kind of life. In this it contrasts with circumcision, which could do no more than initiate into a system of law. The preposition 'into' is significant, for it almost seems as if Paul regarded the Christian life as located in Christ. He uses the same formula in 1 C. 10.2 of the Israelites baptized into Moses. On the other hand, it is not impossible that the expression here is intended to convey the idea of baptism in the name of Christ (cf. Burton). **have put on Christ:** this is a favourite metaphor of Paul's (cf. Rom. 13.12; Eph. 4.24; Col. 3.12f.). But here (and in Rom. 13.14) is his most daring use of it, in which he likens Christ himself to a garment. The expression conveys a striking suggestion of the closeness which exists between Christ and the believer. Those who put on Christ can do no other than act in accordance with the Spirit of Christ. In the Romans passage mentioned above (13.14), the putting on of Christ is antithetical to making provision for the flesh, which supports the contention that the metaphor conveys an essentially new kind of life. Everything has now to be related to Christ.

28. neither Jew nor Greek: in the world of Paul's day the distinction was deep-seated. It was one of the marvels of Christianity to overcome it. Paul is not expressing a hope, but a fact. To make all Greeks become Jews in order to enjoy the privileges of the gospel would only propagate a distinction which has already been done away in Christ. This specific case illustrates equally well the general abolition of all racial barriers—a lesson of vital relevance to the mid-twentieth century. In Christ there are neither Europeans nor Asiatics, Africans or Chinese, or any other racial groups as such. In Christ there is a new bond which leaps over colour, culture, and customs.

neither slave nor free: social distinctions have always been serious obstacles in human relationships. For the Jews the idea of slavery was abhorrent. Consequently they had as much contempt for slaves in particular as for Gentiles in general. Christianity had within it the power to smash the whole system, although many centuries were to pass before it took effect. Paul's immediate approach to the problem was to assert the abolition of the distinction in Christ, even although it continued to be a potent force in the non-Christian world. When masters could learn to treat their slaves as brothers in Christ, the barrier between them was broken. The freeman and the slave both came to Christ in the same way.

neither male nor female: there was particular point in the mention of the absence of distinctions of sex for Jewish readers or those influenced by them. The Jew tended to despise the woman. But the same approach was true of the majority of the Gentile world (Macedonia was an exception). There is no doubt that few outside the Christian Church in Paul's day would have maintained any form of equality of the sexes. The apostle himself drew some distinctions between the sexes as far as their functions within the Church were concerned, but no distinctions over their position in Christ.

you are all one in Christ Jesus: the most important factor for the exegesis of this statement is the meaning of the word 'one'. If all people, to whichever of the previously mentioned classes they belonged, are regarded as on an equal footing, it is because in Christ everyone appears the same, as if one all-inclusive man includes every other Christian. The full force of the masculine gender of *heis* (one) should be retained, for the idea is not of a unified organization, but of a unified personality. The Church is the body and Christ is the Head, in which case the only permissible distinctions are those of function, like the distinction between the hand and the foot. There is no room for a Jew to think that he is any special part of the body, and the same applies to all the other distinctions.

The words 'in Christ Jesus' connect with the same phrase in verse 26. The unity spoken of here is essentially a spiritual unity, inseparably connected with the believer's personal position in Christ.

29. And if you are Christ's: the apostle assumes the truth of his 'if' clause for those whom he is addressing. This clause follows on naturally from verse 28.

then you are Abraham's offspring: Paul here reverts to the discussion which he had introduced at the commencement of the chapter. This, in fact, echoes the thought of verse 7, connected up with the comments on 'offspring' in verses 15ff. This brings Paul's argument to a climax, for Gentiles are Christ's as much as Jews, and both are therefore inheritors of Abraham's promise.

heirs according to promise: there is an indirect allusion to the inheritance historically promised to Abraham, but Paul is no doubt thinking here specifically of justification. It is in this that Abraham's inheritance finds its fulfilment. The main point is that the heirs did not come into their inheritance through the law.

EMERGING INTO SONSHIP 4.1–7

4.1. I mean that . . .: there is no break between this and the preceding verse. This is, in fact, an explanation of Paul's reference to the heirs, prompted, no doubt, by the fear that the Judaizers may have missed the real point.

the heir, as long as he is a child: the apostle, in likening the position of those under the law to that of a minor, again draws attention to the inferiority of their position. The word used for child (*nēpios*), while in legal terminology it could denote a minor (who in Roman law was anyone under twenty-five years of age), is probably here meant to distinguish him from an adult. In either case it represents a person needing to be placed under the protection of others.

no better than a slave: the comparison refers, of course, to freedom of action, not to status. The minor son and the slave alike are under the father's authority. If he were lord of the estate, either because the father is now dead or because the father has put it in trust for him, it would make no difference for the time being.

2. under guardians and trustees: these two words may refer to the successive people to whom a minor was responsible under Roman law, the former until the age of 14 years and the latter until the age of 25 years. But there are difficulties in this view, as the following note shows. Alternatively the words may respectively represent those responsible for the child's person and property (so Burton).

until the date set by the father: under Roman law the fixing of the time limit was out of the father's hands, so Paul must be thinking of some other legal system, intelligible to his readers, which left this to the father's discretion (cf. Ramsay). Although the setting of the illustration is uncertain, the truth behind it is indisputable. The father is in charge of the situation and makes the best possible arrangements for his son, and this serves as an admirable illustration of God's provision for his people. In verse 4 the apostle makes clear the application of 'the time set by the father', for he calls it 'the fullness of time'.

3. So with us: to whom is he now referring? In view of the fact that he proceeds with the first person plural to the end of verse 5, he evidently is thinking here of Christians generally, although, no doubt, with special application to his readers.

when we were children, we were slaves: the apostle now applies his general illustration in a spiritual sense. Sometimes the idea of 'children' is used to describe spiritual immaturity, as in 1 C. 3.1 ('babes in Christ'), but here it has a different connotation, referring to pre-Christian experience. In a sense the application does not fit the illustration, for now the child becomes identified with the slave, because the latter idea is much more appropriate to describe the position of non-Christians. The apostle says, in effect, that we were not even grown-up, we were no better than slaves.

to the elemental spirits of the universe: there are various ways in which the word rendered 'elemental spirits' (*stoicheia*) should be understood. Of the various meanings which were attached to it in Greek writers, two have relevance for its New Testament occurrences. It may mean (a) elementary teaching or rudiments, or (b) as in the present translation, 'spirits'. In the former case it may be understood either of the elementary truths of natural religion or of the elementary rules and regulations, samples of which are cited in verse 10 after a second occurrence of the word. In the latter interpretation, Paul's words would be a reference to the widespread beliefs, which he himself seems to have shared, that spiritual agencies, some good, some evil, affected man's destinies. The contemporary heathen world was in bondage to such spirits, and Paul's description here would have been particularly apt for the pre-Christian position of his Gentile readers. This second usage is rather more favoured by the addition of the genitive 'of the universe' (*tou kosmou*). Elsewhere, Paul refers more than once to 'principalities and powers', by which he also appears to mean spiritual agencies. One difficulty with this view is that there is no evidence that the word *stoicheia* bore this meaning in the first century A.D., although it certainly did at a later period (cf. Burton).

It is not easy to decide between these two alternatives. Verses 9 and 10 would favour rudimentary rules, but would be relevant in that case only to those who had already been subject to them, i.e. Jews. But a wider application to include Gentiles is preferable, in which case the second interpretation must be chosen. It involves Paul in classing all the non-Christian world as being in slavery to powers utterly beyond their control. The implication is that Jews are included and therefore any submission to Jewish scruples would be a return to their former slavery (see verse 9).

4. But when the time had fully come: here the apostle takes up the thought of verse 2 and develops it in a spiritual sense. As in human affairs, a father sets a time limit on his son's minority, so there is a timetable with God. Although the imagery of the opening verses is still hovering in Paul's mind, the analogy really fails at this point. The sending of the Son finds no counterpart in the illustration, only the timing of the closure of the preliminary stage. The timing of Christ's advent was, however, of infinitely greater importance.

The phrase 'had fully come' renders a Greek phrase which literally means 'the fullness of time' (*plērōma tou chronou*), which draws attention to the critical importance of this event. It marked the completion of the old era and the dawn of the new. But what caused Paul to use this expression here? The appropriateness of the time of the advent has often been pointed out. The Jewish world was expectant of the coming of the Messiah. The Roman world, in its rapid spread, had contributed a measure of peace and security, which had been previously unparalleled. It had, moreover, developed communications to a remarkable extent, linking all the strategic centres of the empire with Rome. The Greek language was widely used for trade and communication and supplied an admirable medium for the transmission of the gospel. But it may be questioned how much of these advantages were in Paul's mind when he wrote this statement, however valuable they may be. In the context it is clear that his thought is still centred on servitude to the law and the most reasonable assumption, therefore, is to regard the 'fullness' as the limit of God's testing time under the law, during which the hopelessness of man's servitude was fully demonstrated. Paul is convinced, as the early Christians were generally, that the coming of Christ was not by accident but by divine appointment.

God sent forth his Son: the form of the verb (*exapesteilen*) involves more than just a commissioning. It involves a sending out from a previous state, and must in this case imply the pre-existence of the Son. Such a thought is fully in harmony with Paul's teaching elsewhere (cf. 1 C. 8.6; Phil. 2.6ff.; Col. 1.15ff.). It is appropriate that in this way he draws attention to the filial relationship in view of the analogy used in the previous part of the chapter.

4. born of woman: the striking feature of the Incarnation is the form in which it was effected. In this statement there is the greatest possible contrast with that preceding. The Son of God being born of a woman was the supreme example of his humiliation. Paul is more concerned about this than about a more specific reference to the Virgin Birth (Ridderbos). At the same time the present statement is not out of keeping with that doctrine. The verb can be understood in the sense of becoming. The Son takes up human nature, which he did not possess before. The same verb is used in John's profound statement that the Word became flesh (Jn 1.14), which expresses the same truth in a different way.

born under the law: in the Greek there is an absence of the article, thus drawing attention to law in general, although in the context this cannot be divorced from the Mosaic law, since Jesus was born into a Jewish milieu. The drift of the apostle's argument is that Jesus came into the same environment as those who were finding it impossible to be justified under the law (cf. Bring's discussion here).

5. to redeem those who were under the law: again there is no article in the Greek before 'law', so that Christ's redemptive work reaches beyond the Jewish people, a factor which is, of course, integral to Paul's theology. The idea of redemption has already occurred in 3.13, and the same meaning of deliverance at a definite cost is evident here as there. This present reference to redemption contains no hint of the method by which it was achieved, but in the light of 3.13f. there is no doubt that Paul was here connecting up the redemptive act with the work of Christ on the cross. Redemption has a double aspect: deliverance *from* bondage to the law and deliverance *to* something better—here sonship.

so that we might receive adoption as sons: this is the positive aspect of redemption. It is the ultimate purpose of the Incarnation. The word translated 'adoption' (*huiothesia*) occurs in the New Testament only in the epistles of Paul. In Rom. 8.15 it occurs in a context which also has the 'Abba! Father!' saying, as here in verse 6. In both contexts it clearly denotes not merely sonship but the privileges of sonship. In Christ believers are reinstated into their full status as sons in the family. Paul's thought seems to be that God sent his Son to gain other sons. This involves a remarkable change of status from slavery to sonship.

6. And because you are sons: this appears to give the basis on which the Spirit is given. But realization of the full privileges of sonship can only come through the Spirit. Rather is Paul making clear that adoption and the gift of the Spirit are concomitant. Moreover, verse 5 is stated as a potential, but verse 6 as an actual, experience. The Christian has already experienced the Spirit. That is an indisputable evidence of his sonship. It is significant in this respect that Paul uses the second person plural, although before and after he uses the first person. The change makes a more direct appeal to the experience of his readers.

God has sent the Spirit of his Son: since the same verb is used here as in verse 4, the two actions may be regarded as complementary. The phrase 'Spirit of his Son' is significant because it is used only here in the New Testament, although 'Spirit of Christ' occurs in Rom. 8.9. It is noticeable that in this context the activities of Father, Son, and Spirit are mentioned together. The closeness of the activity of the Spirit and of the Son is evident from the teaching of Jesus himself, when he declared of the Spirit of truth that 'he will not speak on his own authority . . . He will glorify me, for he will take what is mine and declare it to you' (Jn 16.13, 14).
into our hearts: again the apostle returns to the first person plural. Here he wishes to include himself because of the deep reality of his own Christian experience. It is as if Paul has no real desire to maintain the direct approach.
crying, 'Abba! Father!': the combination of an Aramaic and Greek form of the same word suggests some kind of liturgical usage. This is supported by the fact that the double form occurs elsewhere in the New Testament. There must have been some reason for the retention of the Aramaic in writings designed for Greek-speaking peoples. Its occurrence in Rom. 8.15 is closely parallel to this. The other occurrence is in Mk 14.36, where it forms part of the prayer of Jesus in the garden of Gethsemane. In all three cases, therefore, it expresses the prayerful cry of the heart. The most probable explanation of the double form is that a special sacredness attached to the form used by Jesus (i.e. *Abba*), which the early Christians retained together with a translation for those unfamiliar with Aramaic (so Lagrange). The opening words of the Lord's prayer may have had something to do with the sacredness of the form *Abba*, if this were in the original form of the prayer. It is perhaps significant that both here and in the occurrence of the words in Rom. 8.15 the same verb is used. 'Crying' (*krazō*) implies an importunate approach to God, in which the most appropriate basis is an appeal to our filial relationship to God. In both occurrences also the prayer is made through the agency of the Spirit.

7. **So through God:** in placing this phrase first the RSV loses some of the emphasis seen in the Greek text, where it stands last, i.e. after the word 'heir'. Paul means to draw emphatic attention to the fact that any inheritance is entirely due to the gracious action of God. He can never conceive of Christian experience apart from the essential part played by the divine initiative.
no longer a slave, but a son: the thought reverts to verse 1. Christians have acquired a new status. This verse is really a repetition of verse 5 with greater focus on the remarkable transformation. As slavery and sonship are obviously mutually exclusive, so the sons of God cannot be regarded as in bondage to anything.
if a son then a heir: cf. the comment on 3.29. The apostle is strangely attracted to this idea. It occurs in the closely parallel passage in Rom. 8.17, where the even more remarkable statement that we are 'fellow heirs with Christ' occurs. The apostle assumes that adoption into the status of sons carries with it the full privileges of sonship.

Returning to Beggarliness 4.8–11

8. Formerly, when you did not know God: why does Paul go back in thought to the former state of these Galatians, when he has already referred to their sonship? He appears to be doing so by way of warning to focus attention on the folly of their proposed action. The key is found in verse 9. It is noteworthy that Paul describes the pre-Christian state as one of ignorance of God, a description which would not have been so relevant to Jews as to Gentiles. In any case, the next phrase shows clearly that pagans were in mind.

you were in bondage: a continuation of the slave metaphor of the previous section. The same Greek word (*douleuō*) is used for the idea of 'being a slave' and of 'service', because in the ancient world these ideas were often inseparable. But it is significant that in Christ, service can be transformed by love, as Paul points out later in this epistle (5.13).

beings that by nature are no gods: paganism had its gods. Paul does not dispute that fact but he does dispute that they were really gods. He was probably thinking of them as spiritual agencies (i.e. demons). The phrase 'by nature' refers to their essential character. The Gentile world in Paul's day was certainly in bondage in its various religious systems. Its gods were incapable of leading their devotees to freedom. Hence the contrast between Christian liberty and bondage to no-gods could not have been greater.

9. but now that you have come to know God: the strong contrast between the conversion and pre-conversion state is brought out even more distinctly in the Greek than in the English. Neither here nor in verse 8 is there an article with *Theon* (God), and this is no doubt to draw a qualitative contrast with the 'no gods'. They have now come to know one who really is God.

rather be known by God: Paul adds this almost as an afterthought, no doubt because he realized that what he had just stated might give a wrong impression. It was no merit of the Galatians that they had come to know God. The initiative was with God himself. The apostle is not, of course, suggesting that God had acquired a knowledge which he did not previously possess, for the sense of the verb goes beyond theoretical knowledge. True Christian knowledge has both an active and a passive aspect, and Paul makes provision for both in his statement here. To recognize oneself to be the centre of divine attention is one of the profounder aspects of Christian conversion. It is also one of the most humbling. Not only do believers acknowledge God, but he acknowledges them—as sons.

how can you turn back again? After so deep an experience Paul cannot imagine how anyone could desire to revert to the old position. They have already once turned from no-gods to God. Are they now going to turn from God to elemental spirits? Such apostasy seems incredible to the apostle, yet he fears the possibility of it, as verse 11 shows.

the weak and beggarly elemental spirits: the word *stoicheia* (elemental spirits) has been discussed in verse 3. The addition here of two descriptive adjectives is evidently intended to contrast with the knowledge of God. The first adjective stresses the inherent 'feebleness' of their former state, no doubt mainly an allusion to the utter powerlessness of heathendom to assist man in his approach to the true God. The second adjective is even more vivid, coming from a root-meaning 'to crouch or cower', hence to show the qualities of a beggar. Paul could hardly have chosen a more apt description. He is in fact transferring a major characteristic of the devotees of paganism, i.e. a cringing attitude of fear, to the objects of worship themselves.

If the word *stoicheia* means rudiments of religion as shared by all non-Christians, the apostasy would include Jews as well as Gentiles. That this is Paul's intention may seem to be supported by his change from 'no gods' in verse 8 to '*stoicheia*' here, and by the typically Jewish character of the features mentioned in verse 10. It seems most likely, however, that he is viewing the scheme of the Judaizers, however well intentioned it was, to be in effect equivalent to a return to their non-Christian past. Such an idea would be startling to Jewish Christians, but it may well be that Paul intended to startle them.

There can be no denying that he classes all other religious systems outside Christianity as 'weak and beggarly'. To him Christ is the only means of coming to a true knowledge of God.

whose slaves you want to be once more: neither the Judaizers nor the Galatian Christians were probably aware of any desire to be enslaved. And yet Paul makes it clear that they are not only in danger of returning to slavery, but are actually desiring it. His reason for putting it in this form is that, knowing their desire for Jewish legalistic practices and seeing clearly that the consequence of such a desire is relapse into spiritual slavery, he transfers the result to the intention. It is a fitting reminder that those who pursue a course which they know will end in spiritual decline must be held responsible for desiring that decline. The words translated 'once more' (*palin anōthen*) strongly express the completeness of their reversion, as if they wished to begin all over again in heathenism.

10. You observe days, and months, and seasons, and years! These are best regarded as references to Jewish ritual observances, mainly festivals. There were holy days and new moons (months); special festivals, such as Passover and Tabernacles (probably denoted by 'seasons') and a festival connected with the New Year. In other words the Galatian Christians were being urged to bind themselves to the observances of the Jewish calendar. Some features of that calendar were undoubtedly taken over by the Christian Church although adapted to a Christian context (e.g. Passover and Pentecost), but this was entirely different from a rigid legalistic adoption of the Jewish system *en toto*, which seems to be in view here. The verb (*paratēreisthe*) not only supports the idea of rigid observance, but shows it to be currently in practice, since the present indicative is used. It should not be overlooked that heathenism also had its festivals and this aspect of the Judaizers' practices

would, therefore, appeal to the Gentiles. Schlier sees in this verse a reference
to astrological powers.

11. I am afraid: in the Greek text the verb has an object, i.e. *humas* (you),
which expresses with some vividness that the Galatians themselves were the objects
of Paul's fear. Yet the fear had a specific basis, as the following statement shows.
I have laboured in vain: the translation here obscures the fact that after the verb
of fearing the clause is introduced in an emphatic way, i.e. 'lest by any means'. The
verb, which denotes toil with effort (*kopiaō*), is in the perfect tense to draw attention
to what Paul fears may be the permanent result of his past effort. The indicative
rather than the subjunctive suggests that Paul fears it may be a fact rather than a
possibility. For the apostle's reluctance to believe that his work could have been
in vain, cf. 3.4.

A Personal Appeal 4.12–20

12. Brethren, I beseech you: this personal address to them after all the hard
argument preceding shows the real pastoral heart of the apostle. It should be noted
that it does not stand first in the Greek but at the end of the sentence, which gives
it added emphasis. Not only the position of the words but the choice of the verb
strengthens the appeal, for the verb used (*deomai*) expresses greater urgency than
the synonymous *parakaleō* more frequently used by Paul. It is used elsewhere by
him only in Rom. 1.10, where it is associated with a feeling of intense longing, and
three times in the Second Epistle to the Corinthians (cf. 5.20; 8.4; and 10.2), in all
of which a sense of intensity is present. There is no doubt about Paul's feeling over
the Galatians' defection.
become as I am, for I also am become as you are: at first sight this reads like
a riddle, but the solution is found in Paul's own experience. He had been a Jew
bound by the law, but had become as they were at the time of their conversion,
i.e. freed from the scruples of legal observances. His appeal is, therefore, that they
should imitate him in remaining free from such scruples. The strength of the appeal
lies in the fact that Paul knows from experience what the Galatians do not, i.e. the
misery of bondage to Jewish legalism. It is alternatively possible to regard the
second clause as meaning that Paul had virtually become a Gentile among them
and therefore appeals to them on the basis of the sacrifice he has made on their
behalf.
You did me no wrong: why this sudden interjection? It is not easy to say with
any certainty. If stress is put on the aorist tense of the verb, the sense would be—
previously you did not wrong me, but now you do. This would suit the context
and the following words could be understood as an explanation of this absence of
any wrong in the past. Some have supposed that Paul is replying to an assertion of
the Judaizers, i.e. 'we did Paul no harm' (cf. Burton). 'Granted, you did me no
harm, but you are deeply injuring me if you now regard me as an enemy'. Another

interpretation which does not, however, fit so well into the context, is to suppose that 'me' is emphatic, and that Paul is implying that it is Christ, not himself, who has been wronged, or else that it is themselves who have been wronged by their own actions. In view of the next statement, in which Paul refers to their kindness towards him, it seems best to accept the first of these various suggestions as most probable.

13. you know: the way in which Paul introduces the reference to his physical condition while he was among them shows that this was common knowledge among them.

because of a bodily ailment: there is no knowing what the illness was from which Paul was suffering and conjecture seems quite pointless. From verse 15 it would appear that the illness affected Paul's eyesight, while verse 14 suggests that it may have seriously affected his appearance (see comment on next verse). Paul's language here would imply that it was illness that caused him to travel to Galatia, as a result of which he was able to preach to them. This is claimed by Ramsay as a support for the South Galatian theory, since it involves an initial journey to Galatia while Paul was a sick man, and it is difficult to conceive a sick man travelling to North Galatia on account of his illness (see Introduction, p. 26). Of course, even on the South Galatian theory the journey from Perga on the coast across the Taurus Mountains to Antioch was by no means easy, but the nature of Paul's illness may have called for the greater altitudes of the Antioch district.

I preached the gospel to you at first: there have been two interpretations of the word translated 'at first' (*proteron*). It can either mean 'formerly', or 'former of two'. In the latter sense it would require two former visits, and this would support the contention for a North Galatian destination according to Lightfoot. It seems better to suppose that Paul refers here only to an early visit in comparison with his present dealings with them.

14. though my condition was a trial: the Greek statement is more vivid than this and may be literally represented as follows: 'and the trial of yours in my flesh you did not scorn or despise.' In this form it fixes attention on the trial rather than on Paul. In what sense the Galatians found Paul's flesh a trial is impossible to say. It may have been his physical appearance if he was suffering from some malady which disfigured him, or it may have been the trial of having the responsibility of a sick man among them.

you did not scorn or despise me: both these verbs are strong terms, the second literally meaning 'to spit out', used metaphorically as an expression of disgust or revulsion. Why did Paul use such verbs as these? Was there some suggestion in his mind that now the Galatians' attitude had so changed that these verbs could describe them, but that it was not always so? There is such a vast difference between revulsion and reception as an angel that some such explanation seems necessary. It has less probably been suggested that the second verb implies that they might have regarded him as possessed by an evil spirit.

as an angel of God, as Christ Jesus: is there here an allusion to Paul's experience at Lystra where he was supposed to be the god Hermes (Ac. 14.12)? Advocates of the South Galatian theory have sometimes claimed this (cf. Ramsay, Askwith), but it is not certain. What is indisputable is that the Galatians had come to recognize Paul as a messenger of God bringing the good news of Christ Jesus. But the words seem to go further than that, implying that the readers could not have received an angel more courteously or even Christ Jesus himself. This brings up most vividly the contrast with their present attitude towards him.

15. the satisfaction you felt: Paul is referring to the joy with which his teaching and he himself had been received. The word translated 'satisfaction' (*makarismos*) occurs again in the New Testament only in Rom. 4.6, 9, in both cases rendered 'blessing' and referring to the experience of justification apart from works. But here it seems rather a personal pleasure over Paul's presence among them. The rhetorical question clearly implies that the satisfaction has apparently vanished.

For I bear you witness . . .: this statement is intended to illustrate the satisfaction.

if possible: this is added because of Paul's use of metaphorical language. So deeply were the readers in sympathy with Paul at that time that their willingness to help outstripped possibilities.

you would have plucked out your eyes: it has been suggested either that Paul had some eye-disease, and this statement represents the Galatians' deep sympathy for him, or that Paul is citing a proverbial saying denoting a willingness to make any sacrifice on his behalf. There is, however, no evidence that this was a proverbial saying, and the former interpretation is therefore to be preferred.

16. Have I then become your enemy? There is some question about the punctuation here. The sentence is introduced by *hōste*, which would fit better if followed by an exclamation rather than an interrogative, in the sense, 'So I have become your enemy!' In this case the word 'enemy' must be regarded as the Judaizers' own view of Paul, not his own estimate of them. He is most anxious to avoid any feeling of enmity. But if the interrogative is allowed to stand, it suggests that Paul wishes to leave a loop-hole for them to deny the charge.

by telling you the truth: when did this happen? Some suggest that it must have been on a previous visit (cf. Lightfoot, Oepke). If this were true, it would not necessitate the postulation of two former visits on the grounds that the first visit did not result in enmity, for this misconstrues Paul's meaning. The enmity need not be coincident with the telling. But the more probable interpretation is to regard this as a reference to the present letter. In that case Paul is wondering whether by his plain speaking he has created enmity against himself. But some (Lietzmann, Bonnard) take truth as meaning the gospel.

17. They make much of you: the same verb as is used here occurs also in 2 C. 11.2, where RSV renders it 'to feel jealousy for' and something of a similar eager feeling is present here. The Judaizers are evidently in mind, although introduced rather obscurely in the third person. This clearly distinguishes them from the readers whom he has been directly addressing in the previous verses. The idea seems to be that in contrast to Paul's plain speaking the Judaizers are eagerly entreating the Galatians for their support.

for no good purpose: the Greek is abrupt here, equivalent to 'not well' (*kalos*). Behind their enthusiastic regard for you, all is not as fine as it appears on the surface, to give *kalos* its most literal meaning.

they want to shut you out: the apostle does not explain the shutting out process and leaves us to conjecture from what the Judaizers desired to exclude the Galatians. Does he mean excommunication from the church? This would import an alien idea into the context. Is it exclusion from the truth of the gospel? This is not impossible, but a better interpretation is to consider it in relation to Paul. The apostle probably feels that the Judaizers want to cause a rift between the Galatians and himself. This would free them to turn their enthusiasm towards the Judaizers as the last part of this verse suggests.

18. **For a good purpose it is always good to be made much of:** there is a direct contrast here with the 'no good purpose' in verse 17. But what is the good purpose (*kalos*) to which Paul refers? He may, of course, be referring not to a specific purpose, but to a general principle, as much as to say that to be made much of in itself is not to be condemned so long as it is rightly directed. It is possible, on the other hand, to suppose that Paul is thinking of the good purpose, which he had while he was among them and of his enthusiastic interest in them. This would suit well the conclusion of the sentence.

when I am present: this is a reference back to verse 14, to the occasion when they received him as an angel of God. It must have been a bitter disappointment to Paul that the Galatians needed his presence to keep them stable. What Paul experienced has been experienced by innumerable pioneers of the Christian faith.

19. **My little children:** it is astonishing to find Paul using a term (*teknia*) of particular endearment in an epistle which begins without any affectionate greeting, especially as this is the only occasion where this form of address occurs in Paul's epistles. It is found several times in the First Epistle of John, always denoting special warmth of affection. Its use here reveals particular depth of feeling on Paul's part over the Galatian situation, and is especially appropriate to the following metaphor.

with whom I am again in travail: in 1 Th. 2.8, Paul pictures himself as a nurse, while here he is even more daring in his illustration, using the metaphor of child-birth. He thinks of the pain and trouble connected with the delivering of children and transfers the figure to his own relationship to his 'little children'. The fact that he speaks of this travail as repeated shows that the metaphor must not be pressed, although Paul continues the figure in the next clause (see comment). Clearly his purpose is to show that his concern for his converts puts in the shade the attitude of the Judaizers.

until Christ be formed in you! Here there is some confusion in the metaphor, for the purpose as stated here is unexpected. What the apostle probably means is that he was like a mother in travail to bring forth children who would bear the image of Christ in them. The Greek verb (*morphoō*) is connected with the noun (*morphē*), which means essential form rather than outward shape. The idea is therefore of real Christ-like character. The implication is that if the Galatians follow the Judaizers' policy it will not result in Christ being formed in them. This is, in fact, a shrewd and effective touchstone. Any religious system which does not produce the image of Christ in the lives of its people is not thoroughly Christian.

20. I could wish to be present: in expressing a strong desire to be present with them, although stating it in such a way as to indicate its impracticability, the apostle strives to alleviate some of the antagonism which he fears that his previous words have created. It is another one of his intensely human flashes, which often reveal more of his true character than his reasoned arguments.

to change my tone: does this mean that he regrets what he has just said? If he really felt he had overstated his case he would not have sent the letter. What he means is that he regrets that his present tone is necessary and longs to see them face to face, because he is confident that he will find them co-operative and he will, therefore, be able to change his tone. It is evident that Paul has no love of an aggressive approach. He prefers the method of personal appeal where that is practical.

for I am perplexed about you: the verb here used means 'to be at a loss' or 'to be at one's wits' end', which vividly reflects the tension in the apostle's mind. His strong desire is to be warm-hearted towards them. He cannot bear the thought of them regarding him as their enemy. Yet in the present situation he is perplexed to know how to avoid it.

AN ALLEGORICAL APPEAL 4.21–31

21. Tell me: another direct, almost conversational, appeal to the readers, as if Paul resolves in his perplexity to find some means of alleviating the situation. His argument begins on ground that is common between himself and his readers, i.e. acceptance of the authority of the books of the law.

you who desire to be under law: already in verse 9 he has referred to them wanting to be slaves of the elementary spirits, and although the present expression is less provocative, it still draws attention to a desire which was rather the result than the cause of their policy. There is little doubt that the Judaizers' genuine desire was to conform to God's pattern and that they believed that this involved being under the law. The desire, however laudable in itself, would, nevertheless, be wrongly implemented in Paul's view.

do you not hear the law? This may refer to the public reading of Scripture which formed a regular part of early Christian worship, or it may be understood in the extended sense of not only hearing but also obeying. In all probability it is the latter sense which is required. It is as if Paul were saying to them, 'You claim to be under the law, but are you listening to what the law says about the present situation?'

22. For it is written: there is special point in the use of this authoritative formula after the apostle has appealed to them to listen. It also sheds light upon his allegorical approach to the interpretation of Scripture. It is evident that Paul regarded this method as carrying with it full authority. The present phrase could, of course, be understood as no more than a reference to the contents of the law, but the apostle is more concerned about the significance than the facts of this story of Abraham's household. He proceeds as if he assumes that his readers, converted from paganism as these were, would be familiar with the facts. The account is given in Gen. 16 and 17.

one by a slave and one by a free woman: in the Greek the definite articles are used to denote those mentioned in Scripture. It is important to note that Paul does not at first mention them by name, because he wishes rather to draw attention to the categories to which they belonged. The word used for 'slave' means literally 'maidservant' (*paidiskē*), but since in patriarchal times all servants were virtually slaves, the contrast here is legitimate.

23. But the son of the slave: the introduction of this further statement with the adversative particle 'but' (*alla*) is intended to bring out a deeper contrast between these two sons of Abraham. It was not merely a difference in the status of their respective mothers, but also in the circumstances of their birth.

according to the flesh: this phrase evidently denotes natural generation and is distinguishable from the method of Isaac's birth in that his was regarded as the result of divine intervention, in what was otherwise a highly improbable situation (i.e. through promise). Ishmael was the result of Abraham's reliance on human planning rather than reliance on God's promise.

24. Now this is an allegory: a more literal rendering would be, 'which kind of things are allegorical'. The present participle of the verb (*allegoreō*) is designed, therefore, to bring out the significance in the present circumstances, not in the historical context.

The allegorizing of Scripture has had various advocates, but this is the clearest example of it in the writings of Paul. It was used extensively by Philo to the detriment of the historical sense. In this respect Paul differs markedly from Philo and from the later Jewish exegetes, for he gives the full historical meaning to the event and deduces almost as of secondary significance the deeper spiritual implication. At the same time Paul means to appeal to Abraham's sons in this allegorical way as more than a useful illustration of a spiritual truth. As an illustration it would have failed to convince the readers of the folly of their ways, but as an allegory it would carry the same authority as the literal meaning, because it conveyed divinely authenticated principles (cf. Bring). As Paul draws them out, these are in full harmony with, although additional to, the historical meaning. Attention to Paul's approach to allegorization would have avoided much fanciful exegesis. It was the

Alexandrians who were renowned for this in the early Church, but the modern period is still not without examples of excess in the same direction.

these women are two covenants: the line of thought transfers from the sons to the mothers, although as yet unmentioned by name. It is surprising that Paul should use the word 'covenant' (*diathēkē*) here without further explanation, for so far in this epistle he has used it only generally of God's negotiations with Abraham (3.17). But he assumes as common knowledge that his readers will at once identify the covenants. The form of the Greek suggests that he is drawing attention to the number of covenants, 'two', in order to contrast them. It is a choice between law and promise; there are no further options.

One is from Mount Sinai: as he has not previously identified the position under the law as a covenant, the apostle chooses this method of doing so, presumably because Sinai was regarded as symbolic of the divine origin of the law. But the connection between Hagar and Sinai is not obvious, and Paul sees the need to make a further identification in the next verse.

bearing children for slavery: here the apostle has in mind the double idea that as Hagar, a slave-girl, could produce children only in a condition of slavery, so the Mosaic law produced slaves to the law. The latter idea has not been specifically mentioned, but is implicit in the opening section of this chapter. It was not unintentional that Paul avoids the assertion that his readers are wanting to become slaves of the law.

she is Hagar: this is added to make unmistakable which of the two women represents the Sinaitic covenant. This was necessary because the Jewish people, proud of their Abrahamic descent, would nevertheless have drawn no such conclusion. To them the law from Sinai was given to the descendants of Abraham through Isaac and had nothing to do with Hagar's descendants. This identification on Paul's part would, therefore, have appeared to them as something of a *tour de force*, and Paul's further explanations show that he is not unmindful of this.

25. Now Hagar is Mount Sinai in Arabia: this statement is difficult in view of verse 24, which has defined Hagar as the 'one *from* Mount Sinai'. Here Paul apparently feels that he has not gone far enough. He must assert some closer connection. It is not that Hagar merely represents the covenant of law given on Mount Sinai; she is to be identified with Mount Sinai itself. Moreover, the significance of locality is brought out specifically by the addition of 'in Arabia'. And yet it is not easy to see what intelligible meaning can be attached to the present statement. This was no doubt the cause of the modification of the text in some MSS to read 'For Sinai is a mountain, in Arabia', omitting altogether the reference to Hagar. But the only conceivable motive for such a statement, if original, would be the fear that Gentile readers would lose the thread of the argument because of their vagueness over geography. But since Paul immediately switches attention to Jerusalem this seems unlikely. The inclusion of Hagar in the text is more intelligible, because it follows naturally from the previous statement.

It has been suggested that Paul may have known of a tribe of nomads in the area of Sinai called Hagarenes (cf. Ps. 83.6 for a tribe of people of this name (cf. Duncan)). But such an inference is precarious. There may well have been some connection in Paul's mind, however, between Mount Sinai and the wilderness to which Hagar fled from Sarah. A wilderness area was in any case a fitting symbol for the barrenness produced by the law. It must be remembered that Paul had himself spent some time in Arabia, although it need not have been in the area of Sinai (see comment on 1.17). But in the last analysis it seems impossible to be quite certain what Paul had in mind in making this statement. The one thing that matters and that is indisputable is the intended connection of Hagar with those under the law and this is the assumption on which the argument proceeds.

she corresponds to: an interesting verb is here used which means 'to line up in the same rank', in a military sense. Its meaning in this context is that Hagar is in the same category as the present Jerusalem.

the present Jerusalem: this is clearly Paul's description of contemporary Judaism, of which Jerusalem was the acknowledged capital.

in slavery with her children: the apostle is possibly thinking of slavery in a double sense. Jerusalem (and Judaism) was under Roman occupation. But his primary thought must be of slavery to law. Pharisaism had so superimposed upon the law a mass of minute regulations that observance of it had become a burden.

26. But the Jerusalem above is free: after the reference to the Jerusalem which is now, the antithesis is unexpected in its allusion to the 'above' Jerusalem. One would have expected 'which is to come'. But the reason why Paul avoids the more precise parallel is clear, for he is still thinking of a present reality, the spiritual Jerusalem which represents tne Christian Church. The use of the word 'above' (*anō*) in describing Jerusalem is probably influenced by pre-Christian notions of what Jerusalem might one day be. The heavenly Jerusalem is an idea which occurs elsewhere in the New Testament (cf. Heb. 12.22; Rev. 3.12; 21.2, 9ff.). It was evidently a figure which would have been meaningful even to Gentile readers.

The freedom of those belonging to this Jerusalem is in marked contrast to slavery under the law and constitutes an antithesis which is integral to the theme of the whole letter.

and she is our mother: it is noticeable that Paul does not state that Sarah corresponds to the 'above' Jerusalem. He takes it for granted. This accounts for the figure of speech being continued in the following verses. The analogy is clarified in verse 28, where 'the children of promise' are referred to as comparable to Isaac. Paul is here thinking of all who are under the new covenant in Christ.

27. For it is written: this is a citation from the LXX of Isa. 54.1. The prophet looks forward to the greater prosperity of the restored Jerusalem as compared with the old. It is a song of rejoicing over barrenness transformed to fruitfulness. Paul sees it, however, as an illustration of the fruitfulness of Sarah as compared with Hagar. But Jerusalem is further an illustration of the fruitfulness of the Christian Church.

O barren one: since this describes one who is contrasted with 'she who hath a husband', it seems likely that Paul regarded the former as a reference to Sarah and the latter as a reference to Hagar. The analogy is clearly imperfect. Moreover, Isaiah makes no reference to either in this context (although Sarah is mentioned in Isa. 51.2). The real point of the quotation is the comparison of the number of children. Sarah's children through Isaac were innumerable as compared with the descendants of Hagar. But Paul has already suggested that Hagar's descendants correspond to contemporary Judaism, and his thought must be that although the Church at present seems to be barren, bereft of all the advantages and glories of Judaism, it would nevertheless be more productive. History has confirmed this application of the Isaianic prophecy, although in Paul's day the Jews may well have questioned it.

28. Now we: some texts have 'you' instead of 'we', but it seems most probable on intrinsic grounds that Paul would include himself among those corresponding to Isaac in his allegory.

brethren: this form of address is particularly relevant here in view of the phrase 'children of promise', which is clearly intended to refer to all Christian believers.
children of promise: in the Greek text the word for promise (*epangelia*) is emphatic by position and must refer back to the references to promise earlier in the epistle.

29. as at that time: in the comparison which Paul makes he refers back to an incident which does not occur in the Old Testament narrative.
flesh ... Spirit: this statement differs significantly from the similar one in verse 23, where the son born according to flesh is contrasted with the Son born according to promise. The change from 'promise' to 'spirit' shows that Paul is thinking of his earlier statements regarding the activity of the Spirit within believers (cf. 3.2ff.; 4.6). In other words, Paul transfers the appropriate expression from the past to the present, from promise to fulfilment.

persecuted: since no such incident is specifically mentioned in Scripture this may be a reference to a Jewish *Haggadah* or Rabbinical enlargement of a narrative. Genesis 21.9 does suggest friction, if not persecution, and friction of the kind mentioned, i.e. involving mocking or scorn, may well have involved some form of persecution (cf. Williams).

so it is now: whatever the explanation of the persecution, Paul uses it to point to a parallel among the Galatians. There must have been something amounting to persecution on the part of the Judaizers (so Burton). There is no need to think of physical persecution, for in the present case it is more likely to have been mental pressures.

30. But what does the scripture say? Paul is about to appeal to a contrast, hence 'but' (*alla*) introduces this rhetorical question. He is determined to answer the Jewish claims from Scripture, which they fully acknowledged. The force of the citation naturally depends on the acceptance of Paul's interpretation of the allegory under discussion.

Cast out: the citation is from Sarah's words in Gen. 21.10. The action which she called for and which was acted upon meant the curbing of Ishmael's hostility towards Isaac, and Paul sees this as symbolic of the contemporary situation. What was needed among the Galatians was equally firm action to prevent freedom giving way to slavery.

shall not inherit: Paul's previous discussion shows that he means by inheritance the fulfilment of the promise to Abraham. He has made abundantly clear that legalism cannot exist side by side with promise, and this is the principle which he finds illustrated in this Old Testament story. When an important principle like liberty in Christ is at stake the Christian position must be as uncompromising as Sarah's demand over Ishmael.

31. So, brethren: in this verse Paul sums up his allegory. In using the word 'brethren' he is once again including all true believers, and clearly excludes those whom he thinks of as children of Hagar.

the slave: it should be noted that the Greek has 'a slave', which draws more pointed attention to the qualitative aspect, i.e. slave children, although when the free woman is referred to an article is used, no doubt because Paul sees a direct connection between the Christian Church and God's specific promise regarding Sarah.

free woman: it is the apostle's firm conviction that Christians are born to freedom, for Christ is the Liberator. This is a matter of experience, and the validity of his identifying them with the children of the free woman would not be questioned.

ETHICAL EXHORTATIONS 5–6.10

CHRISTIAN LIFE AS A LIFE OF FREEDOM 5.1–15

1. There is no break between this verse and the previous one. This is true whether the first statement is connected with 4.31 or with the rest of the present verse, both of which are possible. It is certainly true that we are spiritually children of the free woman only because Christ has set us free. It is equally true that Paul is exhorting his readers to stand fast, having been set free. The AV 'Stand fast therefore in the liberty' is not based on the best MSS.

For freedom Christ has set us free: here there appears at first to be repetition, but undoubtedly Paul means to stress the incongruity of any other result. Christ did not set us free so that we might become slaves again. He intended us to have freedom. Paul sees the tendency of the Galatians as parallel to the position of a slave who had been delivered from slavery, but who did not understand liberty and preferred to submit to another slavery of a different kind. Had they no thought for the one who had set them free?

stand fast therefore: they are exhorted, on the strength of the liberty which Christ has secured for them, to dig their heels in firmly. There is an element of tenacity which should characterize every Christian's hold on his liberty. The use of this word suggests that Paul realizes that their feet are on a slippery path and only resolute action will save the situation. Once their feet begin to give way it is more difficult to reach stability. Now is the time to secure a firm foothold.

do not submit: the verb is passive, meaning 'do not be held in', and the sense must be 'do not allow yourselves to have a yoke clamped on you'. The use of the passive does not excuse the Galatians from responsibility in the matter, although it makes room for an allusion to the real, though unnamed, agents, the Judaizers. Paul pictures them like men trying to place a yoke on an ox, an action which calls for some co-operation on the part of the ox. Let the creature dig in its heels and refuse the yoke and the masters will not find it easy to impose it.

again to a yoke of slavery: the word 'again' (*palin*) refers to their former state, and since it is applied to both Gentiles and Jews, it is clear that Paul regards all pre-Christian states as slavery in some measure. The figure of a yoke is an apt metaphor for bondage, since an animal in a yoke has no alternative but to submit to the will of its master. It is significant that Jesus used the same word for the submission of his followers to him (Mt. 11.29). Not all yokes chafe, but the Judaizers' yoke could only be described as slavery, very different from that of Christ. It is one of the paradoxes of the Christian position that the 'free' are yoked with Christ. It is because Paul recognizes the need for a true estimate of Christian freedom that he devotes the remaining part of this letter to discussing its practical implications.

2. Now I, Paul: on many occasions the apostle appeals to his own position or to his own testimony in the body of his letters with the emphatic words, 'I, Paul' (*egō Paulos*). 2 Corinthians 10.1 is an example parallel to this, in which he introduces almost abruptly an impassioned direct appeal to his readers. There is no doubt that he intends the present statement to be regarded as authoritative. It should be noted that the word translated 'now' is literally 'behold' (*ide*), which is much more expressive than the RSV translation. Only here does it occur in Paul's writings, and it may reasonably be assumed that he uses it to draw attention to a matter of particular importance. It is as if he wants his readers to listen now to a different line of approach, i.e. an intensely personal appeal.

if you receive circumcision: there was no specific mention of circumcision in the doctrinal section of the epistle, but Paul has had it in mind throughout. He has been concentrating on fundamental principles. Now he comes to the matter of great practical urgency. The fact that he expresses himself hypothetically suggests that the Galatians have not yet succumbed to the Judaizers' pressure.

Christ will be of no advantage to you: what Paul means here is that if circumcision is a necessity for salvation Christ's work would be inadequate (cf. Beyer), and, if so, is of no advantage to those who rely on circumcision. To put the matter differently, Gentiles submitting to circumcision are in fact submitting to a legal system from which Christ has freed them. They are undoing his work. In fact they would be nullifying the essential message of the gospel. To the apostle, to whom Christ had come to mean everything, the threatened action of the Galatians is incredible.

3. I testify again: the word 'again' (*palin*) introduces a further consideration which should deter Gentiles from submitting to circumcision. As verse 2 shows what they would lose (nothing less than the benefit of Christ, and no professing Christian could lose more) so this verse shows what they would gain—the unenviable burden of observing the whole law. By placing these negative and positive aspects in such bold juxtaposition, Paul hopes to impress the readers with the utter senselessness of their proposed action. The verb used gives support to this, for it means not merely 'to bear witness' but 'to affirm solemnly'.

he is bound to keep the whole law: a literal rendering of the Greek would be 'he is a debtor to do the whole law', which, when understood metaphorically, refers to an obligation which must be discharged. In Rom. 8.12, Paul uses the same words in relation to Christians. All men have some kind of obligation, but to enter into an undertaking to keep the whole law was to place oneself under an impossible task-master, as Paul had himself experienced. Nor could they opt out of any part of the law if they were seeking justification by this means.

4. You are severed from Christ: the same verb has been used earlier in this epistle to express the annulling of a covenant, but here it has the special sense of separation in view of the following preposition (*apo*). This idea is closely akin to but more vividly expressed than verse 2. It is not merely loss of the benefits of Christ's work that is involved. It is separation from Christ himself—in other words apostasy (v. Bonnard). Such is the unavoidable consequence of adherence to a legal system. Although the apostle has previously spoken as if the matter is still tentative, he here addresses those affected as if it is an accomplished fact. This is to bring home to them more vividly the consequences which must follow their proposed action. Indeed an aorist tense is used, which has the sense, 'You have been discharged from Christ'.

justified by the law: here the phrase 'by the law' stands for 'by the works of the law', as in 2.16, although a different preposition is used. The preposition *en* used here, meaning 'in the sphere of the law', distinguishes this kind of justification from that secured 'in Christ'.

you have fallen away from grace: as in the first clause, so here the verb is an aorist and treats the potential as actual. What Paul means by grace is all that Christ has done for them. It involves God's free favour towards them. It is like turning their back on a free gift. Nothing could be more tragic than this.

5. through the Spirit: as there is no article in the Greek, the word 'Spirit' may refer to man's spirit or to the Holy Spirit. If the former, it would be used in antithesis to 'flesh'; if the latter, it would denote the indwelling Spirit in the believer. The two concepts merge in experience. It should be noted that there is also no preposition to express 'through', and the notion of agency is not therefore so strong as in the next phrase. It is the same construction as in 3.3.

by faith: Paul returns to the theme of faith which he has emphasized so much in the earlier part of the epistle. The last mention was in 3.26. The apostle is anxious lest they should forget their basis of acceptance and so he refers to his own position.

we wait for: the change of person from second to first emphasizes the contrast between Paul (and all who share his point of view) and those who are following a legalistic course. The verb indicates more than mere waiting. It conveys the idea of eager expectation (cf. Rom. 8.19, 23, 25).

the hope of righteousness: clearly 'righteousness' is the object of the hope. Neither word has an article in the Greek and they are therefore best regarded as qualitative, i.e. the hoped-for kind of righteousness. But why does Paul put it in this way? Is it merely a hope? The answer lies in the meaning of the word 'hope' (*elpis*). It is not simply a pious wish as it has come to mean in modern English usage: rather it is a strong assurance. This transforms Paul's words to mean that in contrast to the Galatians' threatened return to bondage, he was eagerly looking forward to the full possession of that righteousness which he had inherited by faith.

6. For in Christ Jesus: here Paul defines clearly whom he means to indicate by the 'we' in verse 5. The phrase 'in Christ Jesus' is more expressive than the adjective Christian, for there is a sense of 'abiding in', which is particularly relevant to Paul's purpose here. Such mystic union cannot be obtained through external means.

neither circumcision nor uncircumcision is of any avail: the verb when used of persons means 'to have power', but when used of things 'to be serviceable'. But serviceable for what? Surely for attaining righteousness, as referred to in verse 5. The apostle wishes to make clear that there is no more virtue in being in a state of uncircumcision than of circumcision. It is simply irrelevant in Christ. This statement shows expressively the tremendous emancipation which has taken place in Paul's mind.

but faith working through love: the combination of faith and love is highly significant. Faith in the abstract is not enough. Here Paul's mind dwells on the ethical aspect of Christian faith. It must work (*energeō*), and the activity must be in a particular manner, i.e. through the agency of love. So far in this letter Paul has not mentioned the noun 'love' (*agapē*). Moreover, the verb 'to love' has occurred only once, and that to express God's love to us. But three times in this chapter he refers to 'love' in believers. This verse on its own merits would show that Paul is not out of harmony with James' doctrine of faith plus works (Jas 2.14ff.). For the use of the same verb earlier in this epistle to describe the divine working in man, cf. 2.8; 3.5.

7. You were running well: previously, in 2.2, Paul has used the athletic metaphor. Now he uses it again to describe the former Christian state of his readers. Like athletes in the first flush of the race, they had pressed on finely, but something had since happened. Their early progress has not been maintained.

who hindered you from obeying the truth? The verb in its root-meaning was used of breaking up roads in a military operation, and hence came to have the derived meaning of obstructing. It may be, therefore, that Paul mixes his metaphors here. A serious obstruction has arisen in the path of obedience. The apostle puts the matter in the form of a question in order to challenge the readers. But it may also be that the athletic metaphor is still in mind, and that Paul is thinking of the rules of the race which all competitors must obey. In that case the hindrance is someone who has caused them to disobey these rules. No doubt he has the Judaizers in mind in all this, but his main purpose at this juncture is to point out the utter folly of stopping short before the goal is reached.

8. This persuasion: there may be a play on words between this word and the verb 'obey' in the last verse, since the roots are connected. The word 'persuasion' suggests that Paul is thinking of the Judaizers as using some persuasive method of getting the Galatians to disobey what they know to be the truth.

him who called you: this is characteristic of Paul. So conscious was he of his own divine calling that he cannot imagine Christians who do not constantly think of God's call to them. Had they done so, they would never have allowed anyone to draw them away. The source of their 'persuasion' was hostile to God's purpose for them, as is made clear in the next verse.

9. A little yeast: this is a proverbial saying, for Paul cites it also in 1 C. 5.6, where it refers, as here, to the permeating effect of an adverse influence. A very similar metaphor is used in one of the parables of Jesus (cf. Mt. 13.33), although in this case the influence appears to be good rather than harmful. The use of the imagery of the small amount of yeast to describe the adverse teaching of the Judaizers suggests that, so far, they had had little apparent success, but the apostle sees the potential danger of their teaching, particularly owing to its insidious character (cf. Bring).

the whole lump: once the principle was accepted that circumcision was necessary for Gentile Christians Paul sees clearly that none of the Christians would be unaffected. He shows an insight which has often been sadly lacking in Christian history. The insidious permeation of wrong doctrines and wrong practices has all too often not been realized until too late to avoid the corruption of whole communities. In recent times the rooting out of the offending 'leaven' has been made infinitely more difficult because of the contemporary notion that anything savouring of heresy-hunting must be avoided at all costs. The apostle was no heresy-hunter, but he had an acute perception of the disastrous consequences of unchecked wrong.

10. I have confidence in the Lord: the 'I' is emphatic because of the contrast which the apostle is wanting to stress, as much as to say, 'although I have been speaking to you in a straight manner, I myself am confident over you'. Paul's confidence (*pepoitha*) is directly contrasted with the 'persuasion' (*peismonē*, from the same root) of the Judaizers. He demonstrates the superiority of his own confidence by adding the words 'in the Lord' (*en Kuriō*). If the Galatians allow the Judaizers to persuade them, they will be relying, on the contrary, on themselves. For Paul, no firmer basis for confidence could be found than in Christ.

that you will take no other view than mine: the words in the Greek are less explicit than this translation suggests. A literal rendering would be, 'that you mind no other thing', which can either be understood as it is translated here, or as a vague reference to their former position when they first became Christians to which they were to add nothing else. Both would amount to much the same thing.

he who is troubling you: the same expression was used in 1.7, except that there the reference is to more than one. In view of this, too much should not be made of the singular here. If Paul momentarily thinks of an individual it is only as a representative of the whole. Moreover the real point of his allusion is to warn all the Galatians of the judgment which will fall on any who distract them from the truth.

will bear his judgment: the verb means 'to carry as a burden', the same verb as is used twice in the next chapter (verses 2 and 5) for the carrying of one's own and other people's loads, and in 6.17 of Paul's bearing the marks of Jesus. Nowhere elsewhere in the New Testament is the word used as here of the bearing of judgment. Paul thinks of the heavy weight which will press down on those who are seeking to impose a load of legalism on these Christians. The word 'judgment' (*krima*) refers evidently to God's judgment, not man's.

whoever he is: although somewhat vague Paul's reference is really all-inclusive. This means that there are no exemptions from the judgment, no matter what status is claimed. Is he here thinking of the Judaizers' claims to represent those 'who are reputed to be pillars'? It may well be so (cf. Lietzmann, Oepke).

11. But if I, brethren, still preach circumcision: by putting his proposition in an if-clause, Paul is anticipating that some are asserting that in his preaching he favoured circumcision. They may even have heard of the circumcision of Timothy, if it had already happened (see Introduction). This is always a more insidious approach on the part of opponents than a direct opposition. To claim Paul's support for a practice which he was actually opposed to was bound to confuse the issue for the unwary. Here the apostle takes up the charge in order to show its illogical character. Note the use of 'brethren' to give his statement the quality of a personal appeal.

why am I still persecuted? Paul assumes that his readers will know what he has already endured for the sake of the gospel, particularly at the hands of the Jews. Had he still been an ardent supporter of Jewish ritual requirements, he would not have been so strongly persecuted as he had been. His experience refutes the charge being brought against him.

the stumbling-block of the cross: in 1 C. 1.23 Paul uses the same word 'stumbling-block' (*skandalon*) of the Jewish attitude towards the cross. There was an offence in the cross, as the apostle has already implied in chapter 3, in the passage respecting the curse of the law. It was unthinkable for the Jew that their Messiah could ever suffer the utter ignominy of crucifixion, and since this, and not circumcision, had been the real theme of Paul's preaching Jewish persecution was highly intelligible.

has been removed: the same verb as is used in 5.4 and in 3.17. In 5.4 the severance is between those addressed and Christ. But here there is an imagined (though incredible) severance between the cross and its stumbling-block.

12. **those who unsettle you:** only here does Paul use this verb, which means 'to stir up'. It occurs in Ac. 17.6 in the sense of turning the world upside-down. The apostle thinks of the creation of an unstable situation by these false teachers. They are having a disastrous effect upon the readers. No wonder Paul's reaction is so violent.

would mutilate themselves: the bitterness of Paul's feelings comes to expression in a somewhat coarse wish that the circumcisers would turn their knives upon themselves. In all probability Paul may be thinking of the practice of some heathen priests (like those of Cybele) who emasculated themselves as a sign of devotion. The apostle evidently feels that the Gentiles would not be able to differentiate between circumcision and mutilation, for the former had lost for them what significance it had possessed for the Jew. Self-mutilation under the law was a basis for excommunication (Dt. 23.1). The whole expression reflects deep disgust on the apostle's part.

13. **For you were called to freedom, brethren:** again the personal address is emphasized and the emphatic pronoun is used, no doubt to heighten the contrast with the previous attack on the instigators. The reference to freedom echoes verse 1 and the appeal to their calling echoes verse 8 (cf. also 1.6). The use of the aorist sets the whole action in the past and points to the fact that the Galatians had already experienced this freedom, although it would seem that they had not recognized the true nature of it. The ethical implications of freedom, which Paul deals with in the next portion of the epistle, are a vital part of his whole discussion. The freedom for which he is contending is not a theoretical matter, but intensely practical.

only do not use: the verb is missing from the Greek which is, therefore, more vivid than the English. A literal rendering might be 'only as regards the freedom, not for an opportunity . . .'. The abruptness suggests a sudden realization on Paul's part of the possibility that the Galatians' liberty might degenerate to licence.

as an opportunity: the word used here (*aphormē*) is a military word for 'a base of operations'. It is used several times by Paul in the sense, as here, of a 'convenient occasion'. Flesh is represented as an opportunist ever ready to seize any suitable occasion to exert itself.

flesh: already in the epistle there has been the conflict between Spirit and flesh, and the next portion particularly concentrates on this theme from a practical point of view. It is the mention of 'flesh' which seems to spark off the detailed discussion. But why think of 'flesh' as the main opponent of freedom? Why not 'law', or even 'sin', as in Rom. 7.8? The choice of the word 'flesh' is significant because it sums up the impelling motive of the natural man, the moral bias of the man who is not energized by the Spirit.

but through love: just previously (in verse 6) Paul has linked faith and love, and now he links freedom and love. Both faith and freedom may become warped, when divorced from the warmth of love.

be servants of one another: the choice of verbs here is intentional to qualify the idea of Christian freedom, i.e. the readers had not been called to bondage to the law but to servitude to each other. Of course, love takes the sting out of this new kind of bondage, but the whole idea is the antithesis of licence. True love must be mutual and cannot put its own interests first. The idea of loving service as a characteristic of Christian liberty has never been entirely absent from the Christian Church, but in many periods of its history the evidence of it has been weak. This fundamental principle is as much a lesson for our own age as for the first century. An important feature of Christian service is its mutual character. No-one is to be so superior that he claims exemption from the demands of loving service.

14. For the whole law: this is a justification for the preceding statement. Paul's train of thought seems to be that freedom needs love and that love is supported out of the law. The phrase 'the whole law' points to the unity of the law, in the light of which a piecemeal approach is quite inadequate.

in one word: a contrast is clearly intended between 'one' word and the whole law. This concentration of law into the concept of love would have sounded strange to the ears of the legalists with whom Paul is contending, although they acknowledged the importance of the statement which Paul quotes.

'You shall love your neighbour as yourself': cited from Lev. 19.18. Compare also Lk. 10.27, where it is cited as one part of the essence of the law by a lawyer in answer to a question put by Jesus. The idea of good neighbourliness as a requirement of law was clearly of current importance among the Jews. No doubt Paul realized that even Judaizers would assent to this. In a Christian setting love for one's neighbour would mean much more, because of the new conception of love which Jesus had brought. The whole verse emphasizes that Paul is not adverse to law, but wishes to draw out its positive contribution.

15. But if you bite and devour one another: as an antithesis to love this statement is striking. The apostle thinks of a pack of wild animals flying at each other's throats. It is a vivid representation not only of utter disorder, but also of mutual destruction. The policy enjoined by the Judaizers could lead only to dissension of the bitterest kind, for it must arouse passions which are unrestrained by the influence of love. The picture painted is so far removed from the ideal Christian community that the incongruity of the situation must have forcibly struck the readers. It should be noted that Paul tactfully expresses the idea in a hypothetical form.

take heed, or literally 'watch out'. The prospect of the devourers themselves being devoured is unexpected, but requires vigilance if it is to be avoided. It is a challenging example of the Golden Rule being used in a disastrous and negative way. No-one willingly desires to be devoured and yet the action of these Galatians was heading in that direction.

CHRISTIAN LIFE AS LIFE IN THE SPIRIT 5.16-26

16. But I say: this familiar introductory phrase of the apostle is never used in a purely formal way. In 3.17 and 4.1 it is used to introduce a further explanation of what has already been said. Here and in 5.2 it draws attention to Paul's personal appeal to his readers.

walk by the Spirit: some understand 'spirit' here in its general sense of the spiritual life as opposed to the flesh. But the expression has more force if the reference is to the Spirit of God, especially as this fits better into the immediate context. The idea of the Christian life as a walk is frequent in the New Testament. It should be noted that the tense of the imperative (present) shows that Paul is not exhorting them to do what they have not done before; rather he urges them to 'keep on walking by the Spirit'.

do not gratify: in the Greek the verb is in the future indicative, which gives a more forceful sense than the imperative. Those who walk by the Spirit will definitely not (emphatic) fulfil the desires of the flesh. This is an assured result of the Spirit-life.

desires: this word (*epithumia*) is generally used in the sense of longing for forbidden things, but not exclusively, as the next verse shows that it can be used of the Spirit's desires. When associated, as here, with 'flesh' its most dominant sense is to denote 'passion'.

17. For the desires of the flesh: this expression is not identical to that of verse 16, for the use of the cognate verb here (*epithumeō*) brings the more active side of the lust of the flesh. It lusts against the Spirit because it has no outlet for its energies along the path of the Spirit. It can only be in direct opposition.

the desires of the Spirit: as in the previous phrase, so here the statement is active. The Spirit is the subject in the same way as the flesh. The antithesis is as complete in literary form as it is in actual fact.

are opposed: the verb denotes hostility, from the root-idea of two things lying opposite to one another. In Paul's view, spirit and flesh are irreconcilable adversaries.

to prevent you from doing what you would: here the Greek (a *hina* clause. suggests a purpose clause, which would mean that the opposition between flesh and Spirit is in order to prevent (so Burton). But if this is so there is some obscurity about the meaning of the last phrase, which may be literally rendered 'whatever things you wish'. Does this refer to good things or bad things or both? It would be most natural to suppose that bad things are in mind and that the Spirit is conceived of as having the distinctive purpose of restraining the desires of the flesh. But since the opposition is mutual it is not impossible that the idea of flesh aiming to prevent the fulfilment of the good desires of the Spirit may also be in mind. This, however, is less likely in view of Paul's deep conviction that the Spirit is more powerful than the flesh. The *hina* could, on the other hand, be regarded as expressing result, which is rather less difficult because it avoids attributing purpose to a state of continuous opposition. Where a condition of conflict exists a loss of freedom of action is the inevitable result (cf. Bonnard).

18. **led by the Spirit:** here the Spirit is regarded as a guide, to whom the believer is expected to submit himself. Such a conception of the Spirit's activity is much more personal than the expression 'walking in the Spirit' in verse 16. It should be noted that in this verse the distinction is not between Spirit and flesh, but Spirit and law. What was the reason for this change in view of the fact that the immediate context concerns flesh? In all probability Paul was afraid that the Galatians would assume that only two alternatives existed. It may have been thought that rejection of legalism must lead to antinomianism, with its consequent licence. But the apostle inserts the present statement to correct this false impression. There is a third option. The Spirit is antithetical to both law (in the sense of legalism) and flesh. By this Paul is not, of course, placing law and flesh in the same category, but he is showing that in relation to Spirit they have one thing in common, i.e. opposition to the Spirit-controlled life. The idea of leading by the Spirit occurs also in Rom. 8.14, where it is said to be the badge of sonship.

not under the law: both here and in the preceding phrase the article is missing in the Greek, which would suggest general principles rather than specific examples. Yet in the case of law, the specific Mosaic law is never far from Paul's thoughts in this epistle. It may be expressed as follows. Legalism and spiritual life do not mix, as is clear from the distinction between the Mosaic era and the era of the Spirit.

19. **works of the flesh:** it is rather surprising to find Paul using the word 'works' in conjunction with 'flesh', for in the four previous references to works in this epistle it is related to the law. This is unexpected after the reference to law in verse 18, but it nevertheless brings out most strongly the practical outworking of life which is lived under the domination of the flesh. It is significant that 'works' are regarded sufficiently comprehensively to include not only overt deeds but also attitudes, as the following list shows. The detailed list also shows that there is a distinction in Paul's mind between 'works of the flesh' and 'works of the law', the latter denoting 'obedience to given statutes'.

are plain, i.e. they are the kind of things which are well known to everyone. There is not likely to be dispute about them. Libertinism cannot be pursued in secret.

immorality, impurity, licentiousness: the list is introduced in the Greek by a relative (*hatina*) which draws special attention to the qualitative aspect. The list itself is a selection to illustrate the kind of things to be expected from the activity of the flesh. The first three are all sins of sensuality. But why begin with these? It may be because of the prevalence and apparentness of them in Paul's time. They were much in evidence in the pagan background from which the Galatians had come. Indeed they were sanctioned in the rites of pagan worship. 'Immorality' (*porneia*) refers to a particular instance of the more general 'impurity' (*akatharsia*), which, although it can sometimes denote ritual impurity, here refers to moral impurity. The third word of the trio (*aselgeia*) means literally wantonness generally, but is no doubt here used of looseness in sexual relationships. In modern times the increase in these sensual sins and their disastrous effect on social relationships need no illustration. The movement known as the New Morality comes perilously near to sanctioning these sins which Paul so uncompromisingly classes as opposed to life in the Spirit. It would be a sad thing for the world and a sadder thing for the Church if it were ever assumed that free sexual expression could be excluded from the works of the flesh.

20. idolatry, sorcery: the connection of immorality and idolatry in Paul's mind is not far to seek. The two were closely knit in contemporary paganism, especially in much pagan worship. Sorcery or witchcraft, which was also a prevalent contemporary practice, is here represented by a word (*pharmakeia*) which means 'use of medicine or drugs', but which has the derived meaning of the use of drugs for magical purposes. It should be remembered that the dividing line between medicine and magic was not clear-cut in those days, any more than it still is in many tribal cultures. It is significant that Acts records a case of Paul having to deal with an opponent of the gospel who was classed as a sorcerer (13.4ff.). No doubt Elymas was not the only one of this prevalent class of people with whom Paul had clashed. Both idolatry and sorcery were thus examples of the sins of pagan worship, the first providing an inadequate substitute for God and the second counterfeiting the works of the Spirit.

20, 21. enmity, strife . . . envy: the next eight form a self-contained group which may be said to describe social evils. Some (e.g. Lightfoot) see an ascending scale of intensity after the general term 'enmity' at the head of the list. But this is probably reading too much into the arrangement of the list. Paul is no doubt led from one thought to the next within the general category of enmity, which stands first. There are four words which describe strife, the first two and then later on 'dissension' and 'party-spirit'. 'Enmity' is general hostility, 'strife' is more overt, stressing the idea of wrangling, 'dissensions' (the word *dichostasia* means 'standing apart') drawing attention to the formation of hostile splinter groups, while 'party spirit', which comes from the same word as 'heresy' (*hairesis*), refers to the development of various conflicting opinions. The general impression created by these words is one of chaos.

The other four 'works of the flesh' in this part of the list are all attitudes of mind which result in actions implicating other people in the community. Perhaps the most unpleasant of these is the first, 'jealousy', for the same word also means 'zeal', and the idea in this context must be 'perverted zeal'. This word coupled with the eighth word, 'envy', make a formidable pair. These two are still the deadliest enemies of the higher life of the Christian community. The other two in the group, 'anger' and 'selfishness', are very general human failings. The first, which in the Greek is expressed in the plural (*thumoi*), describes outbursts of anger rather than a settled attitude (Burton). The word 'selfishness' does not give quite the full sense of the Greek (*eritheia*), which rather denotes 'ambition, self-seeking', i.e. a particularly anti-social form of selfishness. Maybe the apostle is thinking of the striving of one leading member of a community to oust out all rivals and to gain supporters by fair means or foul, but rivalry is basic to all levels of society and this idea need not be confined to the leadership.

It is worth noting that four of the sins mentioned in this list of eight occur also in 2 C. 12.20 (jealousy, anger, selfishness, and quarrelling (=strife)). Paul fears that he will find these in evidence, together with four other closely allied vices, when he visits the Corinthians. It is possible in view of this and in view of the occurrence of other ethical lists in Paul and other New Testament writers that the apostle is reflecting a list or lists which were in current use among the popular moralists of his day. For a comment on such lists, cf. B. S. Easton, *The Pastoral Epistles*, 1948, pp. 197–202.

21. drunkenness, carousing: the whole list closes with sins of intemperance, which were also not only prevalent but sanctioned by various heathen forms of worship. In Rom. 13.13 Paul mentioned them together in conjunction with some of the other evils mentioned here. In that passage the apostle exhorts his readers to make no provision for the flesh to gratify its desires and thus the idea is closely parallel to the present passage. In view of the necessity for constant repetition of this warning against intemperance it is not surprising to find that one of the negative qualifications of a bishop is that he should not be a drunkard (1 Tim. 3.3; Tit. 1.17).

and the like: this is clearly added by Paul to show that he has intentionally been selective for the purpose of illustrating his point. The works of the flesh are this kind of thing and from these examples it should be possible to recognize others. A modern list of samples would need to be little different if at all from Paul's.

I warn you, as I warned you before: the verb used in each part of this statement means 'to say beforehand', with a derived meaning 'to declare'. Presumably the previous occasion to which he refers was the instruction given during his missionary work among them.

shall not inherit the kingdom of God: the warning is severe. The Jews would mostly have agreed with Paul's warning, for their moral standards were considerably higher than those of the Gentile world. Gentiles would certainly need a higher ethic when they embraced Christianity, but Paul is convinced that such could be found, apart from a legalistic rule, in the life in the Spirit. The word 'kingdom' refers to the reign of God which was to take place at the end of the present age, but it may also include a present realization as it seems to have done in the teaching of our Lord. This statement shows that although Paul did not make much of the kingdom teaching in his epistles, yet when he does refer to it it is full of significance and of obvious importance in his thinking. Similar statements to the present one, which bring out the ethical demands of the kingdom, may be found in 1 C. 6.9f. and Eph. 5.5.

22. But the fruit of the Spirit: the change from 'works' to 'fruit' is important because it shifts the emphasis away from human endeavour. The imagery used is particularly suggestive to convey the idea of spiritual growth, in striking contrast to the deterioration which follows the activities of the flesh. It is significant that Paul uses the singular 'fruit' rather than the plural, because the latter would suggest a number of variegated products, whereas his real aim is to show the various aspects of the one harvest. Not one of those qualities which Paul names can be isolated and treated as an end in itself. The metaphor of fruit, which is frequently used in the teaching of Jesus, is found on a few other occasions in Paul's epistles, the most interesting of which is Eph. 5.9, where it occurs, as here, immediately after a reference to the ethical character of the kingdom. It seems certain that in the apostle's mind there was a definite distinction between the fruit of the Spirit and the spiritual gifts (*charismata*) mentioned in the First Epistle to the Corinthians (so Ridderbos). In the latter the endowments were for special tasks and were not therefore shared by all alike. But the fruit of the Spirit is the normal product of every believer led by the Spirit.

As with the list of works of the flesh, so with this list it is impossible to place too much emphasis on the precise order of each individual item. Nevertheless two observations may be made. The first three are undoubtedly placed in a significant order at the head of the list. Moreover, these three deal with inward qualities which mainly affect the self, although they cannot be divorced from the Christian reaching out; the final six are more socially orientated. Yet this must be regarded as only a rough classification.

love: few would dispute Paul's choice of love as being primary. It is in harmony with his great hymn of love in 1 C. 13. It is at the heart of the gospel. Paul has already had something to say about it in this epistle, both of Christ's love to man (2.20) and of man's own love (5.6). Christian love was vastly different from the contemporary notion of love, which was inextricably bound up with carnal passion, because it is patterned on the love of Christ to man. Both his love and ours are the product of the same Spirit.

joy, peace: joy is especially characteristic of Paul's letter to the Philippians, but it occurs also in several other letters. In this letter it is mentioned only here. Several times Paul uses the expression 'the God of peace', which indicates the kind of peace for which he looks. Cf. 1 C. 7.15, where he applies this to domestic relationships by remarking that God has called us to peace. This peace is very different from the general notion of peace, for it is an inward possession which brings with it serenity of mind. It contrasts vividly with the chaotic 'works of the flesh'. These first three

qualities are completely alien to the very atmosphere which 'flesh' produces.
patience: the word contains the idea of 'endurance', which gives a stronger
content than the word 'patience'. Nevertheless, the main emphasis here is on a
passive quality—bearing up under the stresses and strains of life. This is a quality
seen most vividly in a social context.

kindness, goodness: the first of these words can denote goodness, but always in
the New Testament it signifies 'kindness'. The second word can also mean both
goodness and kindness. Indeed, there appears to be little distinction between the
two words. Nevertheless, it would be unlike Paul in a list of this kind to use two
synonymous words without intending some distinction. It is just possible, therefore,
that 'goodness' is conceived to be more active than 'kindness'.

faithfulness: this translates the Greek word *pistis*, which has already played an
important part in the earlier portion of the epistle in the sense of 'faith in God'.
But since faith is a basic requirement in man's approach to God it cannot be
regarded as part of the fruit of the Spirit in the same way as the other virtues
mentioned. The word must therefore mean 'trustworthiness', either in the sense of
fidelity to standards of truth or in the sense of reliability in dealings with others
(cf. Burton).

23. gentleness: this word (*prautēs*) conveys the idea of mildness, which is seen
in a willingness to submit to the will of God. The AV rendering ('meekness') has
often been misunderstood because it has been assumed that this implied a spineless
lack of resistance even to those things which are evil. But this is not the meaning
of the word. It is the counterpart of 'anger' in the other list. It is not a natural
quality, otherwise it would not have been included in the fruit of the Spirit. It
needs spiritual cultivation. The development of it leads to harmony and not
discord. It is for that reason a potent factor in the elimination of those sins of strife
so prominent in the former list. Cf. Burton's lexical discussion here.

self-control, i.e. mastery over the desires of the self. The corresponding verb is
used in 1 C. 7.9 of control of sexual desires, but the noun in the present context
unquestionably has a wider connotation. In the Spirit-directed life self must keep
its proper place. Self-control, however, does not mean self-negation, but a true
estimate of the function of self in the noblest form of life. There can be no better
example than our Lord himself, who never emphasized his own will and yet never
failed to impress the power of his personality upon others. The Spirit reproduces
in the believer the same kind of balanced view of self.

against such there is no law: the apostle returns to his theme of law because he
probably has in mind the Judaizers' insistence that a legal system is the only hope
of restraining the works of the flesh by condemning them. But Paul wishes to point
out that the Spirit-life is a real alternative because there is no need for any restraining law. The word 'law' is general here, although Paul may well have been thinking
of the Mosaic law. In one sense, if under the legal system men had shown the
qualities enumerated in this list, there would have been no need for the law's

condemnation. The fruit of the Spirit is, therefore, the positive answer to the legalist's challenge to the Galatians.

24. And those who belong to Christ Jesus: there is a close connection between this verse and the last. As contrasted with a legal system Christ has introduced an entirely new relationship. Flesh has been overcome by a new allegiance, indeed a new ownership. It should be noted that there is an article in the Greek before Christ Jesus, drawing attention to the title 'the Messiah', which would be of particular significance in Paul's discussion with the Judaizers.

have crucified the flesh: the verb points to a completed action in the past and might most naturally refer to conversion. Some see the aorist as referring to the finality of the act rather than to the specific occasion, and this is a justifiable interpretation. It is significant that the crucifying act is said to have been carried out by those in Christ, i.e. the verb is put in the active. By way of contrast, when Paul is dealing with his own continuous experience in 2.20 he uses the same verb in the passive. The active voice in this present context emphasizes the believers' responsibility, although Paul would have been the first to admit that the crucifying of the flesh with its passions and desires, is possible only by identification with the crucified Christ. The list in verses 19 and 20 has already sufficiently illustrated what Paul has in mind. The fruit of the Spirit is so antithetical to the operations of the flesh that something drastic must be done to them, i.e. they must be crucified. In itself the first word (*pathēma*) is neutral and is in fact often used by Paul in the sense of suffering, but the 'strong feeling' is clearly used in a bad sense as the context shows, and the article which is used with both words in the Greek denotes those passions and desires which particularly belong to the flesh.

25. If we live by the Spirit: the 'if' clause is rhetorical and might be rendered, 'Since we live by the Spirit'. The matter is not in doubt, but forms the basis of Paul's appeal. Life in the Spirit carries with it unavoidable responsibilities.

let us also walk by the Spirit: there is clearly a distinction in Paul's mind between 'living' and 'walking', the latter requiring a constant application, while the former expresses an abiding fellowship. The Christian believer has a different kind of life compared with those under the domination of flesh. But the practical application of this new life is not automatic. It requires some perseverance, just as a child who is learning to walk needs persistence. The metaphor is suggestive, for the same Spirit who gives life gives both strength and guidance throughout life's journey.

26. Let us have no self-conceit: Paul continues his exhortation with three negative aspects, all of which are an indication of what he means by walking in the Spirit. It is like picking one's way along a path filled with pot-holes. There are many things to avoid such as these three. They are probably selected to give as direct an antithesis to the strife engendered by the flesh as possible. A more literal rendering of the Greek here would be, 'Let us not *become* vainglorious people', i.e. let us not depart from the standard of humility set before us.

no provoking: a word, used only here in the New Testament, which literally means 'to call forth', hence 'to challenge'. Where the Spirit controls there are no combats among people because all are led by the same Spirit.

no envy: here the verb is used which corresponds to the noun used in verse 21, which suggests that Paul's aim is to show how the works of the flesh must be actively resisted. It is tragic that church life has often been wrecked through failure to observe the responsibilities of walking in the Spirit.

CHRISTIAN LIFE IN ITS RESPONSIBILITY TO OTHERS 6.1–10

6.1. Brethren, if a man . . .: there is no break between this verse and the last, for this gives a particular example of the general principles already enunciated. The repetition of 'brethren' reflects Paul's anxiety to keep his exhortations on a personal plane. He intends to treat his readers, in spite of his great concern over their present condition, in accordance with his own principles. The if-clause (*ean*) puts the proposition in a tentative form, and the general character of this hypothesis is emphasized by the use of 'man' instead of 'brother', although the man is presumably a Christian.

overtaken: the element of surprise is dominant in this word in this context, i.e. overtaken or seized unawares. It is the unexpected occasions when Christians fall which are most difficult to deal with and which tend to call forth harsh criticism from fellow-believers.

trespass: the word means literally 'to step aside', and may have been chosen because of its appropriateness to Paul's thought of the Christian life as a walk by the Spirit (5.16).

you who are spiritual: Paul is thinking of a distinct contrast between those who obey the dictates of the Spirit and those who do not. There is no question here of an exclusive group of believers more spiritual than others. This quality of spirituality is meant for all Christians. In the Greek, there is an emphasis on 'you', which heightens the contrast.

restore: the tense is present drawing attention to the continuity of the action. Restoration is generally not a single act, but a persistent procedure.

spirit of gentleness: the interpretation of this phrase will depend on whether the divine or the human spirit is in mind. If the former, the meaning would be 'through the aid of the Holy Spirit with the result of gentleness'; if the latter, 'through a gentility of spirit'. In Paul's own thought there was probably little difference, for the human spirit of the believer was conceived to be energized by the Holy Spirit. Restoration is delicate work and requires a tender approach. Rebuke or condemnation, however necessary in their place, are poor aids when a man is down.

Look to yourself: the change from plural to singular should be noted. Self-examination can only be individual. The verb used (*skopeō*) means more than just seeing; it involves a steady consideration, like looking at a target before releasing a shot.

lest you too be tempted: this may be regarded as expressing either the object or the purpose of the verb 'look'. As the object it would restrict the sphere of self-examination to areas of possible temptation. As the purpose of the verb, the clause would suggest that self-examination will avoid the temptation to fall into the same kind of trespass as the offending brother. It is significant that Paul refers to temptation rather than to sin, although it is the sin to which the temptation might lead which is to be avoided. No doubt Paul considered that self-examination could and should lead to the avoidance of a situation which, in this case, would lead to temptation.

2. Bear one another's burdens: while this is a general injunction, it no doubt had a particular reference to the case just mentioned. A Christian falls to a surprise temptation and immediately other Christians are to seek ways and means of restoring the fallen brother. His burden has become theirs. The principle enunciated is one of the most profound aspects of Christian fellowship. Because the Christian community is closely knit in Christ, what affects one member must affect the whole, a principle more than once illustrated elsewhere by the apostle under the figure of the body (cf. 1 C. 12.12ff.). In the Greek of this statement the first word is 'of one another' (*allēlōn*), which therefore carries special emphasis.

fulfil: the most probable reading is aorist, although there is some strong support for the future. The aorist reinforces the completeness of the fulfilment, which is also stressed by its compound form (*anaplēroō*).

the law of Christ: in all probability some connection exists between 'burdens' and 'law', for Paul has had experience of the burden of the Mosaic law and has been at such pains to dissuade the Galatians from accepting any such burdens. But he is dealing here with burdens and law of a different kind. The burdens are human burdens and the law is Christ's. Undoubtedly the expression 'law of Christ' is meant to contrast with the system of legalism as a religious principle. It involves submission to a Person rather than to a code. It seems better to take it in this sense than to suggest that 'law' here refers to any specific commandments or precepts of Jesus. All that Christ has become to the believer incurs a new kind of obligation upon him. As Christ bore the burdens of others, so the believer must do the same. This is the 'law' of true Christian relationships.

3. For if any one: the conjunction shows a close connection with the previous statement. Bearing other people's burdens involves self-sacrifice, and this is utterly incompatible with a sense of self-importance. Although the apostle expresses the matter indefinitely, he is probably thinking of some specific individual or individuals who had too high a self-esteem.

thinks: the same verb is used here as occurs in chapter 2 of 'those of repute', although here with a different sense; hence 'thinks' rather than 'seems'.

something ... nothing: the English translation obscures the emphatic juxtaposition of these two words. The contrast could not have been more vividly expressed. There appear to be no grades between. No believer has a right to regard himself as any more than nothing, i.e. in his own right, for he owes everything to Christ. This contrasts strongly with the Pharisaic concept of self-righteousness.

deceives himself: the verb, which occurs nowhere else in the New Testament, means to deceive one's own mind. The apostle implies that any believer who claims to be 'something' is filling his mind with fantasies.

4. But let each one test: the examination is an individual responsibility. No Christians are set up as official testers. The word for testing (*dokimazō*) is characteristic of Paul, who accounts for all the New Testament occurrences except four. Its primary application is for the testing of metals to see whether they are pure. This makes an apt metaphor for tests of moral worth.

his own work: two observations may be made here. The subject of examination is to be work which is tangible enough to provide a fairly objective basis. This is much more satisfactory than being called upon to test one's influence, although the latter is affected by one's activity. There is, of course, the difficulty of finding suitable standards against which to test our work, but Paul does not explicitly help us here. But he does so implicitly by evidently assuming that a Spirit-led life will have available spiritual means of assessment. The second worthwhile observation is that each is exhorted to concentrate on his own, not on the work of others. Much unpleasant criticism would have been avoided had this injunction been more closely obeyed.

and then: the result stated presupposes that the testing referred to has proved successful.

his reason to boast will be in himself alone: a literal rendering of the Greek would be, 'in respect to himself alone he will have the ground for glorying', which brings the emphasis more specifically on 'himself' (*heauton*). The word rendered 'reason to boast' (*kauchēma*) is another characteristic Pauline expression (cf. Rom. 4.2; 1 C. 9.15). This is not intended to be a sanction for boasting, but rather a focus on individual responsibility. In the last analysis each man is answerable for himself, not for others, and in view of verse 3 it would seem that Paul assumes that no-one has any real ground for boasting, since 'all believers are nothing'.

not in his neighbour: in the Greek the expression is very general, i.e. in respect of the other, which suggests any other besides oneself.

5. For each man will have to bear his own load: this is not a contradiction of verse 2, for a different type of burden is in mind. In the former verse it is a question of some crushing weight which unexpectedly descends on the person concerned and is completely outside his control. But here it is the general load which all must carry, like a hiker equipped with the bare minimum. There are certain responsibilities which cannot be shelved on to others. Each, for instance, must bear the burden of his own sinful bias, the infirmity of the flesh. In many ways this verse supplies the key to verse 2, for only those who know the measure of their own weaknesses are qualified to share the burdens of others. Here is the paradox of human sympathy. Those are best able to sustain another who have proved their own power to be sustained in trials of their own. It is suggestive that the same word used here for load (*phortion*) is used by Jesus of the burden of his yoke, which he himself describes as light (Mt. 11.30).

GENERAL EXHORTATIONS

6. Let him who is taught: the idea here is of oral teaching, and reflects the wide use made of catechesis in the early Church. This statement comes rather abruptly after the opening section of this chapter and raises the problem whether any connection exists with what precedes, whether it stands as an isolated statement or whether it introduces the next section. There is a connecting particle in the Greek (*de*) which presupposes some connection with what precedes, although that connection is not obvious on the surface. If it arises out of verse 5 it may introduce a necessary modification to avoid any misapprehension. That each man should bear his own burden does not exempt the taught having responsibilities towards the teacher. But the precise connection can be determined only when the meaning of this verse as a whole has been determined.

the word: this is the content of the catechesis and must therefore refer to the whole content of the Christian message. It would, of course, include a Christian interpretation of the Old Testament but would mainly consist of the positive aspects of Christian doctrine, a development, no doubt, from Paul's mission preaching to them. There is no certain knowledge whether there was a fixed form in which oral instruction was given, but it is highly probable. What is here most in view, however, is not the teacher's subject matter, but the teacher-pupil relationship.

share all good things: it is important to decide the precise meaning of the verb used here (i.e. *koinōneō*). Its root-meaning is 'to be a partner in or with'. This would suggest a partnership between teacher and taught, but it still remains to decide in what sense this partnership operates. It is generally supposed that the sharing involves the financial support of the teacher, and this may well fit in with the context (cf. Lightfoot, Bonnard, Bring).

Did the apostle fear lest his statement in the previous verse might be taken by the Galatians in the wrong way? Would they say that their instructors must bear their own financial load and so cease to support them? There is much to be said for this interpretation. Not only does it fit the context; it also suits the expression 'all good things'. Moreover, it would be an appropriate injunction for a people who had come from a heathen environment in which there was no custom of financial support for religious instructors. And yet the term 'good things' could be otherwise interpreted in a spiritual sense, and this would be more in keeping with the spiritual outlook of the epistle as a whole. In this case the emphasis must be placed on the term 'all'. It is the comprehensiveness of spiritual fellowship between teacher and taught which, under this interpretation, is mainly in mind. Perhaps the ambiguity of the statement is intentional to provide for both interpretations.

7. Do not be deceived: what is the connection of thought which causes the apostle to introduce this warning? It would appear reasonable to suppose that he is thinking of the implications of a failure to assume one's proper responsibilities. The idea that a Christian who does not have the right kind of fellowship with his instructor is comparable to one who mocks God seems rather too severe. It is better, therefore, to assume a looser connection with verse 6 and to maintain that Paul's mind moves to a rather different aspect of human responsibility.

God is not mocked: the absence of the article in the Greek word for God shows that it is intended to be taken qualitatively. God is not the kind who is susceptible to mocking. He understands perfectly and it is futile in the extreme to treat his judgments with contempt.

for whatever a man sows: this is certainly a proverbial saying. The metaphorical use of sowing and reaping not only finds parallels in extra-biblical writings, but particularly in the parables of Jesus. The proverb states an inexorable natural law. The harvest bears a direct relationship to the seed sown. No farmer would dispute this principle, but in the moral sphere some may be so self-deceived as to believe otherwise, and this even applies to Christians.

8. For he who sows to his own flesh: Paul applies the metaphor by identifying two different kinds of soil, flesh, and spirit, which have already been shown to be antithetical (cf. 5.16f.). In this case the soil affects the harvest rather than the seed, but although the metaphor becomes slightly mixed, the principle is undoubtedly the same. Flesh cannot produce spiritual results, and the Spirit will always produce results in harmony with his own nature. There is no doubt that Paul intended the emphasis to fall on the words 'his own' (*heautou*), as contrasted with 'the Spirit' in the second half of the verse. In the former case it is integral to the man; in the latter it is a gift from God. The expression 'to sow to a thing' (Greek *eis*) is used only in this context and in the interpretation of the parable of the sower (Mt. 13.20; Mk 4.18). In the latter case, the preposition denotes the direction in which the seed fell, i.e. towards the thorny area. If the same obtains here it must mean, in a metaphorical sense, that flesh is the sphere in which a man sows with the additional idea of direction. Paul is thinking of a man's life which is lived as if 'flesh' and its interests are the ultimate destiny.

reap corruption: the metaphor is vivid here, for who in his senses would ever bother to harvest a field of decaying matter, but the very incongruity of the idea serves to draw attention to the foolishness of those who sow to the flesh. As a contrast to eternal life in the next clause, 'corruption' stands for that which results in death.

he who sows to the Spirit: since this is an exact counterpart to the phrase 'to his own flesh', it must refer to a man whose intentions are directed towards the Spirit-dominated life.

will from the Spirit reap eternal life: the whole clause is exactly parallel in form to the first. As 'into the Spirit' corresponds to 'into the flesh', so 'from the Spirit' is parallel to 'from the flesh'; and 'corruption' to 'eternal life'. Yet the metaphor of the soil is more appropriate to the flesh than to the Spirit. It is a bold idea on Paul's part to apply it to the Spirit, but he wishes to bring out the incalculable advantage of embedding the seed of one's moral life in the Spirit of God. A spiritual harvest more surely follows right principles of sowing than a natural harvest.

The concept of eternal life is not as frequent in Paul as in John. In this context Paul gives no direct definitions of its meaning, but since he uses the term in antithesis to 'corruption' it may be inferred that his major stress is on the incorruptibility of the Christian's inheritance. This does not, of course, exhaust the meaning of the term, which also has a positive content, i.e. all the positive qualities of 'life' in all its fullness. The future tense suggests that Paul is mainly concerned with the ultimate harvest, and this is also supported by the following verse.

9. And let us not grow weary in well-doing: a similar statement occurs in 2 Th. 3.13, but there it is a direct exhortation in the second person. Here the apostle includes himself, for he knows that he is not immune to discouragement. The danger of sowing in the wrong soil is reasonably plain, but the danger of spoiling good work by losing heart is more subtle. Paul may have been thinking that life in the flesh may in its immediate effects seem more attractive, because the Christian path so often involves hardship, and this tends sometimes to undermine morale. When a man tires while he is doing fine things it means that he has temporarily lost his real sense of values.

in due season we shall reap: literally this should read 'in its own season', which clearly means the time of harvest. Metaphorically speaking, there is an appointed time for the spiritual reaping.

lose heart: a different verb is used here (*ekluō*), which contains the idea of fatigue. The figure is probably of reapers in a cornfield, perhaps under the blazing sun, who need to brace themselves for the task if the harvest is to be gathered. Those who become enfeebled will never achieve their end. Paul expresses the condition here by means of a participle to show that it is an integral part of reaping.

10. So then: Paul here uses a characteristic formula to draw out the logical consequence of what he has just said (*ara oun*). No other New Testament writer uses it.

as we have opportunity: this expression assumes that the opportunity is present, in which case 'as' (*hōs*) might be rendered 'while'. The word for opportunity (*kairon*), the same as in verse 9 translated 'season', points to the appropriate period of sowing corresponding to the appropriate time for reaping already referred to. The implication is that during the present life opportunities for doing good are constant.

let us do good to all men: the exhortation is general and should be characteristic of all Christians. But what does Paul mean by 'good' (literally 'the good' (*to agathon*))? In the previous verse 'well-doing' is derived from a different word (*kalon*), which more generally draws attention to the outward manifestation of goodness. But the distinction cannot be pressed too far. There is possibly a connection here with verse 6 where the plural 'good things' (*agathois*) occurs. Probably in both cases spiritual and material benefits may be in mind, although in both the spiritual predominate.

and especially: whereas the previous statement is surprisingly comprehensive, including 'all men' without barriers of race, status, or culture, the apostle wishes to press home a specific application of this principle. Responsibility towards other Christians is greater than towards other people generally.

those who are of the household of faith: there are other New Testament examples of the metaphor of a house to represent the Church of God (cf. Eph. 2.19; 1 Tim. 3.15; 1 Pet. 4.17). Here the imagery is more specifically of the members of a household, all together forming a unit. The genitive 'of faith' must then be regarded as descriptive. The distinguishing mark of the members of the Christian household is faith. This is better than treating faith as personified. On the other hand the Greek possesses the article, which could possibly refer to the content of belief, i.e. doctrine. But the present expression appears to be little more than a colourful description of all true Christian believers (cf. Cole).

The apostle is here touching on an important principle of Christian behaviour. If Christians neglect one another they will have little thought for the needs of non-Christians. Material distress among any members of the Christian family affects the whole family. The reality of the doctrine of the union of all in Christ sees to that. For this very reason, Christians have always been in the vanguard of schemes for social alleviation, although it must be admitted that organized Christianity has not infrequently lamentably failed to face up to its responsibility even towards its own members. No doubt Paul is here thinking of individual action rather than corporate action, since a body of people can never act corporately on any higher plane than its individual members.

CONCLUSION 6.11–18

11. See with what large letters, etc.: at this point the apostle may have taken the pen from the amanuensis and have added the concluding remarks in his own handwriting. If so, he felt it to be necessary to draw special attention to this, no doubt because the change of script would have been noticed only by the reader when the epistle was read aloud, and even he might well have overlooked the significance of the change. But why did Paul conclude in his own hand? According to this interpretation it would presumably have been designed to bring a warm touch to the concluding appeal to the readers. The largeness of the letters would then be in contrast to the smaller and neater script of the amanuensis. But there is no specific reference to an amanuensis here, and it is therefore not impossible that the whole epistle was written in his own hand. In that case his reference to it here would need to be understood in a different way. The largeness of hand would emphasize the intensity and earnestness of his thought in much the same way as block capitals are sometimes now used to arrest attention. It is difficult to choose between this latter theory and the amanuensis proposition. The verb 'I am writing' is in the aorist in Greek (*egrapsa*), which would most naturally refer to what precedes, although it is sometimes used of what is currently being written. Moreover, the epistle as a whole does not read like a dictated epistle, although the force of this argument would naturally be nullified if the amanuensis had reproduced precisely Paul's own statements. If 2 Th. 3.17 is regarded as a norm, it was evidently Paul's practice to take the pen at the conclusion. On the whole there would seem rather more in favour of this view than the other.

Did Paul intend to close at this point and then decide to add a concluding summarizing appeal? In all probability he did.

12. It is those who want: a more literal translation would read, 'as many as want', which makes it rather more general and yet all-inclusive. Paul's aim is to draw attention to one characteristic of all who insist on circumcision, i.e. their desire to create an impression.

to make a good showing in the flesh: the verb occurs only here in the New Testament and implies a desire to put on a fair face. The emphasis is on outward appearance as if God formed his estimates according to purely external measurements. But the key to the verb is in the accompanying phrase. 'Flesh' must once again be regarded as antithetical to Spirit, and Paul returns to his earlier contention that circumcision belongs to the former rather than to the latter. To the Jewish mind which had not been liberated from legalism, the finest outward display of a man's serious intentions towards piety was his willingness to submit to circumcision. This is what Paul means by a 'good showing'.

compel: the same word as used in 2.14 of Peter's action in insisting on Jewish conditions of fellowship with Gentiles. It is a strong word, which underlines the seriousness of the threat with which Paul is dealing. The Galatians may not yet have yielded, but the pressure upon them is considerable.

only in order that they may not be persecuted: the Judaizers are striving for a compromise between the non-Christian Jewish position of orthodox Judaism and the non-Jewish Christian position of Paul. They feared persecution from the orthodox party and yet their policy brought them into direct opposition to Paul. **for the cross of Christ:** in 5.11 Paul refers to the stumbling-block of the cross, and it would seem from both these references that the Judaizers were ignoring or even opposing the essentially Christian doctrine of the cross. Of course, they would avoid persecution if they insisted on circumcision and removed the offence of the cross. It is possible, however, that these Judaizers, if they were Christians at all, were attempting to avert the antagonism of Jews to the gospel message by showing their willingness to make Gentiles submit to Jewish scruples. Paul sees that even if they still retain the doctrine of the cross, their policy, in fact, nullifies it. Hence his own emphasis upon it in verse 14.

13. For even those who receive circumcision: Paul is probably echoing here an objection from the Judaizers that their motive was not to escape persecution but to uphold the law. They had no doubt convinced themselves of this altruistic motive, but Paul points out that not even the circumcised keep the law (cf. Munck, 87f.).

do not themselves keep the law: this can be understood in various ways. The most natural would seem to be that they cannot keep the law because its demands are impossible (so Duncan). Paul is not then criticizing them for failure to keep the law, but for failure to recognize their inability to do so. Had they recognized this failure they would certainly not have insisted on Gentiles attempting to do what they themselves had failed to do. This is better than supposing that Paul knew of any specific instances of their failure, or that he knew that they had not tried to keep the law (cf. Lightfoot, Williams).

but they desire, etc.: this is almost a repetition of the first part of verse 12, although the differences are worth noting. There they were trying to compel: here Paul softens it to desire. There the purpose was to make a good showing; here to glory in the flesh. This latter change is significant, as Paul wishes to contrast this glorying with a glorying in an infinitely superior subject. The most that the Judaizers would be able to glory in would be an increase in adherents to Israel, which they supposed would be pleasing to God.

14. But far be it from me: Paul's characteristic phrase of strong rejection occurs here with the dative of the person to express the alien character of any other object of glorying except the cross.

except in the cross of our Lord Jesus Christ: in no more conclusive way could Paul express the centrality of the cross in his thinking than by exalting it as the sole object of his boasting. He does not enter here, any more than elsewhere in the epistle, upon a discussion of the work of Christ. For him it is the key to man's salvation, and he assumes that his readers will know what he means when he refers to it. It clearly stands for much more than the mere historical fact that Jesus was crucified. It stands for the whole significance of the event, not only for mankind in general but for Paul in particular. He could understand how the cross was a stumbling-block for Jews, but he could never understand how Christians could ever fail to see it as their greatest glory. It may well be that a major part of the weakness of much of the witness of the modern Church lies in a failure to boast in the cross, whether or not its opponents treat this message with contempt or hostility.

by which: the cross is here regarded as the instrument through which a remarkable transformation of Paul's relationship with the world has been made. He probable thinks of Christ's crucifixion as a pattern for the crucifixion of self, as he does in 2.20. An alternative understanding of the Greek could justify the translation 'through whom' (so Ellicott), thus relating the crucifixion of the world to the agency of Christ. It amounts to the same, for the activity of Christ is inseparable from his cross.

the world: here the apostle means the order of material creation and everything under its sway, independent of the control of the Holy Spirit. 'The world' has thus a moral connotation in so far as it is adverse to the perfect pattern of the Creator for his creation.

crucified to me: this is a vivid method of stating that the natural world as such has ceased to have any claims upon him. Crucifixion is a strange figure in this context, but Paul is no doubt regarding it as an act of finality in order to show that something more is needed than a mere lessening of attraction in regard to the world. It must be dealt a death-blow as far as Paul is concerned. It may at first seem that this is far too drastic. Surely the world has much that is worth preserving? But Paul's uncompromising approach is the only effective one. When the world had died to him and he to the world, he could discover real life. He could then look out on the natural order from a different point of view, as verse 15 shows. Henceforth his aims are spiritual and what the natural man regards as gain are for him refuse (cf. Phil. 3.8).

15. neither circumcision . . . nor uncircumcision: in harmony with his general argument Paul asserts the irrelevance of the circumcision issue. The statement is extremely compressed, but Paul's present thought must be interpreted in the light of verse 14. He is giving a reason for his boasting in the cross, i.e. because through it has emerged a new creation. But he must again exclude circumcision as a basis for boasting and with it he links uncircumcision in case the Gentiles should find pride in their uncircumcised state.

a new creation: the same expression as here is found in 2 C. 5.7, where it probably means 'a new creature'. Here, however, the idea seems to be the totality of the renewal effected by Christ. Whatever man might do to earn salvation, of which circumcision is a conspicuous example, he could never succeed. He needed not only to be crucified with Christ, but also to be recreated. Christians should remember, according to Paul's line of argument, that nothing they had ever done, nor ever would do, nor any privileges they thought they possessed, contributed in any way to the new creation. It was all God's work.

16. Peace and mercy: in Ps. 125.5 occurs the phrase, 'peace shall be upon Israel', and there is little doubt that Paul is echoing this Psalm. Nonetheless he has modified the Psalmist's thought, which contrasts the crooked ways of the wicked with Israel as typical of those who trust in the Lord. He contrasts those who trust in circumcision with those who rely upon Christ. Moreover, the addition of 'mercy' is interesting. It would be more general to place mercy before peace, which is the result of an act of divine mercy as it is in 1 Tim. 1.2; 2 Tim. 1.2; 2 Jn 3; and Jude 2. Perhaps the apostle makes the addition because he wants to show that in the Christian sense 'peace' is different from the Psalmist's use of it. It is the peace of those who have thrown themselves on the mercy of God.

all who walk by this rule: since the verb has already occurred in 5.25 of the believer's walk by the Spirit, it is clear that Paul intends the same meaning here. The key to Paul's precise meaning lies in the interpretation of the word rendered 'rule' (*kanōn*). He uses the word, which literally means 'a straight edge', in the sense of a 'principle', and he must mean the principle enunciated in the previous two verses, i.e. the central importance of the cross.

the Israel of God: there are two ways in which this can be understood. It can refer to the faithful Israelites, thus distinguishing them from Israel as a whole, or it can refer to all Christians as the New Israel. The phrase occurs nowhere else in the New Testament and so there are no parallels to which to appeal for a decision. Since 'Israel'·seems to refer to the same people as 'all who walk by this rule', the second interpretation seems preferable. No doubt Paul introduces this reference to Israel not only because he is echoing it from the Psalm, but also because he wants to assure the Galatians that they will not forfeit the benefits of being part of the true Israel by refusing circumcision.

17. Henceforth let no man trouble me: this statement seems rather abruptly introduced as a parting remark. It appears that Paul had made his last strong appeal and realizes that nothing further can be done but to leave the matter with his readers. He hopes that no-one will cause further trouble to him. It may be that this is Paul's tactful way of finishing on a note of personal appeal, as much as to say 'have a thought for all the trouble you have already caused me and shame upon you if you cause me any more'.

for I bear on my body: what the apostle carries in a physical sense is given as a reason why they should cease troubling him. This appears to be an allusion to his present circumstances. It is noticeable that Paul uses 'body' not 'flesh', which would carry an undesired connotation.

the marks of Jesus: Ramsay has suggested that this is an allusion to the branding of slaves as a sign of ownership, in which case Paul is thinking metaphorically of the badge of Jesus upon him, perhaps in contrast to the badge of circumcision carried by the legalists (so Bengel). But this is not the best interpretation. 2 Corinthians 4.10 supplies a suitable parallel. After speaking of being 'persecuted' and 'struck down', he mentions carrying in the body the death of Jesus, an expression so closely parallel to the present statement that it seems inescapable that Paul meant the same thing in both cases. This being so, the marks of Jesus would be the scars of persecution. Some of the Galatians had seen those scars. They were the marks of Jesus in the sense that they had been incurred in the cause of Jesus. They were evidence that Paul owed allegiance to Jesus. In view of those scars, the Galatians should avoid any further harrying.

18. The grace of our Lord Jesus Christ: it is usual for Paul to begin and end his epistles with a reference to grace. For a similar phrase to that used here, cf. Rom. 16.20; Phil. 4.23.

be with your spirit: it is significant that Paul mentions the 'spirit' at this juncture in this epistle, for he has had much to say about the Holy Spirit and this makes a fitting conclusion. He treats the Galatians as spiritual people. Cf. Phil. 4.23; 2 Tim. 4.22, for the same expression.

brethren: this adds warmth to the parting greeting. It does not occur in any other of Paul's epistolary conclusions.

Amen: apart from this, only that to the Romans of Paul's epistles ends with an Amen. It was no formal habit with Paul. He means to add weight to his conclusion. It was intended as a prayer—'so let it be'.

APPENDIX

NOTE A: THE CENTRALITY OF CHRIST IN THE EPISTLE

It is generally supposed that the keynote to this epistle is justification by faith, and there is no denying the prominence given to this important theme. Yet the most dominating feature is the centrality of Christ in the theology of the epistle. This latter, of course, includes the former, but justification can only be fully understood when the nature of the justifier is in clear focus. Although in all Paul's epistles Christ is much spoken of, yet in none other is the mention of Christ so all-pervasive. It is a rewarding study to consider the light that this epistle throws on Paul's Christology. It may be wondered what value attaches to this kind of study for a single epistle, for it might be objected that the resultant study would tend to be one-sided. Not only is such a fear without basis in the case of this epistle, but the importance of the epistle for its spontaneity warrants a separate study. Since, as we have seen, even the most liberal critics of Paul have left this epistle to him because it bears the strong marks of his powerful personality, it is clearly of first-rate importance to study its Christology. At the same time a caution needs to be entered in case it should be assumed that a complete Pauline Christology can be found here. Truth is many-sided, and cannot be contained within the confines of one brief epistle.

Personal Relationship

The reader of this epistle will not progress far before he realizes that the author is a man of deep conviction about the place Christ holds in his own life. Indeed, this appears indirectly in the first verse, when Paul speaks of his apostleship. It is of utmost importance for him to establish the divine origin of his office, but it is significant in this respect that he couples Jesus Christ with God the Father. In his vision on the Damascus road it was Christ who addressed him and who identified himself so closely with his people that he charged Saul of Tarsus with persecuting him rather than them. This was the beginning of a new relationship which became completely Christ-centred.

This deep conviction recurs in 1.12, although in this case it is not Paul's office but his gospel which is in mind. The message is every whit as important as the messenger. It was the apostle's consciousness of his calling in Christ which invested his message with a special authority. What he preached was about Christ, and had been imparted by a special revelation. With such a gospel as that it is no wonder that Christ was set so prominently at the heart of everything he did or thought.

The major statement relating to Paul's consciousness of Christ is found in 2.20, where he not only identifies himself with the crucified Christ, but declares that

Christ now lives within him. More will be said later about the apostle's doctrine of a mystic union between believers and Christ, but this transference of Christ's death and resurrection to his own spiritual experience is strongly characteristic of his thinking. He could not conceive of life apart from Christ, but he knew only too well that there had to be a mortification of the flesh. He had learnt the deep secret of the cross of Christ in his own spiritual experience. There is no doubt that this experience coloured his whole approach to theological thinking, and is particularly apparent in his handling of the Galatian situation. The idea of crucifixion with Christ would have been quite alien to religious legalists, while the attempt to obtain justification by works of the law could find no place in an experience like Paul's.

The deep impression of the crucified Christ on Paul's own soul could not fail to affect his preaching. In fact, he reminds the Galatians that he had placarded the crucified Christ before them (3.1), clearly as the central feature of his message. Paul's words suggest that any influence which could cause the substitution of any other object must be due to an adverse beguiling influence. Paul was so conscious of Christ that he had no desire to proclaim anything else but Christ and him crucified, as he reminded the Corinthians (1 C. 2.2).

Later on in the epistle, the apostle reminds his readers that they had received him initially 'as an angel of God, as Christ Jesus' (4.14). Does this suggest that Paul bore so closely the imprint of his master that the Galatians regarded him as an embodiment of Christ, his true representative? This may be reading too much into the reference, but the close personal connection between Paul and Jesus Christ is unmistakable.

When he is expressing his confidence in the outcome of his pleadings with the readers he makes clear that the basis of his confidence is 'in the Lord' (5.10). Here is a man whose own opinions count less than Christ. He feels that his conviction is not based on his own wishful feeling, but on his relationship to Christ. This is another example of the influence of a man's experience of Christ on his mental and spiritual convictions.

The crucifixion theme as a personal experience is reiterated in 6.14, where the apostle asserts that he glories only in the cross, because it is the instrument by which he is crucified to the world and the world to him. There is a close parallel with 2.20, but in the present case the reference to the world is significant, for there is a clear antithesis between Christ and the world. For Paul, Christ has taken the place which was previously occupied by the world in his consciousness. This does not mean that he became other-worldly, but that he ceased to be under the damaging influence of a world controlled by adverse powers. The principles of Christ were powerful enough to supplant the normal principles of the world and the guarantee that they could do so was found in the cross of Christ.

At the close of this epistle (6.17) the apostle suddenly states that he bears in his body 'the marks of Jesus'. His physical condition was in itself a testimony of what

Jesus Christ meant to him. He had suffered much for Christ's sake, so much so that he conceives of Christ suffering in him. The marks of Jesus were a testimony that all could see.

MYSTICAL UNION

One of the most characteristic facets of Paul's Christology is the phrase 'in Christ' and its corresponding expressions. This epistle is not without considerable emphasis on this aspect of the believer's experience.

There has been much discussion of the meaning of the preposition 'in' (Greek *en*) in the phrase under review, but even although it may carry with it different shades of meaning according to its context the general idea of a close inward relationship is always present. It undoubtedly expresses a high view of Christ. For Paul to conceive of him as a person in whom not only faith but believers themselves might be grounded, he must have recognized a relationship which could never have existed between two purely human persons. The concept of being 'in Christ' at once, therefore, draws attention to the uniqueness of Christ. The various usages of this concept in this epistle will illustrate different aspects of that uniqueness.

The first occurrence is in 1.22, where the apostle refers to the churches of Judea which are in Christ. This is a much more suggestive manner of speaking than if Paul had spoken of the churches of Christ. There is more than the idea of ownership in mind. In some sense these churches, as all essentially Christian churches, were rooted in Christ. He was their basis and their life. There was more than an external attachment. The phrase is not a synonym for 'Christian' as it is generally understood. It involved a definite personal relationship between the group of believers as a body and Christ.

A further aspect of the same idea occurs in 2.4, although here it is specifically related to freedom. The thought is that those who are 'in Christ' are now in a position of freedom. The two concepts are inseparable. The idea of 'bondage' and the idea of being 'in Christ' are for Paul mutually exclusive. This is closely linked with the corresponding statement in 5.1, which makes clear that Christ is the active agent in securing our freedom. The peculiar richness of the present expression is brought out by the incongruity of any parallel idea when another agent is substituted. For instance, in spite of all that the slaves owed to William Wilberforce for their freedom, none would have referred to the freedom which he had 'in Wilberforce'. But the preposition which is so conspicuously out of place for Wilberforce is perfectly adapted to Christ, for two reasons. Not only is the freedom gained in Christ of a totally different order in that it is essentially spiritual, but the agent is immeasurably superior in that he is capable of sustaining a spiritual relationship with those whom he has freed. This latter condition could be fulfilled only by one who was more than human, and again points to the high Christology of the apostle.

The third occurrence of the phrase is in 2.17, where it relates to justification. It is significant that in 2.16 Paul speaks of being justified by faith in Christ, but does not use the formula *en Christo*. In this case the emphasis is upon the appropriation of the benefits of Christ's work by faith. In 2.17 the statement becomes contracted to 'justified in Christ', and in this case there can be no doubt that 'in Christ' expresses the spiritual position of those who have put their faith in Christ, as a result of which they are justified. The phrase thus sums up the result of Christ's work for believers in a direction towards God. It is to be noticed that Paul is using the phrase in a hypothetical question which posits an endeavour to become justified in Christ, which in the nature of the case is impossible, for justification, as Paul shows, is not by human effort but by faith.

In the course of his discussion of Abraham's faith in chapter 3, the apostle explains that the blessing which accompanied Abraham's faith is shared by Gentiles 'in Christ Jesus' (3.14). This may be a concise way of saying that Gentiles who become members of the Christian Church will share the same spiritual heritage as the Jews. But it probably means more than that. The blessing promised to Abraham reached its fulfilment only in Christ and those incorporated in him must naturally share in the inheritance. The believers' mystic oneness with Christ is no doubt in Paul's thought, and this for him is the deep spiritual principle which enables him to abolish any distinction in his mind between Jew and Gentile. The latter could not lay any firmer claim on Abraham's blessing by means of circumcision than he already enjoys in Christ.

A further development of the relationship is found in 3.26 where Paul equates the sons of God with those 'in Christ Jesus'. The latter phrase may relate to 'faith' rather than to 'sons of God', but it seems to make better sense if taken with 'sons of God'. When a man believes, he is then in Christ Jesus, and this invests him with a new status before God. He may now be said to be 'in the family', although even this analogy falls short. The true children of God are not those who could claim physical descent from Abraham, as Jews believed, but those who were in a position of faith in Christ. This at once broadened the basis of sonship and at the same time excluded mere formal relationship from the qualification required. No amount of circumcising of Gentiles could introduce them into God's family without the exercise of personal faith. The new relationship 'in Christ' introduced a new element not only in man's approach to God, but in men's attitude to each other. This is expressed succinctly in 3.28—'you are all one in Christ Jesus'. In this statement in which 'in Christ Jesus' is the basis of unity, it follows that all who are 'in Christ' must have a close relationship to each other. Any means whereby Jew and Greek, slave and free man, male and female could in the ancient world of Paul's day achieve any sense of unity was nothing short of miraculous. This demonstrates that 'in Christ' was no mere formula, but a powerful principle which could overcome all barriers.

The remaining occurrence of the phrase is found in 5.6, where it is once again used to overthrow the distinction between circumcision and uncircumcision. Such a distinction, Paul argues, simply does not exist 'in Christ Jesus'. In place of it, faith works through love. Because of the frequency with which Paul uses the phrase, its extraordinary character is all too often missed. There was no other force of such potency as this which could so effectively abolish age-old and deep-rooted distinctions which had hardened into prejudice. To be 'in Christ' was to be in possession of an entirely new way of looking at things.

More could be said about the same idea of our mystical union with Christ expressed in rather different ways in this epistle. For instance, there is the same mystical idea in Paul's metaphor of putting on Christ (3.27), or in the use of the child-bearing imagery in 4.19, or in Paul's claim that Christ lives within him (2.20). For him Christ had become life's centre.

REDEMPTIVE WORK

There are many references in this epistle to the work of Christ and particularly to the meaning of the cross. The opening salutation (1.3-5) which begins in the usual way leads into a statement concerning the purpose of Christ's coming. (a) He is said to have given himself, so drawing attention to the voluntary character of his self-giving. (b) At the same time, this self-giving is said to have been according to the will of God. Both these aspects are characteristic of Paul's theology and throw further light upon his Christology. What Christ voluntarily did was what God had willed, and any cleavage between them was unthinkable to Paul. The self-giving of Christ is further said (c) to be 'for our sins', reminiscent of the similar statement in 1 C. 15.3. In the latter case Paul is clearly citing a statement of Christian doctrine which he had received, and there is no denying that this interpretation of the death of Christ was not only a dominant feature of early Christian belief but also was deeply impressed upon the mind of the apostle. There is no developed theory of the Atonement in either of these statements, but there is certainly the beginning of an interpretation. No theory can possibly be satisfactory which does not explain the connection between the death of Christ and man's sins. A fourth assertion is (d) that the purpose of Christ's work was to deliver from the present evil age. Here the apostle is thinking of Christ as a powerful victor over the present order, freeing those who were captives to that order. This was a fitting introduction to an epistle which was to battle for the freedom of the Galatian Christians.

There is a passing reference in 1.6 to the grace of Christ, and this must not be overlooked in considering Paul's Christology, for the Christian's calling is the result of Christ's unmerited favour and not the result of any merit on man's part. Paul conceives of all that Christ has done as being grounded in grace. In the classic statement in 2.20, after asserting that he himself has been crucified with Christ, Paul once again refers to the self-giving of Christ on his behalf. The significance of this statement is that the self-giving proceeded from the love of Christ, an important element in the Atonement.

In the next verse (2.21) the apostle bases his argument on the assumption that any religious principle which empties Christ's death of its purpose must be false. It was his deep conviction, shared indeed by all the apostolic preachers and writers, that the cross was no unfortunate accident, but was undertaken with a specific purpose. Paul would never have agreed with any doctrine of the Atonement which regarded the cross as a cause of disillusionment for Christ. It was never planned to be useless, an unnecessary tragedy.

In chapter 3 there is a more developed discussion of the meaning of what Christ came to do, coming into focus particularly in verse 13—'Christ redeemed us from the curse of the law, having become a curse for us'. The idea of redemption is frequently met in Paul's epistles, but only here is that redemption said to be from the curse of the law. The whole statement is fraught with mystery, since it is difficult to conceive in what sense the righteous Christ could actually become a curse, or in what sense by so doing he could deliver those who were already under a curse. Whatever might be the full explanation it seems inescapable that Paul intends us to understand that in some way the effectiveness of Christ's work was due to his close identification with the sin of man. The present statement is parallel to that of 2 C. 5.21, in which Christ is said to have been made sin for our sakes although he himself was sinless. There can be no doubt that in Paul's theology Christ took the place of the sinner. At the close of chapter 3 the apostle shows that the special function of law came to an end with the advent of Christ, thus demonstrating that Christ's coming marked a crucial stage in human history (3.24).

The idea of redemption recurs in 4.4, where it is related again to those under the law. The most significant statement here is that Christ's ability to redeem those under law is due to his being himself born under the law. This shows the essential connection between the manner of his coming and his ultimate purpose. It needed one who was completely identified with those whom he intended to deliver. It is to be noted also that in the present statement Paul once again shows his acute awareness of the divine overruling of the advent of Christ, for it happened at the precise time of God's own choosing. There was no question in Paul's mind of accidental happenings. The whole process of redemption was perfectly planned. The granting of freedom through Christ (5.1) is another way of expressing the idea of deliverance already noted in previous statements, although here the concept is more positive. Christ not only delivers from bondage but delivers to freedom.

In the concluding portion of the letter (6.11–18) there are two further references to the cross, which shows the dominance of the theme in the apostle's mind. In 6.12 he speaks of those who wish to avoid persecution for the cross of Christ, which suggests that there is an inevitable offence in the cross, a theme which he develops elsewhere (cf. 1 C. 1). But in 6.14 he comes to his own attitude towards it in which he declares it to be his sole object of boasting and the reason given is the effectiveness of the cross in dealing with the world. From this it would seem reasonable to conclude that there was an inward effect of Christ's work on the cross which transformed Paul's thoughts about the world, conceived here again in an adverse moral sense. It is a strong statement that the world is crucified to Paul, but it vividly expresses the powerful effect of the atonement on his whole approach to things. It is no wonder that he could write to the Philippians that he had come to regard all his former advantages as mere refuse (Phil. 3.8). Paul never lost the wonder of the atoning death of Christ.

Christ as the Essence of the Gospel

Paul sometimes refers to 'my gospel', but he never means the message which he has himself created. He always means 'the gospel of Christ' (cf. 1.6ff.). He was not proclaiming any human philosophy ('man's gospel', 1.12), but a revelation of Christ. Just as his whole life was centred on Christ, so was his message. It is Christ alone who must be the object of faith, reiterated three times in 2.16. It was Christ whom Paul had placarded before the Galatians as crucified (3.1). It was to believers in Christ that everything promised in the Scriptures to men of faith would be fulfilled (3.22).

Whatever other themes found place in Paul's preaching were subordinate to this. As to the charge that he preached circumcision, he is quick to dispute it (5.11).

Christ in Christian Life and Service

It was Paul's desire in all his service for Christ to become a servant of Christ. He makes no claim to this title in his opening remarks as he does in some of his letters (cf. Rom. 1.1; Phil. 1.1), but he takes it for granted in 1.10. He was not trying to please men but God. His allegiance was to Christ, whose bondservant he was. Not only did he maintain this for himself, but he assumed it as a norm for others.

The depth of Paul's sense of responsibility towards others is most vividly seen where he uses the metaphor of maternal travailing (4.19), longing that Christ might be formed in his readers. This is all the more striking when it is remembered that there were so many other things that Paul must also have desired for them. In a pagan environment, he might have expressed the wish that they might have wisdom in dealing with the many problems that confronted them, or that they might have a developed social responsibility, or that they might manifest evangelistic zeal. But his dominating desire for them was for Christlikeness, for he knew that this would embrace all the others. A group of Christians in whom Christ had evidently been formed would prove the most powerfully effective agent for the propagation of the faith and for the reform of society as a whole.

Christian believers certainly had a direct ethical responsibility as Paul shows in chapter 5. There are works of the flesh which must have no place and there are fruits of the Spirit which must appear (5.19-24). Particularly will there be mutual concern among Christians. Envy is a special danger and must be watched (5.26). If a fellow-believer should fall, the Christlike spirit is seen in a spirit of gentleness in dealing with him. If a brother is bearing burdens it is part of the law of Christ, here conceived as the normal principle of Christian living, for others to relieve him (6.2). It is equally part of that law for a man to refuse to overestimate his own importance (6.3, 4). The practical character of Paul's Christology could not have been more succinctly stated. When a man is Christ's he must adopt Christ's principles of action and not his own.

Belonging to Christ may entail persecution (5.11; 6.12). It may involve bearing the marks of Christ (6.17). But it is abundantly worth while.

NOTE B: THE SOURCE OF OPPOSITION AT GALATIA

It has been assumed in the discussion on the purpose of the epistle and throughout the commentary that the troublemakers were Jewish Christians who were trying to persuade Gentile Christians to embrace Judaism as well as Christianity. It would appear to account for all the facts reasonably well. But two alternative theories have been proposed which deserve mention, even although they do not carry conviction.

It is unlikely that these Judaizers were commissioned by the Jerusalem apostles, although they were laying claim to their authority (cf. Schoep's discussion, 74ff.). A modification of this view is that the Judaizers were themselves Gentiles as Munck (87ff.) maintained. But Jewish Christians seem more probable.

The first theory is that the troublers were non-Christian Jews who saw in the Gentile Christian Church an opportunity to win over proselytes to Judaism. In this case Paul's purpose is to warn the Gentiles against such proselytism. Yet it is much more probable that Jewish Christian activity is in mind since Acts makes clear that such activity caused trouble in the Antiochene Church, and it is a reasonable deduction from this that Gentile churches, which had been founded as a result of the missionary activity based on Antioch, would also be affected. Whether or not the Jewish Christian attempts would have been regarded favourably by the local Jews is not known, but is not an unreasonable conjecture. Nevertheless, the animosity of the Jews was frequently stirred up by Christianity drawing away a number of proselytes on which their own hopes of expansion were pinned, and this must not be lost sight of in assessing the possible sympathy between Judaism and Jewish Christianity. The above view was held by Kirsopp Lake (*Beginnings of Christianity*, edited F. Jackson and K. Lake, Vol. V (1933), 215.

The other theory which must be mentioned is Ropes' idea that the troublers included a group of Gentile perfectionists. Such people would regard themselves as superior to law and would therefore claim a type of freedom which was alien to Christianity. In support of the theory it has been maintained that Paul was concerned not to separate Gentile Christians from Judaism, otherwise he would not have appealed to Abraham in the course of his argument. But this position cannot be maintained, for there is no suggestion that the Gentile Christians were in danger of severing connection with Judaism. Moreover, it was certainly not perfectionists who were urging circumcision upon the Gentiles.

INDEX